TEXT AND INTERPRETATION AS
CATEGORIES OF THEOLOGICAL THINKING

WERNER G. JEANROND

Text and Interpretation as Categories of Theological Thinking

Translated by
THOMAS J. WILSON

Wipf & Stock
PUBLISHERS
Eugene, Oregon

Wipf and Stock Publishers
199 W 8th Ave, Suite 3
Eugene, OR 97401

Text and Interpretation as Categories of Theological Thinking
By Jeanrond, Werner G.
Copyright©1986 Gill and Macmillan Ltd
ISBN: 1-59752-436-0
Publication date 10/21/2005
Previously published by Crossroad, 1986

For
Käthe, Robert and Hans-Josef Jeanrond
in gratitude

Table of Contents

List of Abbreviations	xi
Translator's Foreword	xiii
Introduction	xv

Chapter I
Interpretation as Category of Theological Thinking

1. Introduction	1
2. The Fundamental Importance of Interpretation for Theology	1
a) Texts as Provocation of Theological Thinking	3
b) The Necessity of a Theological Theory of Interpretation	4
3. Towards a Definition of 'Interpretation' after Hans-Georg Gadamer's Philosophical Hermeneutics	8
a) Gadamer's Concept of the Process of Understanding	9
(1) Philosophical Hermeneutics or Hermeneutical Philosophy	9
(2) Understanding as Understanding of Texts	12
(3) Understanding and Interpretation	12
(4) The Essence of Hermeneutical Experience	18
(5) The Linguisticality and Universality of Hermeneutical Experience	19
(6) Truth in Hermeneutical Experience	20
(7) Conclusion	21
b) Critique of Gadamer's Optimistic Concept of Understanding	22
(1) The Problem of Language and of Misunderstandings	22

	(2) The Problem of Inadequate Understanding	27
	(3) The Problem of Hermeneutical Conversation	31
	(4) Conclusion and Further Delineation of the Task	34

4. Further Precision in the Elaboration of the Concept of 'Interpretation' through Paul Ricoeur's Theory of Interpretation 37
   a) The Contours of a Theory of Interpretation in Ricoeur 38
      (1) Hermeneutics as the Path of a Philosophy of Reflection 38
      (2) Symbols, Metaphors, Texts: Language and Interpretation 40
      (3) The Autonomy of the Text: Distanciation as a Prerequisite for Appropriation 44
      (4) The Conflict of Interpretation: Sense and Reference 46
      (5) Appropriation: Understanding and Explanation 49
      (6) Suspicion and Retrieval: Criticism in Ricoeur and Gadamer 52
      (7) Conclusion 55
   b) Critique of Ricoeur's Model of Interpretation 56
      (1) The Problem of Text Sense and Text Reference 56
      (2) The Problem Posed by the Dialectic of Reception 61
      (3) The Problem of Interpretative Pluralism 62
      (4) Conclusion and Delineation of the Task 63

5. Interpretation and Assessment 64
   a) The Horizon of Understanding and Assessment 65
      (1) Thematic Critique 65
      (2) Critique of the Situation 66
      (3) The Necessity for Assessment 68
   b) The Three Dimensions of Interpretation: Understanding — Explanation — Assessment 68
   c) The Dimension of Assessment 69
   d) On the Universality of Interpretation 71

ix

Chapter II
Text as Category of Theological Thinking

1. Introduction   73
2. Theology: Science of the Sentence or of the Text?   74
3. Reflections on Text Linguistics   75
   a) Text Linguistics and the Theory of Interpretation   75
   b) The Dynamic Structure of the Text   79
      (1) On Sense and Meaning in the Text   79
      (2) On the Textuality of Texts   81
   c) The Dynamic Structure of Text and Reading   82
      (1) Text and Reading in the Model of Communication   82
      (2) The Theme-Rheme Structure in the Text   85
      (3) The Complexity of the Text   88
   d) Theological Disclosure of the Sense of Texts   90
      (1) Textual Determination Exemplified by the Book of Genesis   91
      (2) The Significance of the Reading Situation for Reception: The New Testament Canon as an Example   92

4. Text and Text Genres   94
   a) Reflections on the Style of a Text   94
   b) Text Genres   97
      (1) Essence and Function of Text Genres   97
      (2) The Hierarchy of Functions in the Text   100
   c) Theological Text Genres   100

5. Reading and Reading Genres   104
   a) Aspects of a Theory of Reading   105
      (1) Wolfgang Iser's Theory of Reading   106
      (2) Stanley Fish's Theory of Reading   110
      (3) Criticism and Plurality of Readings   113
   b) Reading as Style-Related Activity   114
   c) Reading Genres   116
   d) Theological Reading Genres   118

6. Reading Pluralism and Reader Responsibility: Criteria for an Ethic of Theological Interpretation   120
   a) Text Interpretation as Basic Christian Activity   121

    b) Possible Functions of Reading Biblical Texts   123
        (1) The Problem of Cemented Selection   123
        (2) The Problem of Assessment   124
    c) The Responsibility of Theological Text
        Interpretation   128

Chapter III
Text and Interpretation as Categories of Theological Thinking

1. Introduction   129

2. From Hermeneutical Theology to Theological Hermeneutics: David Tracy's Theological Theory of Interpretation   130
    a) The Hermeneutical Character of Theology   131
    b) Claim and Interpretation of Classic Texts   133
        (1) Tracy's Concept of the Classic   133
        (2) Tracy's Theory of Interpretation   134
        (3) Critical Appreciation of Tracy's Theory of Interpretation   135
        (4) Reflections on the Nature of the Classic   140
    c) Interpretational Theology as Revisionist Theology   142
        (1) Tracy's Religious Interpretation Perspectives   143
        (2) Tracy's Christian Interpretation Perspectives   145
        (3) Tracy's Concept of Revisionist Theology   147
    d) The Hermeneutical Claim of Theological Thinking   149

3. Hermeneutics and Theology: Retrospective and Prospective   150

Notes   155

Bibliography   183

Index of Names   192

Index of Subjects   194

ABBREVIATIONS

AI	*The Analogical Imagination*
BRO	*Blessed Rage for Order*
Ci	*The Conflict of Interpretation*
Freud	*Freud and Philosophy*
HaHS	*Hermeneutics and the Human Sciences*
HuI	*Hermeneutik und Ideologiekritik*
Iser	*The Act of Reading*
IT	*Interpretation Theory*
PhH	*Philosophical Hermeneutics*
RAS	*Reason in the Age of Science*
SE	*The Symbolism of Evil*
TM	*Truth and Method*
TM/WM	German original of TM
tr.	translator/translated by
tr.T.W.	translated by T. J. Wilson. This abbreviation is often used for quotations where the translator has departed from the standard English translation in order to maintain consistency with his translation of the context. Key German words have sometimes been inserted in quotations. When not otherwise stated, quotations are translated by T.W.

Translator's Foreword

It often occurred to me that the assertion: 'The *word* became flesh and dwelt among us' might perhaps more suitably read: 'The *text* became flesh and dwelt among us'! It was therefore a pleasant surprise to find a theologican thematising the 'text' and an even more pleasant one to be invited to co-operate in making this study available to an English-speaking readership.

But a theology to be constructed around the notion of 'text' will presumably run into the same type of difficulty as does a philosophy with similar aspirations, i.e. speechlessness, or worse, the temptation to invent a 'jargon of authenticity'. For, it might be argued, the basic notions in the *Oxford Dictionary* and in *Duden* are derived from a 'stone ontology' rather than a 'text ontology'. They are based on the conviction that the basic mental operation is one which says something about something out there — about a substance, a plant for example, or indeed a human being understood on the model of 'corporalia'. Reality consists of things to be known, i.e. asserted, and not of texts or a text to be read. Our culture and our so-called common sense have so conditioned us to this abstraction — logocentrism — and all that goes with it that we forget our existential immersion in the historical stream of consciousness. This, like any consciousness, looks forwards and backwards. It is this creative looking which establishes meaningful connections. And since reality is nothing if not meaningful, it is this tying up, this 'texere' which creates the text of reality. In the absence of categories derived from this 'text', we are 'speechless' in certain fundamental dimensions of our being.

Revelation has no choice but to insert itself into this 'text'. It can only be understood as basic — ontological — textuality and depends on the help of textual categories. Hence the importance of 'text' and 'interpretation' as 'categories' of *theological* thinking.

Having had occasion as a philosopher to go hat in hand to the literary critics in search of a text definition, I have some concept of the difficulty involved. Werner Jeanrond has been much more successful in his quest. His study, drawing from linguistics and hermeneutics, offers a lucid if technical presentation of reading theories and theories of textuality.

He has checked the accuracy of my translation, particularly in regard to such words as *Sinn, Bedeutung* and *Deuten*. He has also helped me in the time-consuming task of tracking down and substituting existing translations of German works quoted, and for all of this I am very grateful.

Furthermore, we have discussed together such 'trivial' matters as the use of the definite article. I was tempted to use it to qualify 'Categories of Theological Thinking' and only omitted it because I felt that it was understood, i.e. implicitly there. The *Oxford Dictionary* lists under 'category': 'one of the divisions in a classification'. Here, any such conception would be misleading. In this book textual thinking is precisely *not* a division of the classification, theological thinking! Though the author in using the word 'category' wishes to remain within the confines of ordinary language, because of its philosophical provenance it is hard to escape philosophical overtones. We are reminded of the (linguistic) derivation of the categories in Aristotle and Kant (both of whom seem to operate on the level of the sentence in such derivation). Progenital concepts (*Stammbegriffe*) like causality, unity, reality, possibility are, in Kant, apriori enabling conditions for experiencing things around us. In Aristotle categories are comprehensive principles: ultimately we talk about things in terms of substance and accidents. For both Kant and Aristotle categories have to do with the founding aspects of reality as we know it. More recently, the text of reality is for Heidegger that which enables, transcendentally grounds, the interpretation of the printed text before me. Also for W. Jeanrond categories are comprehensive principles. Text and interpretation as basic modes of access to reality, theological or otherwise, allow such derived modes as the sentence to emerge. The book deals with *the* fundamental categories of theological thinking. We are implicitly in the tradition of Aristotle, Kant, Heidegger.

Thomas J. Wilson

Introduction

In a twofold sense theology is a text-centred science. On the one hand talking about God and reflection on it are accomplished in linguistic texts. On the other hand such discourse and reflection take their orientation from linguistic productions of a textual nature emerging from the tradition of this discourse. Christian theology interprets the texts of the Bible and the experiential statements of those who have formed the Christian tradition, who have developed it or continue to do so — these statements of experience which have become crystallised into texts. Again the interpretation of all texts has itself a textual character. In other words: theology produces texts when it reflects on texts. To say that theology is enmeshed in language is not sufficient; theology is enmeshed in texts: texts are the manner in which theological thinking is accomplished. This insight rests on the knowledge which has emerged in text linguistics according to which the leading paradigms of linguistic usage do not consist of the word or the proposition but rather the text. The importance of this knowledge for theological thought deserves to be investigated because it could indeed happen that, viewed from the perspective of textuality, theological thought and discourse are open to a new understanding, just as literary science turns anew to the text as paradigm, away from the fragmented discussion about individual propositions within a text, a discussion which as such is outside the frame of reference of the text. The limitation implied by such a propositional reading would constitute a betrayal of the text which of course lays claim to be more than the sum total of single statements strung together in a 'text'.

In relation to theology this means: we have to consider whether our reading of biblical texts, of texts from the Christian tradition and of dogmatic texts, was not and is not too much oriented on the sentence and verse. We have to ask ourselves furthermore whether our reading as a result does not require a critical referral to the textuality of texts and we have to consider that new theological thoughts also appear as text arrangements which in their turn require to be read.[1]

Without a doubt neither 'talking about God' nor its systematic definition confine themselves to the interpretation of texts, whether traditional or contemporary. This 'talking about God' speculates, questions, generates problems, systematises also, moves therefore outside the ambit of the textual basis. But it is itself never free from the generation of its own text, and it is continually spurred on by texts to reconsider, further develop or think to their logical conclusions the thoughts of tradition. It is therefore continually invited to involve itself with texts. Theology therefore has no choice but to engage systematically in the interpretation of texts.

Two possible procedures suggest themselves for a study of the implications of these considerations. One could on the one hand assemble, criticise and further develop the different theological outlines of a theory of interpretation. Or one could, on the other hand, start off with a general discussion about an appropriate theory of text interpretation with the help of which one could then subject to critical scrutiny the theological suggestions for text interpretation which are already in existence. I have decided in favour of this second possibility because it is the only one which makes it possible to start off with a suggestion for a total outline of text interpretation which alone can do justice to the already mentioned insight into the textual character of all theological statements. This outline of a text interpretation will be further developed in the course of our study (Chapter II).

The present work studies therefore the conditions and methodological procedures of theological interpretation of texts. In Chapter I a new concept of interpretation is presented. The point of departure for our study is the debate about the view of philosophical hermeneutics taken by Hans-Georg Gadamer and the criticism of this as a universal concept of understanding. Its weak points have been sufficiently investigated and widely discussed. The debate over Gadamer's suggested hermeneutics confines itself, however, for the most part to historical elaborations and critical reflections. In this work therefore we do not propose to offer a further history of hermeneutics or a review of Gadamer; the present study strives rather in the first instance to give a further development of the theory of the understanding of texts in order to ground theological text interpretation in an appropriate foundational theory.[2]

The controversy about the methodological implications of a theory of understanding has up to the present failed to encourage a reflective return to the process and actual achievement of the understanding of texts. The controversy has on the contrary distorted such a return. It is our purpose to show here that the transcendental character of hermeneutical reflection not only does not preclude a reflection on method but that on the contrary this transcendental character always simultaneously grounds it and requires it. But how can a general theory of text interpretation be described? I propose to develop such a thory in which interpretation encompasses three dimensions which are to be distinguished but not separated: *understanding, explanation and assessment.* In a responsible interpretation which tries as far as possible to do justice to the text, it cannot be merely a question of an innocent fusion of the horizons of the reader and of the text. Rather, every understanding of the text must be verified in the accompanying explanation of the coherence of the text and of its claim to make sense as Paul Ricoeur has convincingly shown. But the explanation dimension of every text interpretation has not yet taken into account the human responsibility of assessment. The fullness of textual *meaning (Bedeutung)* disclosed in the understanding-explaining process is in continual need of being *assessed (gedeutet werden).* It is in the act of assessing textual sense that every interpretation finds at once its consistence and its vulnerability; the latter invites to new efforts at interpretation and accordingly underlines the in principle open-ended character of every interpretation.

How the interpretation of written linguistic texts — and here we are dealing only with written textuality[3] — how such interpretation discloses sense will be discussed in Chapter II. In this connection it is to be shown that methodical text interpretation, far from diminishing the transcendental status of the theory of interpretation, must actually co-found this status. For it is only a methodological reflection on the textuality of texts which allows us to critically assess the appropriateness of any interpretational theory in relation to its object. Every theory of text understanding must critically scrutinise the text theory which underlies it. It must derive its legitimacy from this; otherwise it is useless. Since we are here endeavouring to achieve an adequate theory of textual understanding of a theological nature, theological texts will constitute the concrete matter under investigation, with the help of which our general text theory is to be illustrated.[4] We shall show furthermore that text and reading stand in a dialectical relationship to each other. Finally, the theory of reading formulated in this chapter points to a dialectic of a threefold structure between text, text genre and text style on the one hand and reading, reading genre and reading style on the other.

This assessment and characterisation of our general theory of interpretation on the basis of its possible methodical contribution lead us in Chapter III of this work to specifically theological texts and theological interpretation theory as such. Text and interpretation emerge as universal thinking categories in which theological thinking is also in principle accomplished.

The programme of this study, which we have just outlined, forces us to delimitations and a certain onesidedness of reflection which require some justification: ultimately I am concerned neither with making a new contribution to the discussion concerning a universal hermeneutics nor with making an unqualified defence of formalistic approaches to the work of theology. Rather should the discussions of hermeneutical thought and formalistic working methods make a contribution to the fundamental improvement of theological thinking. Theological thinking is accomplished not in isolation but in the context of contemporary debates about truth and the knowledge of truth. Martin Heidegger has highlighted the connection between interpretation and truth, between understanding of sense *(Sinn)* and truth.[5] Where is the theological contribution towards the disclosure of truth to be found today? This is a question which we can pose in connection with Heidegger and clarify in dialogue with the methodologies of the other sciences. Then it becomes clear that theology possesses a special affinity on the one hand with the philosophical hermeneutics which had emerged in the Romantic movement from previous theological reflection on the interpretation of biblical texts,[6] and on the other hand with the philological sciences (sciences of literature and language) which concern themselves especially with texts, textuality of texts and reception of texts. Theology must learn from these sciences. But this does not entail either competition or sublation of theological thinking into philosophical and philological thinking. Theological thinking stands rather in a correlative relationship to these lines of thought. Accordingly the work we are engaged in is not in a position either to adequately discuss the problems of other modes of thought or to solve them. Nevertheless it is the aim of our study to make a contribution, a decidedly theological contribution to the discussion regarding a general theory of text and of interpretation.

CHAPTER I

Interpretation as Category of Theological Thinking

1. Introduction

It is the aim of this chapter to outline a general theory of text interpretation which will make it possible to adequately describe the process of theological thinking of a textual nature *(Textdenken)*. First the significance of interpretation for theology will be studied and then an effort will be made, in critical discussion with the philosophical hermeneutics of Hans-Georg Gadamer and with Paul Ricoeur's theory of interpretation, to arrive at an interpretation theory which can be equally accountable both to the text and to the recipient[1] who is postulated by every text. The theory of interpretation which is outlined in this chapter must then in Chapter II be subjected to new scrutiny in the light of the concept of text which is to be discussed in that chapter. Finally in Chapter III our theory must be developed with a view to its significance for responsible application to theological texts. In spite of this division of our work the problem of a specifically theological text interpretation is to be introduced already at the beginning of this first chapter in order that this problem can move in unison with the main thrust of our work not only implicitly but rather in a constant, explicit and exemplary fashion. Finally the question about the aptitude of this theory of interpretation for a comprehensive theory of theology is to be posed even at this early stage.

2. The Fundamental Importance of Interpretation for Theology

Attention was drawn, already in this book's introduction, to the nature of theology as a specifically textual science. This observation must now be clarified.

2 Interpretation and Theological Thinking

The literal meaning of theology is: 'Talking about God'. 'Talking about God', however, is always to be found in its own particular tradition which is mediated by oral and written texts. What theological dictionaries in an effort to define a Christian theology characterise as 'the listening [!] of the believer to the authentic revelation of God's word as it took place in history, the scientifically methodical effort to understand it and the reflective development of the object of such knowledge'[2] implies already a characteristic of textual mediation which, however, must be made explicit. On the basis of certain written canonical texts, the so-called 'word' revelation, theology reflects on the God who is known through such revelation. The historical revelation of God in Jesus Christ has taken on text character to the extent that human beings have linguistically borne witness to it and handed it down. The Christian tradition consists not of words of propositional fragments which have been thrown together at random but rather of several collections of texts and of these the canonical text collections of the Old and New Testaments take precedence. Christians of all generations have disclosed the revelation of God from these texts so that the first task of a reflection on the Christian faith, the first task of Christian theology, must consist in the opening up of its texts in a reflection which looks for possible revelation.[3] And indeed theologians of all generations have repeatedly set about accomplishing this task. Here the decisive question has already been, from which points of view the foundational texts of Christianity are to be approached: do the texts themselves give sufficient clues to their interpretation *(sola scriptura)* or is recourse to some additional instance outside of the texts also necessary which would serve as a key to the meaning of the texts (tradition)?[4] It is in both cases undeniable that the texts constitute the decisive carriers of mediation for the Christian faith.

The texts spur on the faith community which reads them to the disclosure of the truth of faith and the community of readers/hearers must continually ask itself whether it responsibly receives the potential for provocation proper to the texts and if it reflects this in the thought which guides its actions. The indications here outlined are now to be further developed in the next two stages of the development of our thought.

a) Texts as Provocation of Theological Thinking

Not every discourse about God has texts of tradition as its basis. Christian theology continually transcends its textual origins through its production of narrative, speculation and systematisation. But Christian theology which takes seriously its foundation in Jesus Christ through the texts which bear witness to him continually returns to these foundations in order to further develop its thought from this standpoint. Without wishing to discuss at this point already the detailed catalogue of exegetical tasks which confronts us, it is possible even here to formulate two main theses concerning the work of theology: i) formally speaking, theology is challenged by the texts which have been handed down, to the extent that they must be continually seen as worthy of disclosure because of the potential for sense *(Sinn)* which they contain;[5] and ii) the consideration of these original provocations arising from the text must take pride of place in the task of theological self-reflection — that is to say in fundamental theology.[6]

To refuse to consider the primacy of textual understanding would mean to expose oneself right from the beginning to the possibility of denying the importance of that which constitutes the sustaining sources of Christian theological thought, namely the texts. As against this, surely every instance of Christian theological thinking, whether reflected or unreflected, develops its conceptuality through critical consideration of these texts. Theological concepts such as God's Covenant, the Kingdom of God, the Cross, the Resurrection, the Parousia, these are not to be gleaned in their originality apart from their textual appearance in the Bible as everyone would have to admit, even if these concepts can be further developed in areas of thought which go beyond the biblical text.

One must therefore hold on to the insight that Christian theology, in its concrete questioning, receives from texts inspirations for reflective action. In this sense one can agree with Helmut Peukert who sees contemporary theology challenged in the new situation of dialogue 'to give an account of its basic conceptions, i.e. its understanding of reality, and its access to it, as well as of the possibility of speaking intelligibly about it'.[7] Peukert formulates accordingly two theses: he states first of all 'that the Judeo-Christian tradition is concerned with reality experienced in the foundational and limit experiences of communicative action and with the modes of communicative action still possible in response to these experiences'. He states secondly 'that a *fundamental theology* can and must be developed, as a *theory* of this communicative action of approaching death in anamnetic solidarity and of the reality experienced and disclosed in it'.[8] Unfortunately Peukert does not demonstrate in what follows which theory will serve his purpose of securing that the texts bearing testimony to the experience of the reality of God in the Judeo-Christian tradition are adequately interpreted. He intends to preserve his 'proposal of a conception of fundamental theology from hermeneutic näiveté...',[9] and he requires that a fundamental theology should give an account of the way in which theoretical reflection in theology is linked up methodologically to basic communicative actions, or to the foundational actions of subjects themselves'.[10] Peukert does not, however, further consider under which conditions such fundamental communicative actions as text production, text tradition and text reception function and whether or how theological interpretation is distinguished from other types of interpretation. But he does proffer at the end of his otherwise helpful book the observation that

> a fundamental theology which is developed as a theory of communicative action through the paradox of anamnetic solidarity is faced with the task of developing a hermeneutics of the history of religion in connection with a theory of the development of human consciousness and action as a whole.[11]

Peukert's achievement lies then in his insistence upon the fact that theology is to be understood fundamentally as a theory of communicative practice, and his oversight lies in his continuing to withhold from this theory of theology the decisive chapters on text understanding and text interpretation.[12] These chapters must accordingly be supplied by us. Nevertheless, we can see from this first reflection of a 'fundamental theological' nature the manner in which theological and here especially biblical texts are in principle capable of eliciting provocation. Biblical texts challenge their readers to a new reflection on their thought and practice, to renewed conversion. But this connection between text interpretation and reflection on practice requires further analysis of a fundamental nature.

b) The Necessity of a Theological Theory of Interpretation

Texts can only provoke a new reflection on thinking and practice, i.e. conversion, when they are received, that is to say read or heard.[13] The reading of texts is accordingly the process in which a recipient discloses a text under the aspect of its provocation, allows it to achieve expression. This process, the process of reception or reading, is foundational for theology: in the first place theology draws its original dynamic from the disclosure of texts which have been handed down; in the second place the reception of these biblical textual traditions has itself left texts behind it which both bear testimony to the reception of the biblical texts at a particular point in time (historical dimension) and also influence the future acts of reception (effective historical dimension). Theological reception of texts can accordingly only be fully elucidated when on the one hand the process of reception itself is in its structure analysed and disclosed and when on the other hand every process of reception is understood as entangled in effective historical relations. Without such enlightenment of a two dimensional nature, theological text reception would have to remain uncritical and that in turn would signify that theology as a whole would deal with texts on a dubious basis. And as a result it could never move forward to patterns of activity which would be publicly transparent and capable of standing up to critical reflection.

Thus theology requires a theory of interpretation for two reasons: in order to remind itself of its cognitional basis, its dealing with its textual provocations, and in order to supply criteria which make it possible to publicly justify this dealing with texts.

This insight is not new, on the contrary it is as old as the conscious exercise of theology itself. Origen, Irenaeus and Augustine, for instance, have very profoundly reflected on their dealing with biblical texts and have made known their criteria; Luther and the Council of Trent were at pains to lay bare their differing textual understanding; and up to the present day all theologians find themselves challenged to say which criteria guide their dealing with biblical texts and texts of the Christian tradition.¹⁴ The present work finds itself also in this tradition of interpretative self-reflection. It is its aim to study and present the manner in which theological interpretation today can be publicly accountable and what are the consequences of such a theory of interpretation for the self-understanding of theology in general. In so doing this study tries to respond to the urgent plea to the theologian

> to show the appropriateness of his own categories (and, by implication, the categories of the later tradition) to the meanings expressed in that collection of texts called the Hebrew and Christian scriptures. In this case, it becomes imperative for the theologian to seek an adequate method of interpretation for texts.¹⁵

But where is the novelty of this requirement relative to the traditional, historical-critical bible exegesis? The historical-critical exegesis is at pains to determine the genesis of a text, its environment and its *Sitz im Leben* within this environment, its formal structures and sub-structures (literary unity, principles of composition) and sometimes also its first effects, in order in this way to supply critical standards for a later theological interpretation. The following division of labour has developed in theology: the exegetes critically prepare the text from the point of view of form, genre, redaction and context and, thus elaborated, give it over to the systematic and practical theologians who interpret it with a view to the needs of the modern reader, either in liturgical or systematic-theological genres. With this the text specialists feel themselves relieved of the interpretative problem, and the interpreters of the specifically textual problems, and each group feels itself set free for its respective special tasks. Such is the appearance of a typified, simplified model of contemporary theological division of labour.¹⁶ In this manner of proceeding, however, certain text and interpretation dimensions get lost from view and certain textual and interpretational assumptions of a theoretical nature which often run counter to the needs of a complex text reception get silently and implicitly accepted. Thus exegetes work rather linguistically and historically whilst systematic theologians tend to work rather synchronically and speculatively. A text is considered to be understood exegetically when the historical circumstances of its coming to be have been sufficiently clarified and a key has been found to its linguistic competence, and a text is considered to be theologically received when it is sufficiently embedded in a total system of theological assertions. But in this way the basic hermeneutical problem of understanding texts and especially ancient traditional texts today does not receive sufficient attention.[17] The phenomenon of the textuality of texts, i.e. that texts are more than a stringing together of single assertions, is thus not recognised. Essential semantic connections *(Sinnzusammenhänge)* get lost, when primary theological consideration is given to single assertions, bible verses and dogmatic statements instead of textual unities. Furthermore the premise of the task division which restricts responsibility to the language of a text or the interpretation of a text can lead to fundamental interpretational short circuits with devastating effects for the totality of theological thought. Finally the absence of historical-critical discussion of texts, among their interpreters, leads to seductive illusions of perfection in interpretation. These illusions, being by nature exclusive and dogmatic, reject in principle future semantic disclosures of texts.[18]

Even though such hermeneutical problems — they are by no means exhaustively listed here — are also repeatedly recognised by contemporary theological interpreters and even though they have provoked the call for theological interpretation and with this for closer co-operation or personal union of exegesis and theology,[19] nevertheless a 'theological hermeneutics, which relates the proclamation to discourse as a communicative practice and the text of the bible in interpretation to the context of contemporary society is... not really yet in view'.[20] Naturally this holds also for a theological theory of interpretation which aims as well at the interpretation of non-biblical traditional texts of Christianity such as creedal texts, dogmatic texts and liturgical texts.

The novelty of a call for a theological theory of interpretation does not accordingly lie in the endeavour to find new perspectives with the help of which biblical texts are to be interpreted — such as the existential, narrative, rhetoric and transcendental perspectives — but rather in the efforts to reflect on the process and assumptions of theological text interpretation in a *fundamental* manner. In this respect, the significant works on theological hermeneutics which have been produced in the last few decades are not to be overlooked. However, it is our aim in the first place to search for a *universal* theory of the process of interpretation which precedes and grounds them all and which puts us in a position, for the first time, to determine the place and value of *concrete* theological-hermeneutical perspectives — as, for example, those of Bultmann, Barth, Rahner, or Ebeling. In this sense we must distinguish between a theory of interpretation as basic theory on the one hand, and concrete suggestions for specific theological attitudes of reception, on the other hand.

In the following sections of this chapter we shall therefore endeavour to develop a general theory of interpretation of a type which can also function as a basic theory for theological interpretation.

3. Towards a Definition of 'Interpretation' after Hans-Georg Gadamer's Philosophical Hermeneutics

With the appearance of Hans-Georg Gadamer's book, *Truth and Method: Outlines of a Philosophical Hermeneutics* (first German edition, 1960)[21] the discussion concerning the essence and function of hermeneutical experience won and holds to the present day the status of a cardinal point in the self reflection of the human sciences, as is indicated by the ongoing reception and criticism of Gadamer's opus. *Truth and Method,* as well as the shorter writings which followed it, has elevated the hermeneutical problem to the focal point of critical scientific discussion. Whereas hermeneutics in earlier times was understood as the art of theological-exegetical understanding and was later expanded, more especially by Schleiermacher, to a universal theory of understanding, being finally raised by Dilthey to the theoretical position of foundation of the human sciences, hermeneutics matures in Gadamer to the status of a fundamental theory of knowledge which precedes and is universally at work in all methodical efforts to know, whether these are conscious of it or not. In this case Gadamer speaks of the universal aspect of philosophical hermeneutics.[22]

The universal aspect of hermeneutics and the transmethodical,

Towards a Definition of 'Interpretation' 9

apriori cognitional claim connected with it have called forth agreement and sharpest contradiction. We wish to begin our effort at a definition of the concept of 'interpretation' with an analysis of this critical discussion. We first of all introduce Gadamer's concept of the process of understanding and the problems this raises, and then assess his contribution with the help of the philosophical and text critical objections which can be brought against it.

a) Gadamer's Concept of the Process of Understanding

(1) Philosophical Hermeneutics or Hermeneutical Philosophy

Both in *Truth and Method* and in his shorter writings Gadamer strives to show how, of its nature, understanding is always ahead of every type of methodical science; accordingly it resists any attempt 'to change it into a method of science'.[23] He never calls into question, however, the fact that there exist several specific forms of understanding which certainly possess their own methodical character, as for example biblical and philosophical hermeneutics.[24] But what primarily merits Gadamer's attention is the hermeneutical phenomenon as such, that is, the fundamental determination of human hermeneutical experience. Philosophy is the place where such basic or total meaning occurs. 'Philosophy has to do with the whole'.[25] In philosophy the person as thinker renders an account to her/himself of her/his thought; this is an ongoing, openended process. 'In it is realized not only the conversation which each of us conducts with ourselves in thinking but also the conversation in which we are all caught up together *(begriffen)* and never cease to be caught up — whether one says philosophy is dead or not.'[26] Philosophy is best capable of achieving its aim of satisfying 'the exigence of reason for unity' and of fulfilling 'the task of self-understanding on the part of human beings with regard to themselves'[27] to the extent that it reflects on that human experience which is essentially directed at universally shared understanding, that is the hermeneutical experience.

> The hermeneutics that I characterise as philosophic is not introduced as a new procedure of interpretation or explication. Basically it only describes what always happens

wherever an interpretation is convincing and successful. For, understanding is more than the adroit application of a skill [this sentence tr. T.W.]. It always harvests a broadened and deepened self-understanding. But that means hermeneutics is philosophy, and as philosophy it is practical philosophy.[28]

And Gadamer continues:

> Hermeneutics has to do with a theoretical attitude towards the practice of interpretation, the interpretation of texts, but also in relation to the experiences interpreted in them and in our communicatively unfolded orientations in the world.... So it appears to me, heightened theoretic awareness about the experience of understanding and the practice of understanding, like philosophical hermeneutics and one's own self-understanding, are inseparable.[29]

In his hermeneutical reflections Gadamer is concerned to define philosophy as hermeneutical in the age of methodical sciences, as is evidenced by this statement of the goals of his research. By the same token, he aims at overcoming the subjectivism and particularism of a self-consciousness which is so constituted that it seeks domination of the world through technological methodology. Gadamer tries to reflect on the common element which the notion of 'theoria' originally expressed:

> to have been given away to something that in virtue of its overwhelming presence is accessible to all in common and that is distinguished in such a way that in contrast to all other goods it is not diminished by being shared and so is not an object of dispute like all other goods but actually gains through participation.[30]

But these observations of Gadamer already give rise to problems, given his hermenetucial-philosophical approach. His aim is not to propose a method but rather to describe what is the case when understanding takes place.[31] Nevertheless he studies these basic states of affairs in *Truth and Method* guided by the understanding of texts. It is with the help of textual understanding that he carries out his transcendental reflection, derives his theoretical insights.

All of those are reflective acquisitions which emerge from 'praxis' and thrive on nothing other than 'praxis'. As an old philologist, I may be forgiven for having exemplified all of that with the help of 'being-in-relation-to-the-text'. In truth the hermeneutical experience is totally enmeshed in the general nature of human 'praxis' which includes essentially, though in secondary fashion, the understanding of the written word. Hermeneutical experience extends as far as the potentiality for speech of intellectual beings may conceivably reach.[32]

Though wishing to make universal statements about hermeneutical experience Gadamer nevertheless contemplates this experience mostly through the specific area of textual understanding which, however, according to his own observations, constitutes rather the object of specific divisions of hermeneutical methodology, even taking into account the fact that these specialised areas have already become constant partners in dialogue with philosophical hermeneutics.[33] It follows that a reciprocal relationship exists between understanding of texts on the one hand and philosophical hermeneutics on the other. But one might legitimately wish to know more precisely how Gadamer can progress from the model of textual understanding to the universal hermeneutical essence of human praxis. This necessitates in the last analysis a critical reconstruction of his model of textual understanding. But according to Gadamer reconstruction is always of its nature methodical.[34] Thus, serious tensions begin to appear here in Gadamer's method of reflection.

Gadamer's philosophical hermeneutics is then a philosophy which — because it is concerned with understanding which we have in common — is hermeneutical and claims for itself the capacity to make universal statements about all specific attempts at understanding; but these universal statements which are hermeneutical in nature can be effected, as Gadamer asserts, without becoming entangled in concrete methodical discussions about the specific activity of understanding texts. In fact, they are by nature more extensive, since they already ground all efforts at methodological elaboration. But here we must ask ourselves, how such general philosophico-hermeneutical meta-insights can be achieved without reference to hermeneutical practice, taking into account the fact that Gadamer — as quoted above — has expressed himself against such a separation.[35]

With this, we have arrived at a first contextualisation and a preliminary awareness of the problem of Gadamer's hermeneutics. The aim of his reflection is 'to open up cognitional opportunities which would otherwise have remained undisclosed'.[36] This disclosure of cognitional opportunities is opposed to the absolute dominance of methodical self-consciousness[37] though it does not decry the immanent validity of the critical methodology of the sciences as such.[38] Furthermore, Gadamer himself is, as we have seen, forced to rely on methodical thought in order to pursue his own reflective path and to allow it to be subjected to critical reconstruction. We shall have occasion to consider this problem in greater detail.

(2) Understanding as Understanding of Texts

Although Gadamer in *Truth and Method* takes aesthetic experience as starting point for his reflection and occasionally returns to it, nevertheless this experience plays a rather subordinate role in the development of his investigations. 'Aesthetics has to be absorbed into hermeneutics.... understanding must be conceived as part of the process of the coming into being of meaning, in which the significance of all statements — those of art and those of everything else that has been transmitted — is formed and made complete.'[39] Accordingly for Gadamer in the second and third part of his work the study of understanding is practically identical with that of the understanding of texts. Gadamer introduces at first the discussion concerning textual understanding since the Romantic period and then goes on to present us with his outline of a theory of hermeneutical experience[40] which it is now our task to discuss here.

(3) Understanding and Interpretation

'... to understand a text always means to apply it to ourselves and to know that, even if it must always be understood in different ways, it is still the same text presenting itself to us in different ways.'[41] Gadamer essentially sums up his concept of understanding in this sentence: 'understanding' is a matter of the application of a text to ourselves. How does this application take place and what is applied?

Gadamer describes the contribution of understanding as 'a sharing of a common meaning'[42] of a text and as acquisition of 'agreement *in content*'.[43] The reader as the person seeking understanding already posesses anticipations of sense, fore-understandings, prejudices which he brings to bear on the text, which in fact open to him in the first instance the possibility of 'conversation with the text'.[44] Accordingly, Gadamer goes so far as to speak of prejudices as 'preconditions for understanding'. He adds the remark however that one has to distinguish between legitimate and illegitimate prejudices.[45] But how one is to make this distinction is not explained by Gadamer. He is, rather, concerned with the rehabilitation of the notions of 'authority' and 'tradition' in this connection. He points out that authority has no immediate connection whatever with obedience but rather with knowledge and that tradition in fact is 'always a dimension of freedom and of history itself'.[46]

> Even the most genuine and solid tradition does not persist by nature because of the inertia of what once existed. It needs to be affirmed, embraced, cultivated. It is, essentially, preservation such as is active in all historical change. But preservation is an act of reason, though an inconspicious one.[47]

Gadamer studies now, with the classical as exemplar, the dimension of tradition, under the aspect of its hermeneutical energies.

> The classical is that which resists historical criticism because its historical dominion, the binding power of its validity that is preserved and handed down, precedes all historical reflection and continues through it.[48]

All engaged in understanding are thus, according to Gadamer, implicated in a web of traditions and classical authorites which find expression in each of us. Reason requires of those engaged in understanding that they know and acknowledge such traditions and authorities. Summing up, Gadamer expresses himself as follows:

Understanding is not to be thought of so much as an action of subjectivity, but as the placing of oneself within a process of tradition, in which past and present are constantly fused. This is what must be expressed in hermeneutical theory, which is far too dominated by the idea of a process, a method.[49]

But how is this mediation between past and present to be conceived of more precisely?

Linking up with Heidegger, Gadamer stresses that the hermeneutical circle, the circle of understanding the whole and the part, 'is not to be dissolved in perfect understanding but on the contrary, is most fully realised in such understanding'.[50] Again the understanding subject does not contribute 'the interplay of the movement of tradition and the movement of the interpreter'[51] but moves in the common ground, connecting it with tradition, from which it gleans the fore-understandings which activate the dialogue with the text. 'Thus the meaning of the connection with tradition, i.e. the element of tradition in our historical, hermeneutical attitude, is fulfilled in the fact that we share fundamental prejudices with tradition.' And again Gadamer emphasises the fact that the understanding person himself is not in a position, of himself, 'to separate in advance the productive prejudices that make understanding possible from the prejudices that hinder understanding and lead to misunderstandings'. This distinction must take place in understanding itself.[52]

Hence, Gadamer again postpones the information about the manner in which he conceives of the critical distinction between productive and destructive prejudices. He proceeds, rather, at present to discuss the importance of the temporal distance which separates the interpreter of a text from the situation in which the text was produced. He emphasises the semantic autonomy of all texts, from which it follows that the meaning of a text constantly transcends the author and that accordingly, the exhaustion of its true meaning has to be thought of as an openended process.[53] Understanding is therefore to be conceived of not merely as a reproductive, but always as a productive attitude as well'.[54] But, in view of the fact that Gadamer has already repeatedly warned us against treating this productive procedure as a contribution of the interpreter, we are entitled to await with curiosity information as to who in fact is capable of the productive procedure of understanding and as to where the source of this orientation may be found.

Gadamer elevates, finally, the temporal distance to the status of a critical norm which contributes the possibility of 'filtering' the true prejudices from the false ones, which lead to misunderstandings.[55] He thus transfers the responsibility for successful understanding onto the unending process itself of the understanding of sense *(Sinnverstehen)*. Accordingly, his description of what happens in understanding rests from the very beginning on the vague reference to the ongoing process of understanding itself and not on a basis which would stand up to criticism. Understanding, as a moving into the process mediated by tradition and its authority, is then reduced to adherence to a movement which promises to filter itself, without saying in what exactly this sieve consists.

What is now to be said of the productive activity of understanding in this obscure process of understanding?

Understanding comes into action in the first instance through the fact that we are, so to speak, engaged in conversation by the text and that our anticipations of meaning, our prejudices, are challenged to measure themselves against the text and thus become open to question. Gadamer recognises in every suspension of judgement — and especially of prejudices — the structure of a question to the text.[56] However, this question is not to be thought of in an unhistorical fashion, but rather as being itself of its nature the product of history which is effective in it. Therefore Gadamer asks for the recognition of the consciousness of the hermeneutical situation, i.e. of *effective-historical* consciousness.[57] Particularly appropriate in describing the hermeneutical situation is the notion of 'horizon'. 'The horizon is the range of vision that includes everything that can be seen from a particular vantage point.'[58] It is, in the last analysis, this definition which enables Gadamer to conceive of understanding as the fusion of the horizon of the present hermeneutical situation with that of the text to be understood.

In the process of understanding there takes place a real fusion of horizons, which means that as the historical

16 Interpretation and Theological Thinking

horizon is projected, it is simultaneously removed. We described the conscious act of this fusion as the task of the effective-historical consciousness.⁵⁹

Understanding is an 'event' (*Geschehen:* process; tr. T.W.),⁶⁰ it is something which we experience,⁶¹ it is a fusion of horizons. But it is evidently not an action. It is accordingly in the tension-laden meeting of horizons that Gadamer places the productive element of understanding. 'The hermeneutical task consists in not covering up this tension by attempting a naïve assimilation but consciously bringing it out.'⁶² Our question regarding the productive element of understanding has thus confronted us with a further problem of Gadamer's concept of understanding: understanding is a process and not an action of the understanding subject. Understanding happens to us rather than through us.⁶³

There arises immediately out of what has been said the question, how then misunderstandings can occur and why texts, in spite of everything, evidently never cease to be subject to wrong interpretations.

But the confusion increases further, when we develop Gadamer's contradictory concept of 'interpretation'. At first we discover that all reading 'is always a kind of reproduction and interpretation'.⁶⁴ Then we continually notice Gadamer's interchangeable use of the concepts of the 'understanding' and the 'interpreting' subject.⁶⁵ And lastly, we detect a considerable confusion of the concepts 'understanding' and 'interpretation' when Gadamer deals with the hermeneutical problem of application.⁶⁶

Gadamer resumes the old insight, according to which the manner in which understanding is achieved has three dimensions: understanding *(intelligere),* interpretation *(explicare),* and application *(applicare).* These mental refinements, formerly referred to as *'subtilitates'* are now considered by Gadamer to be integral parts of the hermeneutical process.⁶⁷ Accordingly, this concept of 'understanding' reaches its climax in application which concludes the fusion of horizons. Application then is conceived not as an afterthought or contingent element in the phenomenon of understanding but rather as determining it apriori and in its totality. 'The interpreter dealing with a traditional text seeks to apply it to himself.... Rather, the interpreter seeks no more than to understand this universal thing, the text; i.e. to understand what this piece of tradition says, what constitutes the meaning [*Sinn;* tr. T. W.] and importance [*Bedeutung;* tr. T. W.] of the text.'⁶⁸

After these definitions it strikes us as even more surprising when Gadamer suddenly reserves the concept of *interpretation* for those efforts which aim at discovering not only the intended but also the hidden sense of the text. The discipline of history is an example of such endeavours. 'Thus it is a basic principle for the historian that tradition is to be interpreted in another sense than the texts of themselves call for. He will always go back behind them and the meaning [*Sinn;* tr. T. W.] they express to enquire into the reality of which they are the involuntary expression'. And finally: 'The concept of interpretation reaches its fulfilment here. Interpretation is necessary where the meaning [*Sinn;* tr. T. W.] of a text cannot be immediately understood. It is necessary wherever one is not prepared to trust what a phenomenon immediately presents to us'.⁶⁹

This confusion of concepts is all the more surprising when Gadamer now proceeds to restore to its rightful place the 'former unity of the hermeneutical disciplines'. Both philologists and historians achieve an application of textual sense in their hermeneutical situation as this is determined by effective history.⁷⁰ We must conclude from the foregoing that application subsumes every particular interpretation in the process of understanding — so that understanding, interpretation and application are after all seen as identical.⁷¹ Later however they are again to be distinguished ⁷² and in the Epilogue to *Truth and Method* reunited when the task of hermeneutics is seen as that of interpretation of the texts of tradition.⁷³ We are here faced with a problem of some importance: Gadamer appears to wish to designate 'textual understanding' as 'interpretation' at least in those instances where texts are not at once intelligible.⁷⁴ We must ask therefore whether textual understanding is subject to a dynamic different from Gadamer's understanding of tradition. (This develops in such a way as to transcend the understanding subject, and even be independent of it and passive relative to it. The subject is expected to 'place itself' within tradition.)⁷⁵ Is there perhaps a distinction between immediate understanding of tradition and mediate interpretation of texts, through which tradition is mediated? Gadamer does not oblige with an answer and so the basis for reflection is obscured for us and likewise the further development of his transcendental reflection on understanding.

(4) The Essence of Hermeneutical Experience

Effective historical consciousness has for Gadamer the structure of experience.[76] Contrary to Hegel, Gadamer emphasises the fact that the dialectic of experience 'is properly achieved not in a conclusive form of knowledge but rather in that openness to experience, which is set free by experience itself'.[77] The productive significance of negative experiences introduces the person experiencing them to an insight into human finitude. 'Experience properly so-called is accordingly experience of one's own historicity'.[78] This applies in a special way to hermeneutical experience which by nature is conscious of being conditioned by its effective history.

> The hermeneutical experience is concerned with what has been transmitted in tradition. But tradition is not simply a process that we learn to know and to be in command of through experience; it is language, i.e. it expresses itself like a 'Thou'. A 'Thou' is not an object, but stands in a relationship with us.[79]

Accordingly, hermeneutical experience does not encounter an object but rather stands in a relationship to tradition, i.e. to the texts which have been handed down. But how? Acknowledgment of tradition requires a basic openness to it. This openness has the structure of a question. The question accordingly opens up the 'relationship' to tradition which Gadamer understands as 'conversation'. 'To conduct a conversation means to allow oneself to be conducted by the object to which the partners in the conversation are directed'.[80] This conversation that 'we ourselves are'[81] aims at the meaning of the text itself.[82]

The linguistic character of the hermeneutical experience requires further reflection.

(5) The Linguisticality and Universality of Hermeneutical Experience

'Language is the middle ground in which understanding and agreement concerning the object take place between two people'.[83] Gadamer is here again reflecting directly on the understanding of texts. 'The text brings an object into language, but the fact that it achieves this is ultimately the work of the interpreter. Both have a share in it'.[84] 'The achievement of the interpreter' must surely signify here the fact that a text can only find expression through the dialogue which is initiated by the interpreter.[85] In this matter according to Gadamer 'written texts present the real hermeneutical task. Writing involves self-alienation. Its overcoming, the reading of the text, is thus the highest task of understanding'.[86] 'The understanding of something written is not a reproduction of something that is past but rather the sharing of a present meaning [*Sinn,* tr. T.W.]'.[87] Gadamer emphasises the semantic autonomy of the written text which offers, with the unfolding of time, the renewed occasion and the energy for hermeneutical dialogue, in this way repeatedly seeking conversation with a reading partner.[88]

Gadamer investigates in the following development of his reflections the relationship between language and content of the hermeneutical dialogue as well as the disclosure of truth which is connected with such dialogue and comes to the following conclusions: 'Linguistic form and content which has been handed down cannot be separated in the hermeneutical experience.'[89] 'From language's relation to the world there follows its specific factuality. Matters of fact come into language'.[90] He emphasises

> that language has its true being only in conversation, in the exercise of understanding between people.... For language, in its nature is the language of conversation, but it acquires its reality only in the process of communicating. That is why it is not a mere means of communication.[91]

And Gadamer never tires of making the point that language does not signify a process either of putting reality at our disposal or of making it predictable. On the contrary 'it is what exists, what man recognises as existent and significant, that is expressed in it'.[92] And it is at this point that his reflections on language reach their climax: 'It is the centre of language alone that, related

20 *Interpretation and Theological Thinking*

to the totality of beings, mediates the finite, historical nature of man to himself and to the world.'[93] *'Being that can be understood is language'*.[94] As a result of this insight into the linguistic character and intelligibility of man's relationship to the world Gadamer asserts that hermeneutics *'is a universal aspect of philosophy'* and not just [!] the methodological basis of the so-called human sciences'[95] and 'that the hermeneutical experience, as the experience of transmitted meaning, has a share in the *immediacy* which has always distinguished the experience of the beautiful as it has that of all evidence of *truth'*.[96] Thus, research into the process of understanding flows over into the disclosure of truth. Understanding is 'genuine experience, that is encounter with something which asserts itself as truth'.[97]

(6) Truth in Hermeneutical Experience

As far as Gadamer's hermeneutical philosophy is concerned this is the point where its circle is completed: his development of the hermeneutical experience is to show how we as human beings are drawn into 'an event of truth' (i.e. 'a coming to pass of truth' *Wahrheitsgeschehen,* as process, tr. T. W.), in which truth mediates itself, comes to pass.[98]

Gadamer returns here to the concept of play as illustration of the happening in which *sense (Sinn)* or truth 'asserts itself'.[99] At the beginning of *Truth and Method* Gadamer already made explicit the notion of play with the help of the experience of art. Here he held that a play has its own dynamic which transcends[100] the intentions of the participants to such an extent that one can say: 'the players are not the subjects of play; instead play merely reaches presentation though the players'[101] and this happens furthermore through constantly renewed repetition. The play is accomplished through its 'transformation into a structure', indeed the play is structure — that is to say 'it is a meaningful whole which can be repeatedly represented as such and the signficance of which can be understood. But the structure is also play, because — despite this theoretical unity — it achieves its full being only each time it is played'.[102] Thus, for example, the identity of a work of art is continually represented in new forms but it does not lose itself in these presentations; on the contrary it is an identity which is mediated in the renewed temporal interpretations, that is to say in the activity of the hermeneutical experience it is revealed as semantic truth *(Sinnwahrheit)*.[103]

The concept of truth which emerges from Gadamer's reflections may be best characterised as 'revelatory truth'. The play plays the player, that is to say it manifests to him/her his/her otherwise undisclosed *identity*, his/her *meaning (Sinn)*, his/her *truth* in its coming and going.[104] For Gadamer these three concepts, as we have seen, touch on the same phenomenon. To stand consciously in the tradition signifies then to expose oneself consciously to the play which playfully expresses itself to us as truth.[105]

Although the specific constitution of play does not permit 'the player to behave towards the play as if it were an object',[106] we must nevertheless ask ourselves what exactly is being played here, what plays itself out through us, what precisely is this process that playfully releases truth? And who are we, the players? Can we be at ease with Gadamer's observation that: 'in understanding we are drawn into an event of truth and arrive, as it were, too late, if we want to know what we ought to believe'?[107] What corroborates the conviction in us that we are not perhaps manipulated in a playful manner? How do we know whether we are being played with in an authentic rather than in a false manner? Is it really the case that we should treat as truth every insight which imposes itself upon us in the play which constitutes the process of understanding and should we accept it in a spirit of faith? Are the questions addressed to the texts of tradition which impose themselves on us the correct ones and do all texts of tradition really guarantee truth? Is every disclosed textual sense, by the fact of its disclosure alone, guaranteed to be adequate and does every disclosed textual meaning already by that fact uncover truth?

(7) Conclusion

Our presentation of Gadamer's concept of understanding gave rise to questions and developed problems which have to be clarified if the concept of understanding which has just been presented is to make even a partial claim to credibility. For this reason we are resuming our treatment of the questions already posed, and expanding on them through the addition of further

22 Interpretation and Theological Thinking

problematic areas which are significant in the process of handling the line of questioning guiding our research: how can we adequately characterise the interpretation of texts and so come to a responsible concept of interpretation?

b) Critique of Gadamer's Optimistic Concept of Understanding

Gadamer's concept of understanding is based on the belief that understanding, generally speaking, is successful and that we who wish to understand require only to be appropriately open to understanding, so that it can happen to us. This optimistic conception has elicited a lot of criticism. In treating of this criticism however, one must not overlook the fact that essential parts of Gadamer's hermeneutical reflection can certainly be accepted and welcomed. It is, for example, to Gadamer's great credit that he has described understanding as a process experience of the fusion of horizons conditioned by effective historical consciousness.[108] But Gadamer's notion of hermeneutics can only be appropriately appreciated when the problems of this concept are adequately diagnosed, discussed and overcome. The discussion of Gadamer's concept will accompany every stage of this study. Here, however, we must, as a preliminary step, present the points of criticism which we consider essential for our purposes.

(1) The Problem of Language and of Misunderstandings

Gadamer's concept of hermeneutics is optimistic: understanding will always succeed if those trying to understand will only subject themselves to 'the dictate of the text' and remain open to it in a questioning way.[109] This universal aspect of hermeneutics must, however, itself be questioned in the form in which it is presented by Gadamer. It is Jürgen Habermas who has most pointedly formulated such doubt:[110] he welcomes Gadamer's reflective elaboration of hermeneutical self-consciousness and agrees with him in pointing out the dependence of speaking subjects on their language; he calls in question, however, the claim to universality of hermeneutics by analysing the hermeneutical limit experience constituted by the specific case of unintelligible vital expressions. 'Hermeneutical consciousness remains incomplete as long as it has failed to integrate into itself the reflective elaboration of the limit of hermeneutical understanding.'[111] For Habermas such a limit experience is given in the case of pseudo-communication, 'in which a disturbance of communication is not discernible for the participants. In this case it is only somebody coming from outside who notices that one participant misunderstands the other. Pseudo-communication gives rise to a system of misunderstandings which under the misleading appearance created by false consensus fails to be seen through'.[112] In this case Habermas speaks of 'systematically distorted communication'[113] which requires to be clarified through depth hermeneutics. Depth hermeneutics demands 'a systematic fore-understanding, which extends to languages as a whole, whereas on the contrary hermeneutical understanding takes its origin in each case from a traditionally determined fore-understanding which develops and changes within linguistic communication':[114] Hence Habermas requires 'a theory of communicative competence', which would uncover the pre-conditions for communication and for a possible consensus, to the extent that the theory would analyse the forms of linguistic intersubjectivity and the genesis of their deformations.[115]

Habermas reaches the conclusion:

> Even *the implict knowledge of the pre-conditions of systematically distorted communication* which is really presupposed in the usage of communicative competence characteristic depth hermeneutics — even this is sufficient to put in question the *ontological self-understanding of hermeneutics* which Gadamer, following on Heidegger, makes explicit.[116]

It is therefore not the concern of Habermas to reject Gadamer's concept of understanding in its totality. Rather does he wish to contradict its claim to universality and to demand that a hermeneutics which is critically enlightened in its own regard, 'which differentiates between insight and restriction of vision ... should integrate into itself the meta-hermeneutical knowledge about the conditions of possibility of systematically distorted communication'.[117] With this Habermas contradicts especially Gadamer's contention that understanding, of itself so to speak, mediates itself linguistically through the authority of tradition and in this manner plays itself in, in a 'non violent' fashion.[118] Habermas also sees as endangered Gadamer's criterion of truth which governs the prevailing understanding of meaning and he offers the following corrective: 'Truth is that special coercion which leads to unforced universal acknowledgement; this however is connected with an ideal situation of discourse and that means a form of life in which free, uncoerced communication is possible'.[119]

In his response Gadamer refuses to acknowledge the validity of Habermas's criticism.[120] He counters with the remark that his aim was simply to highlight possibilities of knowledge in hermeneutical reflection and not to elaborate a criterion of truth.[121] For him the aim of hermeneutics is simply 'to integrate into the unity of linguistic interpretation of the world that which one encounters as unintelligible or as not universally 'intelligible', or as 'intelligible' only to the initiated'.[122] And he finds it totally unacceptable that Habermas would speak of forced communication even in such cases 'where love, choice of model, respectfulness, stabilise readily accepted superiority and subordination'.[123] He accuses Habermas himself here of dogmatic prejudice 'in relation to what "reason" signifies among ordinary mortals.'[124] Accordingly Gadamer's universal aim is to make understanding possible and even to facilitate opportunities of communication where these are still wanting.[125]

Repudiating Habermas's criticism, Gadamer accuses him of being blind to the claim to reflection of his (Gadamer's) analyses: Habermas would not acknowledge the meaning of application which he, Gadamer, sought to highlight as a structural dimension of all understanding.

> That upon which I have reflected is the mode of procedure of the sciences themselves and how this limits their objectivity. This, one may discover by examining them (it is not something recommended). To acknowledge the productive sense of such limitations, for example in the form of productive prejudices, appears to me to be nothing other than a precept of scientific authenticity for which the philosopher is accountable.[126]

But the problem regarding the manner in which hermeneutical

experience deals with the systematic distortions which threaten it in general and with the danger of false forms of consensus in particular remains unexplained. Gadamer's latest insistence that his concept of understanding as a transcendental and universal reflection is primordial by comparison with all these 'technical' questions[127] is unconvincing. What is more: Habermas has expressed the desirability of an ideologically critical determination of the relationship between language and hermeneutical experience and Gadamer has in the last analysis failed to deliver on this point.[128]

Now Gadamer has — as we have seen — without doubt reflected on the relationship between language and the experience of understanding: *'It is the centre of language,* whence our whole experience of the world, and especially hermeneutical experience unfolds'[129] and *'Being that can be understood is language'.*[130] The reason for this is that 'man's relation to the world is absolutely and fundamentally linguistic and hence intelligible'.[131] Language then for Gadamer is neither a means nor an instrument nor an implement nor a formal force or faculty, 'but rather is the preliminary medium that encompasses all beings insofar as they can be expressed in words,'[132] (The German text does not mention the word 'medium'; tr. T.W.) We encounter the world linguistically and for this reason learning to speak, according to Gadamer, . . . 'does not mean learning to use a preexistent tool for designating a world already somehow familiar to us; it means acquiring a familiarity and acquaintance with the world itself and how it confronts us [is encountered; tr. T. W.].[133]

Gadamer distinguishes three features of the linguistic as such: (1) *'the essential self-forgetfulness that belongs to language* [discourse, *dem Sprechen,* tr. T. W.]'. 'The actual operation of language lets grammar vanish entirely behind what is said in it at any given time.'[134] The German text does not speak of 'grammar', but of language itself (tr. T. W.). (ii) *'The selflessness of language'.* Language is by nature foundational for society which expresses itself in conversation.

> When one enters into dialogue with another person and then is carried along further by the dialogue, it is no longer the will of the individual person, holding itself back or

exposing itself that is determinative. Rather, the law of the subject matter is at issue in the dialogue and elicits statement and counterstatement and in the end plays them into each other.[135]

(iii) *'The universality of language'*. Language is all embracing. 'Hence every dialogue has an inner infinity and no end. One breaks it off... But every such break has an intrinsic relation to the resumption of the dialogue'.[136]

The analysis of the 'middle ground of language' provides for Gadamer the basis of his affirmation of the 'universality of the hermeneutical problem'[137], in other words of the 'universal aspect of hermeneutics'.[138] The recognition of the possible systematic distortions which threaten all potential discourse and the question about possible misunderstanding (which will receive further elaboration below), these elements do not properly justify the calling in question of the universal claim to an understanding of the world but rather the universal claim of Gadamer's description of this phenomenon. We can therefore continue to speak of the universality of the hermeneutical problem but in that case we must always include critique of ideology, the criticism of possibly ideological linguistic usages. Gadamer repeatedly states that such criticism is implied in his concept of understanding. 'Ideological criticism represents only a particular form of hermeneutical reflection, one that seeks to dispel a particular class of prejudice through critique'.[139] And he continues:

> Hermeneutics achieves its actual productivity only when it musters sufficient self-reflection to reflect simultaneously about its own critical endeavours, that is, about its own limitations and the relativity of its own position... In any case, the hermeneutically enlightened consciousness seems to me to establish a higher truth in that it draws itself into its own reflection.[140]

It is surprising how an author who is aiming at clarification of the hermeneutical consciousness fails to take up into this consciousness the possibilities of fundamental distortions of communication. The critique of ideology as demanded by Habermas aims precisely not at 'a particular type of prejudices' but rather in general at those distortions of a language which precede all individual speech acts of that language.

Lastly Gadamer refers to the connection between hermeneutics and rhetoric. Rhetoric is not concerned with manipulation but rather with convincing through arguments, which for Gadamer has nothing in common with arbitrary coercion.

> Even the technical types of formation of public opinion which our industrialised society has developed, always contain at some point or other a dimension of consent. This may be on the part of the consumer who is of course free to withhold it. Or it may be the case — and this is decisive —that it happens through the fact that our mass media are not merely the long arm of a uniform, political will but rather the arena of political exchanges which for their part reflect to some extent the political happenings of society and to some extent determine these.[141]

But precisely this possible and conceivably totalitarian determination of opinion formation is to be illuminated through the very critique of ideology proposed by Habermas. Here Gadamer himself contributes the argument against his optimism in understanding and for the continual necessity of investigating any suspicion of forced consensus.

But how are we to view 'simple' misunderstandings — that is, false interpretations which take place in communication which is not systematically distorted? Is there, according to Gadamer, any possibility at all of a false interpretation?

(2) *The Problem of Inadequate Understanding*

The truth of hermeneutical consciousness is for Gadamer 'the truth of translation'.

> It is higher because it *allows* the foreign to become one's own not by destroying it critically or reproducing it uncritically but by explicating it within one's own horizons with one's own concepts and thus giving it new validity. Translation *allows* what is foreign and what is one's own to merge in a new form by defending the point of the other even if it be opposed to one's own view.[142]

These propositions supply us with a concise definition of that which Gadamer in *Truth and Method* has presented as 'fusion of horizons'. His formulation is also intended here to grasp this understanding as a process: Gadamer speaks of *allowing* the appropriation 'to take place' and of 'giving entry' to the new form.[143] To the extent that this dynamic, which is proper to understanding, is applicable in the form just described, it would naturally constitute a basis for optimism of understanding. For, if in the matter of serious understanding, it is only a question of giving entry to understanding and of allowing it to happen, then there can be no misunderstanding in the proper sense. Understanding would then come about of itself in accordance with the conditions visualised by Gadamer. Either the understanding person opens her/himself to dialogue with the text or does not. That is to say she/he allows understanding to happen or does not. Admittedly understanding is for Gadamer an open-ended process, in which one can participate through one's readiness for conversation. Neither does Gadamer lay claim to definitive understanding. He is concerned with the possibility of getting into the understanding process. But now the question is whether there is such a thing as a false entry into this process, a defective happening of understanding or in Gadamer's words: a coming to consciousness of the wrong energies of understanding, that is to say of those pre-judgments which in consciousness are found adequate but in reality are inadequate.

Heinz Günther Stobbe who has investigated this problem was in a position to show that Gadamer can in no way offer an answer to this question, as a consequence of his particular transcendental-logical approach.

> Hermeneutical reflection can achieve nothing more than to integrate the prejudice *structure* of all understanding into the light of consciousness. The 'adequacy', in other words the truth or falsity of certain empirical prejudices can in no way become a problem for this reflection. It is only in the scientific interpretation of concrete texts that the necessity arises to separate true prejudices from false ones. How this is to come about is not a transcendental-logical but rather a methodo-logical question.[144]

It follows from this that the adequate or inadequate participation of the subject in the process of understanding can only be

Towards a Definition of 'Interpretation' 29

investigated more closely on the level of methodology. Hence Gadamer's philosophical hermeneutics is certainly not in a position to deal with the adequacy of prejudices, a fact which constitutes a fundamental defect for it and calls in question its transcendental and above all its universal significance.

Nevertheless Gadamer always tends to become quite concrete when there is a question of denying the arbitrariness of the interpretation of texts.

> Every assimilation of tradition is historically different: which does not mean that every one represents only an imperfect understanding of it. Rather, every one is the experience of a 'view' of the object itself.

> The paradox that is true of all transmitted material, namely of being one and the same and yet different, proves all interpretation to be, in fact, speculative. Hence hermeneutics has to see through the dogmatism of a 'meaning-in-itself' in just the same way as critical philosophy has seen through the dogmatism of experience.[145]

In what does the experience of the subject matter itself consist, which surely can only receive the concretion in which the sense of a text is understood, individually, in relationship to the understanding ego?[146] Meaning does not exist as 'meaning-in-itself'. At this point Gadamer is in the midst of his elucidation of the method of understanding of meaning as Stobbe rightly remarks and for which he adduces the following quotation from Gadamer:[147]

> A person who is trying to understand a text is always performing an act of projecting. He projects before himself a meaning for the text as a whole as soon as some initial meaning emerges in the text. Again, the latter emerges only because he is reading the text with particular expectations in regard to a certain meaning. The working out of this fore-project, which is constantly revised in terms of what emerges as he penetrates into the meaning, is understanding what is there.[148]

Gadamer attempts therefore to describe how the understanding of a text, as the understanding of sense *(Sinnverstehen)*, unfolds. It is the concern of the understanding person 'to achieve in understanding, an agreement in *content*'[149] and the person is motivated in this direction by the prejudices which have been mediated by effective history to the extent that he/she anticipated meaning, as we have seen above. 'The goal of all communication and understanding is agreement concerning the object. Hence the task of hermeneutics has always been to establish agreement where it had failed to come about or had been disturbed in some way.'[150]

These observations and quotations in relation to Gadamer's concept of understanding do not give a satisfactory answer to our question about the clarification of possible misunderstandings in the process of understanding a text. Gadamer emphasises on the one hand the procedural nature of understanding: it is not at the disposal of the individual understanding. But he emphasises on the other hand the manner in which all understanding is related to the ego. Furthermore he defends himself against the accusation of arbitrariness in the understanding of a text and emphasises the 'matter itself'. But he explains on the other hand that 'the dogmatism of "meaning-in-itself" ' has been unmasked. And finally he affirms the transcendental-logical character of his reflection whilst at the same time descending repeatedly to the level of concrete text interpretation in order to illuminate its method. Hence Stobbe is able to point with justification to the 'transcendental-hermeneutical/methodological ambiguity of his argumentation'.[151]

Gadamer tries to resolve all these inexactitudes in his already mentioned unity of tradition and authority to the extent that in this unity the understanding person becomes the plaything of the process of tradition, which in its handing on mediates itself with an authority that has to be affirmed. In this process of understanding therefore the options are either to participate consciously in it or to descend into unawareness. Conscious participation appears then as follows:

> But a text can begin to speak.... When it does begin to speak, however, it does not simply speak its word, always the same, in lifeless rigidity, but gives ever new answers to the person who questions it and poses new questions to him who answers it. To understand a text is to come to

understand oneself in a kind of dialogue. This contention is confirmed by the fact that the concrete dealing with the text yields understanding only when what is said in the text begins to find expression in the interpreter's own language.[152]

The place in which our question regarding the success or failure of textual understanding might be answered is to be found in the open-ended dialogue with the tradition which mediates itself in texts and their interpretation. It is in this dialogue that the as yet undetermined 'agreement in the matter itself' appears to assert itself.

(3) The Problem of Hermeneutical Conversation

The matter at issue in a text gets expressed in the fusion of the horizons of text and reader as a shared reality and this is achieved in the form of conversation.[153] 'The conversation with the text' functions for Gadamer as something he can use to undermine the claim, made by the monological statements of the sciences, to be able adequately to explain the world. This conversation with the text functions accordingly as 'a critique of the speechlessness which threatens mankind to the extent that man cannot understand himself in the monological language systems of science and therefore of necessity loses his identity.'[154] It is then the function of conversation to develop a communicative form of speech in which we can learn better to understand ourselves. 'Self-understanding is always on-the-way, it is on a path whose completion is a clear impossibility.'[155] The conversation of humankind with its tradition is for Gadamer the inexhaustible source of new instances of self-understanding.

But is it possible in this connection to speak at all of 'conversation' in a meaningful way? Gadamer describes — as we have seen — the contribution of understanding as that process which is precisely not a contribution of the understanding person but which requires only his/her 'joining in the play'. This process, however, must always subordinate itself to the text. 'The matter itself which is at issue — the meaning of the text'[156] comes into its own to the extent that it penetrates the consciousness of the individual engaged in understanding by scaling the ladder of critical exchange with his/her prejudices.

What is the object of this dialogue? Certainly not the text,[157] since this is the conversation partner of the understanding person. Rather is the object of this conversation the interpretation of the text in relation to the situation of the understanding person. It is accordingly that which Gadamer has described as the fusion of horizons. This in turn means that the question regarding adequate understanding of the text is one which for Gadamer cannot be posed. The reason is that as long as the fusion of horizons — that is to say, the conversation — proceeds, in other words as long as interpretations take place (fusions of horizons) the conversation is justified. The conversation is therefore self-justifying.[158]

Wolfhart Pannenberg has elaborated this weak point in Gadamer's presentation with particular clarity and from it has drawn the conclusion that 'this exclusion of the constitutive significance of the objectifying function of the statement for the objectivity of language' makes possible in the first place Gadamer's dichotomy between hermeneutical experience and '"methodical" procedures of natural science which operate with statements'.[159]

It follows that these critical questionings of Gadamer's concept of understanding lead us back to his polemic against the methodical knowledge to which he opposes the understanding that is characteristic of discourse. It is true that he later admits the polemical acuteness of this tension between truth and method. Nevertheless he justifies it again by pointing to the 'warped' reflective self-consciousness of the methodical sciences.[160] To the fight against this self-consciousness (the absolute aspect of which is certainly warped) he sacrifices all methodical thinking and 'creates' conversation as the only transmethodical, apriori and self-justificatory form of the discovery of truth, in the achievement of which, truth is to be thought of not as constant but rather as always capable of being experienced anew. As against this, the ideal of knowledge which is determined by the concept of method consists in the following:

> that we measure out a path of knowledge with such deliberation that it is always possible to retraverse it. The meaning of *methodus* is the path of repeatable traversals. The possibility of repeated traversal of the path already

walked, it is this which constitutes the methodical and characterises the procedure of science. But with this very concept a necessary restriction has taken place of that which can emerge as in any way laying claim to truth. When verifiability in any form whatever constitutes the primary characteristic of truth *(veritas)* then it follows that the standard of measurement for determining knowledge is no longer truth but rather certainty.[161]

But this very conclusion is by no means intelligible.[162] In the first place it is not verifiability which 'constitutes the truth', in other words brings it forth. Rather does verifiability guarantee the truth disclosed in the process of understanding against possible apriori distortions or de facto errors. And finally: is there any way, other than by pointing out the path which has led to the knowledge of this truth, in which the interpreter of the text can convincingly communicate the disclosed truth and subject it to critical discussion? Gadamer himself continually brings into relief stages of this journey when he highlights semantic understanding *(Sinnverstehen)* as locus of the knowledge of truth. Granted, he calls this highlighting a process of bringing to consciousness that which already of its nature happens. But are we not compelled in reading Gadamer's work to follow this path of discovery and in doing so subject it to critical review if we wish to come with him to a critical insight into the matter at issue? From this point of view it is nothing short of paradoxical to say that 'conversation' and 'methodus' must be mutually exclusive. The only conceivable case in which this exclusion would have to take place would be when the dialectical dynamic between text and interpreter is to remain uncritical.

Gadamer writes in his preface to *Truth and Method* that it is not the purpose of his investigations 'to offer a general theory of interpretation and a differential account of its methods' but 'to discover what is common to all modes of understanding and to show that understanding is never subjective behaviour towards a given 'object', but towards its effective history — the history of its influence; in other words, understanding belongs to the being of that which is understood'.[163] It has, however, now emerged that this element, common to all modes of understanding but illustrated with the help of the concrete example of textual understanding, has no choice but to be open to such methodological criticism as arises from this sort of procedure. It is by no means necessary that such criticism should be devastating. On the contrary it must endeavour, in a constructive manner, to achieve insights into the ontological characteristics of hermeneutical conversation and to eliminate from them certain all too pointed considerations of an anti-methodical nature.[164] It may well turn out that Gadamer's concept, once it has been deprived of its claim to universality and reconstructed in a manifestly text critical manner, is in a strong position to make a cognitive claim that can offer the beginnings of a foundation of a universal theory of understanding, at least of texts and works of art. In this study we wish, therefore, to go a little beyond Gadamer in order to come back to him later in a critically constructive manner.

But before we do this we must take account of the extent to which our critical analysis of Gadamer's concept of understanding has advanced our project.

(4) Conclusion and Further Delineation of the Task

Gadamer's description of the manner in which understanding is achieved remains patchy and problematic. Especially disastrous, as has been shown, is the absence of a critical concept of the achievement of understanding itself which would accompany this process, and the absence of a criticism of the contents which are brought to light in it. The activity of the person understanding is confined, according to Gadamer, to affirming the concepts which are to be understood. Thus tradition asserts itself with an uncritical authority. Gadamer's restoration to fame of 'authority' cannot escape the ambiguity which inheres in every concept, even in such concepts as 'understanding', 'tradition' and 'conversation'. It is not a question, however, of denying this ambiguity but rather of accepting it and meeting it with criticism. It goes without saying that every criticism is itself subject to ambiguity. For this reason we must discover ways to accept the basic ambiguity of our acts of reflection and communication in order to achieve insight into this ambiguity and to encounter it critically in the openended process of understanding. Such a critical exchange with the form

Towards a Definition of 'Interpretation' 35

and content of tradition implies decisions from the understanding person which turn him/her into an active — and at the same time fallible — co-operator in the process of the understanding of texts. In order to achieve intelligent results from understanding, that is to say results for which one can take responsibility, nothing short of endless criticism is necessary in countering this fallibility. Therefore it is not sufficient then to point out that understanding is always propelled by prejudices. Rather must it be possible in principle that these prejudices and the various stages of their development in the understanding process, not excluding the ever present pregrasp of interpretative results, be made transparent and thematised for discussion. This holds naturally, even more so, for such textual understanding as constitutes the foundation for the activity of communities, instanced in the case of Christianity by the interpretation of the Bible and of tradition.

Every case of textual understanding which lays claim to public validity must be revisable and surely that also means verifiable. There is therefore constant need of a methodical component. It is not the function of this methodical component to produce truth but to secure critically the process of its disclosure.

It is, however, not only the understanding of the texts themselves but the communicative conditions of such understanding which require to be as far as possible, made transparent. Here it is not a question, as Gadamer fears, of the ideal of 'a completed Enlightenment'[165] but rather of reflection — and following that, a change of distorted praxis. Gadamer is correct when he states relative to Habermas' criticism:

> ... the work of ideology critique has a dialectical structure. It is related to determinate social conditions upon which it has corrective and dismantling effects. It belongs itself then to the social process which it criticises. That is its ineluctible presupposition that cannot be replaced by any scientific pretension.[166]

But it must be allowed then to become effective on this basis.

Claus von Bormann has treated Gadamer's general depreciation of the Englightenment as responsible for the absence of criticism in his concept of understanding. This depreciation of the Englightenment is according to him 'responsible for the fact that the significance of criticism has no place in Gadamer and, with this, science is also excluded. Science, though not the element out of which we live, is nevertheless an element without which life is impossible.' In the seventeenth and eighteenth centuries, 'it is the aim of criticism not to produce truth — at any rate not in all forms of the Enlightenment — rather does it understand itself as critical substantiation of truth possessed beforehand on the basis of common sense'.[167]

Gadamer has succeeded in making understanding recognisable as a significant process and as the aim of human self-perception. Understanding requires however, as we have seen, methods of critical revision and critical — by implication also fallible — decisions on the semantic grasp *(Sinnverstehen)* achieved of the contents of tradition in general and of texts in particular.[168] It must accordingly be our task to supply the 'understanding' presented by Gadamer with the dimensions which should critically accompany it and make it responsible. For this purpose it is appropriate to look for a concept which encompasses all the dimensions of this critical-responsible understanding. I suggest that we choose the word 'interpretation' for this notion. This concept has already been used in a comprehensive sense by Martin Heidegger: as the interpretation of *Dasein*.[169] Certainly even this Latin concept of *'inperpretatio'*, which corresponds with the Greek concept of *'hermenaea'*, is loaded and vague. But precisely because of its methodical implications, which have also been recognised by Gadamer, this concept seems to me to be more appropriate than that of 'understanding'. Interpretation encompasses understanding and its methodical revisions. Accordingly the concept of interpretation — in Gadamer's sense also — does not represent a falling back into an objectivist methodologism but rather encompasses the openended process of understanding together with its methodical and, by the same token, finite, efforts at achieving certitude. This concept also solves the confusions in Gadamer's conceptual usage between understanding and interpretation to the extent that it includes and orders methodical and trans-methodical, that is to say transcendental-reflective, thinking. Finally the concept of interpretation leads us back more modestly to hermeneutical praxis before it proceeds to make universal statements on the basis of such praxis.[170]

In hermeneutical praxis, however, the concept of interpretation is only appropriately and responsibly used when it has been elaborated dialectically for, and with the help of, its respective object. Not the least of the elements responsible for Gadamer's defective concept was the unexplained tension between universal theory and the object of particular interpretation.

We elaborate our concept of interpretation with the help of texts which have been fixed through writing and handed on in tradition. These texts at first 'confront' interpretation and require to be assimilated. Every reflection on the process of appropriation which does not thoroughly see through the object to be appropriated, in other words the text, and which does not also consider this object in the structural aspects of its assimilation requirements must of necessity remain incomplete and inappropriate.

For this reason it is our purpose in the first place to devote our attention to extending the concept of interpretation in order that we may then be in a position to measure this enlarged concept of interpretation against its object, that is to say the text.

4. Further Precision in the Elaboration of the Concept of 'Interpretation' through Paul Ricoeur's Theory of Interpretation

At this point in our reflection on the notion of 'text' and 'interpretation' we have reason to expect help from Paul Ricoeur:
i) Ricoeur strives like Gadamer to reflect upon the foundations of philosophical hermeneutics but he is at variance with Gadamer to the extent that his first concern is not to develop a hermeneutical ontology. On the contrary Ricoeur begins with the hermeneutical elaboration of our linguistic existence. This means that Ricoeur's starting point is both more modest and more realistic than Gadamer's; more modest because he does not start with the enormous project of fundamental hermeneutics but rather with a hermeneutics of the 'I am', and for this reason also more realistic, because it is possible for him to work forward gradually to universal questioning rather than being faced with the task of deriving regional from universal hermeneutics. This as we have seen in Gadamer must lead to all kinds of short circuits.[171]
ii) Ricoeur increasingly works towards an elaboration of the

notion of the text, something which Gadamer has not achieved up to the present. iii) Text and interpretation represent for Ricoeur an inseparable relationship which cannot be conceived of — as in the case of Gadamer — as simply an entering into the process of tradition but rather calls for a methodical elaboration which can responsibly subject itself to public criticism. iv) Ricoeur is therefore not obliged to concern himself with 'truth *or* method' but rather elaborates 'understanding *and* explanation' as steps of the hermeneutical arch which advance philosophical reflection, critically and self-critically.

To what extent Ricoeur's theory of interpretation moves in the direction of the solution of our task or whether it rather leads us to new complexes of problems which must be critically confronted by any theological theory of interpretation, will be considered in the following analysis.

It is, however, appropriate to remark already at this point that it is not the intention of our analysis to offer a complete presentation of Ricoeur's hermeneutical theory, far less of his overall philosophical approach. Here we are confined to investigating Ricoeur's contribution to a more precise concept of interpretation.

a) The Contours of a Theory of Interpretation in Ricoeur

Ricoeur's theory of interpretation is still in process of being developed. The theory is to be gleaned from an abundance of essays which have not as yet led to a complete presentation.[172] For this reason our present effort is confined to delineating the contours of such a theory with the help of some of Ricoeur's important essays.

(1) *Hermeneutics as the Path of a Philosophy of Reflection*

Reflection is the locus of hermeneutics in the process of Ricoeur's philosophy. It is not the concern of this reflection to justify science and duty but rather 'to re-appropriate our effort to exist'. Reflection accordingly is a task: 'We have to recover the act of existing, the positing of the self in all the density of its works.'[173] Ricoeur sums up, by way of definition, that the reflection is not intuition but rather

> ...*the appropriation of our effort to exist and of our desire to be, through the works which bear witness to that effort and that desire.* That is why reflection is more than a mere critique of knowledge and even more than a mere critique of moral judgment; prior to every critique of judgment it reflects upon the act of existing that we deploy in effort and desire.

And for this reason reflection must develop into interpretation

> ...because I cannot grasp the act of existing except in signs scattered in the world. That is why a reflective philosophy must include the results, methods and presuppositions of all the sciences that try to decipher and interpret the signs of man.[174]

As a consequence reflection is accomplished as interpretation of the signs through which man mediates himself to himself. 'Every hermeneutics is thus, explicitly or implicitly, self-understanding by means of understanding others.'[175]

'I am, I think', these are the acts of positing the self and as such the beginning of philosophy.[176] These acts of positing bring ambivalence into philosophical reflection, however, right from the start, both because it is only in adopting the detour of understanding the other that one can become conscious of oneself, and also because distorted interpretations can creep in as a result of this detour. Reflection is language and has a detour leading through language. But language lacks univocity. The apories of interpretations are therefore also the apories of reflection.[177]

Ricoeur concentrates at the beginning of his hermeneutical studies especially on symbols as primordial signs of mankind which mediate man to himself.

> The man who speaks in symbols is first of all a narrator; he transmits an abundance of meaning over which he has little command. This abundance, this density of manifold meaning, is what gives him food for thought and solicits his understanding; interpretation consists less in suppressing ambiguity than in understanding it and in explicating its richness.[178]

40 *Interpretation and Theological Thinking*

'In order to become concrete, i.e. equal to its richest contents, the reflection must become hermeneutic: but there exists no general hermeneutics.' Hermeneutics is, rather, a 'rough' discipline in which an understanding of concrete signs has to be fought for;[179] not, however, with the weapon of polemic but rather with convincing arguments, to be considered now.

But before proceeding, the locus of hermeneutics according to Ricoeur can be made more precise and more clearly defined than it is with Gadamer.

Ricoeur must then reject the formulation of an ontology of understanding in advance because he has decided in favour of the long, indirect and gradated path of knowledge. Heidegger suggested a short cut to the extent that he advised recognition of the primacy of ontological understanding and subordination of historical knowledge to this primacy. According to Ricoeur, Heidegger gives us not the least concrete indication as to the manner in which pure historical understanding is to be derived from this primordial understanding, so that one is forced to ask: 'Is it not better then to begin with the derived forms of understanding and to show in them the signs of their derivation?'[180] Ricoeur starts out on this long journey through the world of symbols and myths.[181] Ontology is, on this journey, nothing more than *'ontologie brisée'*,[182] in other words 'the promised land for a philosophy that begins with language and with reflection; but, like Moses, the speaking and reflecting subject can only glimpse this land before dying.'[183] Ontology, then, for Ricoeur is more in the nature of a leading idea. His position is therefore essentially different from Gadamer's *claim* to a 'hermeneutical ontology'[184] even though common elements as regards the *matter at issue* are by no means absent, as should become evident in what follows.

(2) Symbols, Metaphors, Texts: Language and Interpretation

Symbols. Ricoeur began his path of reflection through the linguistic signs with the symbol. This starting point is by no means accidental for the philosopher Paul Ricoeur but, rather, a necessity. Ricoeur calls it an illusion to seek for a presuppositionless starting point for a philosophy. There is no such thing as a philosophy without presuppositions; a meditation on symbols on the other hand '... starts from speech that has already taken place, and in which everything has already been said in some fashion; it wishes to be thought with its presuppositions. For it, the first task is not to begin, but from the midst of speech, to remember; to remember with a view to beginning.'[185]

By having recourse to the symbol, Ricoeur is at the same time paying tribute to language — more precisely, to the abundance of meaning in language which requires to be decoded. The symbols give the promise of addressing present-day humankind in a new light; this is particularly true in a time of rational thinking, of structuralist coercion into systems and of instrumentalising prescripts. That is expressed by Ricoeur in the following manner. 'The symbol gives rise to thought.'[186] More precisely the symbol calls for interpretation. That is the case not just at the present moment; symbols by their very structure require to be interpreted. This requirement is not to be supplied in an uncritical manner. But neither is it permissible for the criticism to reduce the stature of the symbol. That means for Ricoeur that a critical exposure to the symbol, a second naïvety, must follow on the first naïvety, consisting of immediate exposure to the symbol. In other words this insight entails that we are to think no longer *in* symbols but *with* symbols as starting-point. And taking symbols as starting-point he wishes to elaborate existential concepts. This means furthermore that Ricoeur, conscious of the contingency of the culture in question, which is the source and origin of his reflection, prescribes reflection on this very contingency.[187] The starting-point of such hermeneutical reflection excludes again in the most rigorous manner a universal hermeneutics of an idealistic type which would serve as the basis for conclusions leading back to symbolic interpretation.

'Having recourse to symbols' in philosophy[188] has now, as a matter of fact, something scandalous about it because such a procedure undermines from the outset every effort at achieving univocity as an end product in philosophy and with it all 'objective truth'. For that which characterises the symbol is precisely its ambivalence. *'I define "symbol" as any structure of signification in which a direct, primary and literal meaning designates, in addition, another meaning which is indirect, secondary and figurative and which can be apprehended only through the first'.*[189] That means there is at work in the symbol an overflow of meaning, a surplus of semantic content, in excess of that suggested by the first and literal sense. It is no accident that this ambivalence attaches to the symbol. Rather is the double meaning constitutive for it, 'inasmuch as the analogous sense, the existential sense, is given only in and through the literal sense'.[190] This ambivalence of symbolic language is now transferred into philosophy and imposes on it the burden of not only taking on the conflict of hermeneutical systems within reflection but even of justifying this conflict.[191] So the interpretation of symbols for Ricoeur is not only the beginning of philosophical reflection but also the fundamental proof of its identity as hermeneutics.

Ricoeur, however, does not remain at the stage of interpretation of symbols to which he devoted a large place in his thinking, but broadens the scope of his thought to extend to ambivalence as an essential characteristic of language and to the surplus of meaning contained in linguistic products.[192]

Metaphors. Ricoeur diagnoses a general symbolic function of language: symbolism 'now appears to us to be a meaning effect, observable on the level of discourse, but constructed on the base of a more elementary function of signs.'[193] He has in mind the process of polysemy. This is capable of being described on two levels: on the level of synchrony: words have manifold meanings, and on the level of diachrony: the plurality of meaning is the result of transference of meaning. Both descriptions taken together lead to the lexical designation of a word in any particular case.[194]

With these observations the fullness of meaning of a word in usage is not as yet adequately characterised. It is only the text (Ricoeur speaks frequently of the 'context') which decides the question as to the fullness of meaning of its words. This happens more precisely in the interplay of combination and selection which will be gone into in greater detail below.[195] Ricoeur summarises this as follows:

> The simplest message conveyed by the means of natural language has to be interpreted because all the words are polysemic and take their actual meaning from the connection with a given context and a given audience against the background of a given situation. Interpretation in this broad sense is a process by which we use all the

available contextual determinants to grasp the actual meaning of a given message in a given situation.[196]

How a creative linguistic process can develop out of polysemy becomes evident for Ricoeur, principally and in a manner which is really archetypal, by means of the example of metaphor.[197] Contrary to the custom of ancient rhetoric which used to describe the metaphor with the help of a theory of substitution, Ricoeur wishes to point out that the dynamic of metaphor consists in the fact that it confuses the traditional logical boundaries in order to thus give expression to new similarities which up to then remained unnoted.[198] The life of the metaphor is therefore constituted by the new referential corrections which it produces. But as soon as these new referential corrections become conventional we begin to speak of a 'dead metaphor'.[199]

Ricoeur devotes several studies to the creative function of metaphors and these studies cannot be reported here in detail.[200] It is important however to highlight Ricoeur's insight that metaphor not only explodes prevalent linguistic structures but also conventional 'realities'.[201] This explosion of reality, as Ricoeur could point out, is not, however, accomplished on the level of words but on the level of sentences and of texts: 'a word receives a metaphorical meaning in specific contexts within which they are opposed to other words taken literally.'[202]

Ricoeur characterises metaphors, with Monroe Beardsley, as 'metaphorical twist', and with Gilbert Ryle as 'category mistake'.[203]

> It is in effect, a calculated error, which brings together things that do not go together and by means of this apparent misunderstanding it causes a new, hitherto unnoticed, relation of meaning to spring up between the terms that previous systems of classification had ignored or not allowed.[204]

Hence the study of metaphors leads to two fundamental insights into the human exercise of language: i) the exercise of language is an internal semantic process in which new meanings can be created, and, at the same time, an outwards directed referential process in which our linguistically mediated experiences of reality can be changed; ii) the level of this creative exercise of language is not the word but the text, or the sentences as building material.

Symbols and metaphors[205] require interpretation, they constitute accordingly the stages of Ricoeur's path towards a theory of interpretation. They are not however units of the abstract store of words of the language or of the linguistic system, but they function on the level of discourse, whose linguistic form is the text.

Texts. With this Ricoeur's reflection has reached the level of the text. One can point to a veritably 'increasing significance and centrality of the text in his reflection'.[206] His path of thought might be seen as leading on from interpretaton and appreciation of the individual exercises of linguistic creativity to a general reflection on language as text. Accordingly Ricoeur formulates his thinking:

> ... there are problems of interpretation because there are *texts, written* texts, the autonomy of which (as regards either the intention of the author, or the situation of the work, or the destination to privileged readers) creates specific problems; these problems are usually solved in spoken language by the kind of exchange or intercourse which we call dialogue or conversation. With the written texts, the discourse must speak by itself.[207]

In what follows we wish to consider Ricoeur's theory of *text* interpretation, to analyse and criticise it, without, however, losing sight of its philosophical implications.

(3) *The Autonomy of the Text: Distanciation as a Prerequisite for Appropriation*

Ricoeur's reflection on the relationship between distanciation and appropriation of a text may best be understood from his criticism of Gadamer's concept of the opposition between alienated distance on the one hand and participation on the other.

Gadamer aims at overcoming what he experiences as unsalutary distance from the object of understanding, through a participation in the object of tradition, which is 'effective historically' founded. In this manner he hopes to eliminate all objectivism characteristic of the natural sciences and to restore to the understanding subject the participation in the process of tradition which had thus been alienated. Here, however, as we have already seen above, the question arises as to how it is still possible in this concept of participation to articulate a critique of the object and of 'the process of entering into' this object.[208]

Ricoeur escapes this dilemma, refusing to underrate the distance from the process of transmission — indeed he actually appreciates it as the critical space in which the process of interpretation can be achieved but even goes so far as to uncover in Gadamer's own concept a twofold implicit dynamic of distanciation:

> ... in spite of the general opposition between belonging and alienating distance, the consciousness of effective history contains itself an element of *distance*. The history of effects is precisely what occurs under the condition of historical distance. It is the nearness of the remote; or to say the same thing in other words, it is efficacy at a distance. There is thus a paradox of otherness, a tension between proximity and distance, which is essential to historical consciousness.[209]

And furthermore Ricoeur discovers in Gadamer's concept of the fusion of horizons a dialectic between participation and distanciation, to the extent that this fusion actually receives its dynamic from the mutual assimilation of the distanced horizons.[210]

In order however to be in a position to further penetrate Ricoeur's constructive criticism of Gadamer, we must first of all analyse his concept of constructive distanciation as it is developed especially in his essay 'The Hermeneutical Function of Distanciation'.[211]

Spoken language receives life from the direct immediate exchange of meanings, the ambiguity of which can be relieved through gesticulation and further precision. This possibility of correction is on the other hand absent from language as written. There are three ways in which a written text, as distinct from the spoken one of oral communication, can be characterised as autonomous: writing confers on it a distance from its author, from the original situation of the discourse and from its original addressees. The written text is in principle accessible to every reader who has at his/her disposal the decoding knowledge postulated by the text.[212]

Ricoeur designates such a text as a 'work', in order to highlight that we are dealing here with something more than a mere series of words or sentences.[213] A text is rather in the nature of a composition produced by a conventional and an individual dimension: genre and style respectively. Such a textual production must be understood as a process of distanciation and decontextualisation from which results textual autonomy, making the text susceptible to future appropriations. It is this productive threefold distanciation of the text which makes possible in the first place its universal reception.[214]

In order to draw out the whole richness of these insights we must take a look at the theory of text sense *(Textsinn)* and text meaning *(Textbedeutung)*. This is fundamental for the appropriation of texts which have been distanced in the manner described. It is only then that we shall be in a position to appreciate Ricoeur's theory of interpretation as a whole, to expose its differences from Gadamer's concept of understanding and to express our own critical reflections and suggestions.

(4) The Conflict of Interpretation: Sense and Reference

'Distanciation is one of the constitutive elements of the text as such and it insures that the text requires interpretation.'[215] This summary marks the stage at which Ricoeur's theory of interpretation must confront the conflict of competing theories of interpretation.

Ricoeur has repeatedly given his attention to the spectrum of contemporary interpretation theories and in doing so has tested especially that of Sigmund Freud, as also the theories of Western and Eastern European structuralism, with a view to discovering their constructive suggestions.[216] Here we shall concentrate on the last mentioned debate because in it Ricoeur's linguistic philosophy achieves its own contours, which from now on guide his reflections on text interpretation as philosophical praxis.

Ricoeur does not introduce the debate with structuralism in the frame of mind of one who wishes to emerge as winner. It is rather his intention to integrate certain insights of structuralism, joining them up with his own existential reflection. At the same time he does wish to point out the limits of structuralist thinking.[217]

He begins by considering the 'system' characteristics which take their inspiration from de Saussure. Language is analysed synchronically as a system of signs, whereas diachronically one is interested only in the comparison of later and earlier conditions of the system.[218] The claim is made here that one can arrive at objective knowledge about language independently of the observer and finally, in cases where structuralism behaves like philosophy, that it is possible to push forward to philosophical insights into life in general, in other words to project a universal model of rationality. In such 'system-thinking' there are no absolute points of reference but only relationships of mutual dependence.

> By reason of the definitive nature of the world of signs, the sign itself constitutes nothing other than a difference between the signs and a difference between expression and content which is immanent in every single sign. This double-edged reality remains intact in the realm of the exercise of language.[219]

Structuralist linguistics has accordingly got itself its autonomous object and acquired for itself a 'scientific' gloss but the price is great: such a linguistics considers language only under the aspect of possibility *(langue)* and excludes language as reality, as event *(parole)*. 'In excluding the act of speaking, not only are its external accomplishment and individual contribution excluded but also the free combination, the production of still unknown assertions. But it is precisely here that the essential characteristics of language, its essential determination, lies.'[220] Furthermore, structuralist 'system thinking' excludes history, as well as the primary intention of language which is only to be understood from the standpoint of history, namely to say something about something, i.e. not only to create *possible* but also to mediate *real* meanings *(Bedeutungen)*. 'For us as speakers language is not an object but rather a process of communication; language is that through which and with the help of which we express ourselves and enable things to be expressed.'[221] Language does this not on the level of words, which are the preferred object of structuralist 'system thinking' but rather on the level of discourse. Changing from the level of *langue* to that of *parole* entails at the same time a change from *structure* to *fonction* of speaking, in other words from syntactics (joining together of words) to semantics (the meaning *(Bedeutung)* of statements).[222]

It is on the level of the sentence, and more properly on that of the text, that the statement generally begins.[223] Ricoeur seeks, with the help of Gottlob Frege's terminology[224] to grasp the transcendence of the sign as it assumes the function of bearer of communication of meaning *(Bedeutung)* i.e. the explosion of the system in favour of the historical event. Accordingly 'sense' *(Sinn)* for Ricoeur signifies the ideality of sense; and 'meaning' *(Bedeutung)* the relatedness, the *référence* of the statement to the total concrete reality. And finally the reflection on the notion of *parole* reveals the act-character of language. This reflection reveals also the presence of an option regarding possible meaning *(Bedeutung)* and the new combinations which result from this option. These together with *référence* refer also to the subject who expresses the *parole*.[225]

In language as written the reference of a text is freed in a threefold manner as described avove: the relatedness of a text is now independent of the author who has expressed it, independent also of the possible context in which the text was produced and of the circle of addresses to whom it may have been aimed. It is only in the act of reading that the relatedness of the text is re-created and this happens by and with reference to the reader and his/her world horizons. Thus Ricoeur can summarise as follows: 'reading is the *pharmakon*, the "remedy," by which the meaning of the text is "rescued" from the estrangement of distanciation and put in a new proximity, a proximity which suppresses and preserves the cultural distance and includes the otherness within the ownness.'[226] In the act of reading then, the distanciation of the text is not negated but rather acknowledged and made fruitful to the extent that the text now receives new references to a new world, namely that of the reader.

And here logically the hermeneutical arc of Ricoeur's philosophy of reflection returns to the reflecting subject. It is in this way that the text becomes 'mediation by which we understand ourselves'.[227] The text opens to the reader a new world, a new 'mode-of-being-in-the-world' which changes him/her the reader:

If the reference of the text is the project of a world, then it is not the reader who primarily projects himself. The reader rather is enlarged in his capacity of self-projection by receiving a new mode of being from the text itself.[228]

Having now reflected on the hermeneutical function of the distanciation of written texts, on the dynamic of their appropriation and its aims in the heightened self-understanding of the reflecting person, we are compelled to face the urgent question, how such appropriation proceeds and in what finally lie the advantages of Ricoeur's model of interpretation as against Gadamer's concept of understanding, taking into consideration Ricoeur's intention to learn from the structuralist 'system thinking' once it has been confined within its proper boundaries.

(5) *Appropriation: Understanding and Explanation*

Ricoeur opposes a dialectic of understanding and explanation to Dilthey's dichotomy of the natural sciences that explain and the human sciences that understand. This dialectic is also opposed to Gadamer's polemic in favour of an ontology of understanding, and to the technical rationality of the sciences which would leave nothing unexplained. Ricoeur understands under this dialectic 'the view that explanation and understanding would not constitute mutually exclusive poles, but rather relative moments in a complex process called interpretation'.[229] On the epistemological level, therefore, Ricoeur is concerned to grasp both poles as correlative and to free them from the services of the polemic or conflict — over the claim to being scientific — between the human and the natural sciences.[230] Ontologically this new vision signifies that one can no longer play off against the other the truth of understanding and the truth of explanation from a methodological point of view.

This really general philosophical re-formulation of the two modes of knowledge, now essentially related to each other, has without doubt weighty consequences for a new theory of text interpretation.[231] The reason is that this theory is now extended to the process of structural analysis of the text — that is, to the area which has as its object the analysis of ideal linking of meanings within the acts of language.

Ricoeur admits in several places that he has learned two things from the structuralist analysis of texts: first, a method of explaining the horizontal aspects of the text, that is to say the syntactic and semantic elements and relations which go to make up a text, and secondly, a method of explaining the hierarchical aspects of the texts, in other words the relations between the exercises of language which are combined within the text.[232]

Applying this to the example of narrative genre, following Levi-Strauss, Ricoeur can define the two didactic stages as follows:

> The unities below the sentence enjoy composition as well as those above the sentence; the meaning of the narrative is to be found in the arrangement itself of the elements; the meaning consists in the power of the totality to integrate the unities below it; conversely the meaning of an element is its capacity to enter into relationship with other elements and with the totality of the work; these postulates together define the closure of a narrative; the task of the structural analysis will consist therefore in proceeding to the segmentation (horizontal aspect), and then in establishing the different levels of integration of the parts within the whole (hierarchical aspect).[233]

In other places he summarises this insight in the following manner: 'to explain a narrative is to get hold of this symphonic structure of segmental actions'.[234]

But what is the contribution of such structural-analytical explanation of texts to the total operation of interpretation?

Ricoeur describes the process of interpretation as a dialectical movement, which proceeds from a first naïve understanding, to explanation of the text, in order then to lead back from the explanation to a deepening comprehension so that the explanation appears as mediation between two stages of understanding.[235] To understand a text it is not necessary to understand its author but, rather, understanding must take into account the autonomy of the written text as explained above, a text whose original distanciation invites the reader to a new appropriation. This new appropriation becomes a new event of the text independent of the author etc. This text-event is set in motion in the first place by a preliminary guess of the meaning of the text.

This guess is necessary because the text — as shown above — is a complex figure, characterised by ambivalence which, however, is not constituted in the same way as the polysemy of words or the ambiguity of single sentences.[236] In order to disclose the totality of the text with the help of the individual parts a projection is necessary which takes into account as far as ever possible the conventional and individual characteristics of the text. Such projections are, however, always one-sided, for which reason we must continually hold open the possibility of still other divinatory perspectives. Every text interpretation must be in a position to justify its existence, it must be textually possible, it postulates an explanation of its possibility.[237]

Establishing the possibility of an interpretation demands a structural analysis of the text, which does not however conclude the act of interpretation. Ricoeur compares the polarity between understanding and explanation with the already mentioned polarity of sense *(Sinn)* and reference *(Bedeutung)*. Explanation and sense are however in this case text-internal categories whereas understanding and reference are external to the text. 'The reference expresses the full exteriorization of discourse to the extent that the meaning is not only the ideal object intended by the utterer, but the actual reality aimed at by the utterance.'[238]

On the other hand the various schools of literary criticism are justified already through the autonomous character of written texts because their precise task is to exploit all the different possibilities of textual meanings and their references.

But these stages of interpretation which explain the text must be complemented by procedures which again assemble the parts so that the text forms a totality of communication which is to have the character of an event and which receives its reference from the fact that a new world is opened up to the reader of the text. Ricoeur summarises as follows the process of opening up this reference on the basis of the textual depth semantics disclosed in the phase of explanation:

> The sense of the text is not behind the text, but in front of it. it is not something hidden, but something disclosed. What has to be understood is not the initial situation of discourse, but what points towards a possible world, thanks to the non-ostensive reference of the text. Understanding

has less than ever to do with the author and his situation. It seems to grasp the world-propositions opened up by the reference of the text. To understand a text is to follow its movements from sense to reference: from what it says, to what it talks about. In this process the mediating role played by structural analysis constitutes both the justification of the objective approach and the rectification of the subjective approach to the text.[239]

With this Ricoeur wishes to rescue not only the identity of the text within the process of interpretation (objective side) but also to allow to come fully into its own the act of the reader's participation (subjective side) in this process. He has accordingly gone a step beyond Gadamer and freed the participation in the process of tradition through texts from the strain of sheer 'entering into', and has opened this participation to methical objectifications of the text in a critical manner so that the identity of texts can be firm even in relation to the changing identity of the interpreter. On the other hand the identity of the text remains meaningless if it is not repeatedly re-appropriated. But appropriation does not signify dominion over the text; rather an emptying of the narcissistic ego in favour of a selfhood which develops itself with the help of the text.[240]

Three things happen then in the appropriation of the text: i) the victory over the historical and cultural distance, ii) the fusion of interpretation of texts and self-interpretation, and iii) the development of the text itself into an event.

(6) Suspicion and Retrieval: Criticism in Ricoeur and Gadamer

Ricoeur formulates already in his study on Freud a di-polar concept of interpretation which includes both 'collection of sense' and 'hermeneutics of suspicion'.[241] Marx, Nietzsche and Freud are masters of such suspicion which however does not mean that they are masters of scepticism. Rather, these three philosophers contribute to the fact that 'understanding is hermeneutics: henceforward, to seek such meaning is no longer to spell out the consciousness of meaning, but to *decipher its expressions*.'[242] Thus Ricoeur develops a critical concept of interpretation in the dialectical manner already expounded: a critique of the derivation of sense in the explaining process must accompany the collection of sense in the process of understanding. Similarly, in order to make possible the unfolding of the self, a critique of the ego must accompany all stages of the collection of sense in the self-understanding of the interpreter which takes place through text interpretation. Ricoeur's theory of interpretation is thus, right from the outset, explicitly critical and self-critical. This explicit disposition to criticism characterises Ricoeur's theory over against Gadamer's concept of understanding. It is true that Gadamer is not, as we have seen, explicitly anticritical but he still owes us clear statements regarding the openness to criticism of his model.

Ricoeur acknowledges Gadamer's lack of an explicitly critical approach and nevertheless defends Gadamer against Habermas's global accusation that Gadamer is insensitive in relation to the critique of ideology. In his discriminating examination of Habermas's criticism of Gadamer, Ricoeur poses two questions: i) Can hermeneutical philosophy hold its own in face of the postulates a critique of ideology and if so at what price? ii) Under what conditions is the critique of ideology possible? Can it in the last analysis remain separate from hermeneutical presuppositions?[243]

Ricoeur's *first question* aims at clarifying the place of criticism within hermeneutics. In so questioning he sees, with all due clarity, the dilemma which cripples Gadamer's hermeneutics as consisting in the fact that it is his concept of hermeneutical experience itself which makes difficult the recognition of any critical dimension. The reason for this is that the basic hermeneutical experience in Gadamer involves the rejection of alienation which he sees at work in the objectifying stance of the human sciences, so that the polemics between truth on the one hand and objectifying method on the other hand restrains Gadamer 'from really recognising the critical instance and hence rendering justice to the critique of ideology, which is the modern post-Marxist expression of the critical instance'.[244]

As against that, Ricoeur introduces four suggestions intended to raise Gadamer's hermeneutics to the level of dialogue concerning the place of criticism in this discipline: i) 'distanciation is not a misfortune for hermeneutics but on the contrary constitutes its basic dynamic;[245] ii) hermeneutics must overcome the unsalutary dichotomy between explanation and understanding;[246] iii) texts open up modes of being with projections of a possible reality they contain, and this is especially the case with poetic texts, presenting a criticism of the dominant image of reality;[247] iv) textual understanding is now also self-criticism; this is so because in order to understand, the reader must open her/himself to the text.

> ... it is the matter of the text which gives the reader his dimension of subjectivity; understanding is thus no longer a constitution of which the subject possesses a key.
> ... Reading introduces me to imaginative variation of the *ego*. The metamorphosis of the world in play is also the playful metamorphosis of the *ego*.[248]

Reading then makes a decisive contribution to a criticism of the illusions of the subject. This critical potentiality of the act of reading can however only be effective when distanciation is no longer treated as a taboo but is rather appreciated as a dynamic of new appropriation and self-knowledge. In this manner the critique of false consciousness becomes an integral part of hermeneutics and with this insight a major concern of Habermas's criticism of hermeneutics will have been taken into account.

Ricoeur's *second question* dealt with the relationship between hermeneutics and the critique of ideology. In this respect he reinforces Gadamer's point of view according to which hermeneutics and critique of ideology are mutually penetrating. i) Both hermeneutics and critique of ideology have their basis, in spite of different objects, in a common hermeneutics of finitude which throws a light on the affinity between the concepts of 'prejudice' and 'ideology'.[249] ii) As regards the interest in emancipation in the critical social sciences Ricoeur points out that such interest rests on the same foundation as that of the historical hermeneucital sciences, namely on the level of communicative praxis. And as regards this state of affairs he asks Habermas:

> ... can a critique of distortions be separated from the communicative experience itself, from the place where it begins, where it is real and where it is exemplary? ... Distortions can be criticised only in the name of a *consensus*

which we cannot anticipate merely emptily, in the manner of a regulative idea, unless that idea is exemplified; and one of the very places of exemplification of the ideal of communication is precisely our capacity to overcome cultural distance in the interpretation of works received from the past. He who is unable to reinterpret his past may also be incapable of projecting concretely his interest in emancipation.[250]

iii) In relation to Habermas's demand for a depth hermeneutics which would eliminate pathological distortions of communication, Ricoeur states flatly: 'A depth-hermeneutics is still a hermeneutics, even if it is called meta-hermeneutical.'[251] And Ricoeur asks himself further what, if not the creative renewal of the cultural legacy, can constitute the basis for an emancipatory interest, in view of the continuously different ideological trimmings of social communication. iv) Finally, he emphasises that critique also constitutes a tradition, namely the tradition of emancipatory actions, for example, Israel's Exodus or Jesus' Resurrection. There is no doubt that for Ricoeur there is a difference between a text theory and a theory of institutions and phenomena of domination. But to state that there is an antimony between the interest of reinterpretation of the cultural legacy which has come down to us and the interest in futuristic projections of an emancipated humanity is, according to him, false. 'The moment these two interests become radically separate, then hermeneutics and critique will themselves be no more than ... ideologies!'[252]

The question concerning the openness to criticism of hermeneutics is thus answered in an explicitly positive way by Ricoeur and he asserts the necessity of co-operation with the social sciences in their attempts at critique of ideology. The confrontation between Habermas and Gadamer loses its edge for Ricoeur. The reason is that it now becomes fruitful for philosophical reflection, when its false starting points and antimonies have been unmasked as such.

(7) Conclusion

The effort which we have devoted to studying Ricoeur's theory of interpretation of written texts has decisively advanced our quest for an appropriate concept of interpretation. Both the notion of 'interpretation' and its dialectical partner concept 'text' have been further consolidated, but there are still unresolved problems. In the following critical reflection on Ricoeur's contributions, which we have just discussed, these problems require further illumination from three points of view: i) is Ricoeur's model of 'text sense' and 'text reference' a fruitful one? ii) how can the appropriation of texts together with its accompanying metamorphosis of the reader be more closely determined? iii) how are the limitations and opportunities of interpretative pluralism to be more precisely grasped?

b) **Critique of Ricoeur's Model of Interpretation**

(1) The Problem of Text Sense and Text Reference

Ricoeur's theory of interpretation is, in contrast to Gadamer's philosophical hermeneutic, concerned to orient itself closely on its specific object, the 'text'. Ricoeur always means a written text: 'the text is discourse stabilised by writing'.[253] Such a notion of text is, from the general point of view of literary science, too restricted. As a description of the object of Ricoeur's theory of interpretation however, which is only concerned specifically with written texts, it is justified in view of the fact that he sees the hermeneutical problem as primarily grounded in the distanciation of written texts from the reader. Ricoeur's hermeneutics is accordingly characterised as a hermeneutics of written texts, whereas Gadamer aims at achieving a universal hermeneutics, whose object can be constituted by all linguistic carriers of tradition. But this vagueness of Gadamer's object dilutes his concept of understanding, as we have seen. Accordingly we are quite willing to pay the price for Ricoeur's text hermeneutics, which reflects on a precise object, the written text and its reception (reading), adopting therefore an epistemological rather than an ontological starting point.

Leading ideas for Ricoeur's model of text interpretation are on the side of the text 'sense' *(Sinn)* and 'reference' *(Bedeutung)* and on the side of the reader 'understanding' and 'explanation'. These coordinated conceptual pairs play the role of sponsor in Ricoeur's overcoming Dilthey's dichotomy of the understanding human sciences and the explaining natural sciences, and in the elimination of Gadamer's polemics against trends of methodical explanation within the human sciences. The distinction, understanding of sense on the one hand and explanation of reference on the other, makes it possible for Ricoeur to determine and elucidate the 'ideal sense' of a text and to lead it to its fulfilment as an understood linguistic event.[254] In other words the linguistic structure of a linguistic event needs to be methodically explained in order that the linguistic event be better understood. Gottlob Frege's distinction between 'sense' and 'reference' serves Ricoeur's purposes because it helps him to take up the concerns of structural analysis and employ them in the interpretation of texts, to the extent that the structural analysis of reference subjects the reader's original projection of sense to a durability test carried out on the text in order to make possible a deeper textual understanding.

Although accepting without qualification Ricoeur's concern for methodical control of the various ways in which understanding is achieved and although I see in this his great contribution, superior to that of Gadamer, nevertheless Ricoeur's recourse to Frege's dual notion of 'sense' and 'reference' and his transference of this to the level of the text appears to me to be confusing and in the last analysis erroneous.

Frege, as we know, takes as his starting point the level of the word in his essay 'Über Sinn und Bedeutung'[255] and then moves forward to the level of the sentence. On the level of the sentence he defines 'sense' as thought content, and 'reference' as the truth of the sentence, and in this definition none of the concepts has anything in common with subjective, private *representations*. In the notion of 'thought content' he understands 'not the subjective activity of thinking but rather its objective content which is capable of being the common property of many'.[256] 'It is the striving for truth, then, which propels us in each case from sense to reference.' 'We find ourselves accordingly impelled to acknowledge the *truth value* of a sentence as its reference.'[257] 'Thought' is sense, 'truth value' is object and 'judgment' is for Frege 'not the mere grasping of a thought but rather the acknowledgment of its truth'.[258] In other words judging can 'be conceived of as a movement forward from a thought to its truth value'. 'Our concern can therefore never be restricted to the reference *(Bedeutung)* of a sentence; but it is also true that the mere thought does not of itself give knowledge. Rather is it the case that the thought together with its reference, that is to say with its truth value, constitutes knowledge.'[259] Frege is mainly concerned, therefore, with the cognitional value of a sentence. For him the thought expressed by the sentence, its sense, 'does not deserve less attention than its reference, that is to say its truth value.[260] The reason is that Frege's interest is aimed at grounding equality between sentences in which insights are expressed. And an insight encompasses, according to what has been said, the communicable thought of the sentence as well as its truth value,[261] which is then capable of being compared with the truth value of other thought. — So much for the background to the concepts of 'sense' and 'reference' which have been adopted by Ricoeur.

In Ricoeur these concepts are transferred from the level of the sentence to that of the text, in order to affirm in this manner that the sense ideality *(Sinnidealität)* of texts is not exhausted in subjective representations.[262] Ricoeur finds himself encouraged in this transference also by Husserl, who extends the concept of ideal meaning to all psychical achievements; not only to logical acts but also to acts of knowing, of willing and of feeling. 'For an objective phenomenology, every intentional act without exception must be described from its noematic sides as the correlate of a corresponding noetic act.'[263] Ricoeur's striving for the objectivity of meaning *(Sinn)* is, then, in the last analysis also in accord with the recent literary movements which think of the text as 'a kind of atemporal object, which has, so to speak, cut its ties from all historical development',[264] because in this way the semantic autonomy of the written text is emphasised, which in its turn calls for methodical explanation. To this autonomous and self-contained sense then accrues its reference for the reader, for whom it discloses the world of the text.

Ricoeur's reception of Frege's concepts becomes here, however, independent of Frege: Frege's reference *('Bedeutung')* which is to render the truth value within the system of logic turns into *'référence'*, which roots 'our words and our sentences in reality'.[265] A quotation from Frege follows this sentence: 'it is therefore the striving for truth which in every case impels us to move forward from sense *(Sinn)* to reference *(Bedeutung)*',[266] from which then Ricoeur immediately draws the conclusion: 'this impulsion of (ideal) sense to the (real) *Bedeutung*, to referentiality, is the soul of language *(langage)* itself'.[267] Frege was concerned with logic, Ricoeur is concerned with reference to reality. That indicates a clear extension of Frege's concepts, away from the truth value of the sentence and on to the relation to the reality of the text. Frege's dual notion of 'sense and reference' correspondes to Ricoeur's dual notion of 'ideal sense and reference to reality', keeping in mind however that Ricoeur's reference to reality *(Wirklichkeitsbezug)*, as distinct from Frege's reference *(Bedeutung)*, is, surely, related to the reader's *representational world*: 'If the reference of the text is the project of a world, then it is not the reader who primarily projects himself. The reader rather is enlarged in his capacity of self-projection by receiving a new mode of being from the text itself.'[268]

The greatest difficulty, however, is to be found in Ricoeur's observation: 'To understand a text is to follow its movement from sense to reference: from what it says, to what it talks about,' which postulates a movement from ideal sense to its reference to reality.[269] Are we not dealing here with a relapse into idealism — now admittedly taking its origin from a new standpoint, namely that of structuralist analysis? For how is it possible in any way whatever to conceive of an ideal sense of a text without reference to reality? Is it possible to really separate such reference from the textual constitution of sense which takes place in the act of reading? How would this be at all possible? Would it not be more accurate to say that the sense of a text has two dimensions which are to be distinguished but never separated: namely, an internal texture of references *(Bedeutungsverflechtung)* which, by reason of the nature of the act of reading, build up *simultaneously* a textuality of reference to the world? In this case one should speak of internal propositional references, which together constitute the sense of the text and at the same time the sense of the world for the reader. In Ricoeur's terminology, this would run as follows: the sense of the text is its reference to reality. Frege's dual notion would in that case not be betrayed but rather returned to its rightful place, on the level of the sentence: the sense of a sentence would then be identical with its reference in the text.

And the reference of the text would then be identical with its sense as texture of references and at the same time as reference to reality. There is no other way, in my opinion, in which the problem of idealism present in Ricoeur can, through the division into sense and reference *(référence)* be effectively dealt with.

John B. Thompson draws attention to a further problem of Ricoeur's concept of reference to reality *(référence)* in his critical dialogue with Ricoeur's hermeneutics.[270] Thompson finds fault with the obscurity of the concept of *référence*. According to him, Ricoeur neither explains satisfactorily how an interpreter does or does not succeed in achieving this reference to reality nor what is to be considered as reference to reality and in what situation this can happen. According to Thompson, Ricoeur makes the qualifying statement that an expression develops its reference to reality only in its usage, 'Yet Ricoeur does not clarify the nature of this contextual dependence, nor does he specify the sort of circumstances that are to be regarded as relevant in assessing the success or failure of a referential claim'. It would thus remain unclear how a text would disclose a possible world and how one could decide which world the text would disclose.[271]

Thompson's remarks also have an important bearing on Ricoeur's understanding of truth. The reason for this is that Ricoeur understands by the notion of truth of a text, as we know, the world which is made explicit through the text. But how is one to decide between conflicting claims of truth as long as it has remained unclear how the disclosure of possible worlds opened up by the text is to be thought of?[272]

Our proposal, for its part, does not wish to slip back into intuitive understanding but rather calls for an identification of semantic linking within the text, that is to say the constitution of sense, with all the structural analytical methods available. This identification will preserve the simultaneous referential constitution of sense in the act of reading from exposure to the arbitrariness of the reader. It will bring back the constitution of sense continually to the objectifiable semantic linking *(Bedeutungsverkettung)* within the text. In this manner, it would appear to me that the dialectic of understanding as constitution of sense, and explanation as analysis of semantic linking, are brought to their interpretive completion. In this case the sense would really be disclosed and not concealed, and its disclosure would be a reference to reality, which had as its foundation demonstrable possibilities for constitution within the text.

But there are still two complexes of problems which in Ricoeur's theory remain to be clarified.

(2) The Problem Posed by the Dialectic of Reception

As regards the theory of text interpretation then, we are indebted to Ricoeur for a twofold advance on Gadamer: interpretation has become a complex leading idea of hermeneutical dealings with texts, one which is open to criticism, and the notion of text has matured to the extent that it is a challenge to our understanding of reality, a challenge which is not to be conceptually removed or otherwise eliminated. Methodical explanation and text-centred understanding complement each other in their efforts to comprehend the sense of the text. Interpretation is no longer a selfless moving into the totality of the contextual framework of tradition but rather a critical reflective self-reconstruction of the interpreter in the act of reading.

This act of reading is, however, according to Ricoeur's concept, only set out in outline and is to a certain extent covered over by his theory of appropriation. This reflection on the praxis of reading is an essential part, however, of the theory of reading. Here also a dialectical framework must be the dominant element under pain of allowing the theory of reading to become idealistic and the practice of reading to remain unreflecting so that both would come under ideological suspicion.

To read a text is to interpret it. Ricoeur has come to understand interpretation as a metamorphosis of the narcissistic ego into a new self.[273] This involvement of the reader with the text to be read, in other words the hermeneutical circle of reading, requires us to abandon the quest for objective achievements of interpretation.[274] The dialectic of text and appropriation is to be celebrated as a creative act, but one which does not create independently of the sense of the text but rather re-creates this textual sense. From this point of view the act of reading demands to be thought out more precisely from both poles: namely from that of the requirements of the text postulating its re-creation and also from that of the desire of the reader for a renewal of his/her self; and this must be done with greater exactitude than Ricoeur has demonstrated to date. It is only then that the parallels between text-sense-relationships and reader-sense-projections can be understood both in their dialectical nature and in their process characteristics.

(3) The Problem of Interpretative Pluralism

There remains another question to be put to Ricoeur's theory of interpretation: how does it handle the pluralism of possible readings? Where are the possibilities and limitations of appropriation? Up to the present Ricoeur gave the impression that he attributed to the text a certain uniformity of sense, which one can meet through a pluralism of methods.[275] But can one justify this confidence regarding uniformity of sense by an appeal to the text itself or do texts provoke complex, or rather multiform sense-creations? Ricoeur leaves no room for doubt about the fact that he does not consider an arbitrary handling of the text to be a suitable appropriation of textual sense,[276] but he does not express an opinion as regards the reverse aspect of the problem, namely that of the responsible plurality of possible interpretations, nor does he express an opinion regarding the dialogue concerning such a sense of pluralism.

The existence of such a pluralism of readings is repeatedly suggested, in an implicit fashion, by Ricoeur whenever he reflects on the hermeneutical function of the distanciation of the text from its situation of origin, which exposes textual sense to innumerable acts of reading.

> If the meaning of a text is open to anyone who can read, then it is the omni-temporality of meaning which opens it to unknown readers; and the historicity of reading is the counterpart of this specific omni-temporality. From the moment that the text escapes from its author and from his situation, it also escapes from its original audience. Hence it can procure new readers for itself.[277]

The ever new acts of reading called for by the text constitute, then, a history of reception of the text in question — one could also say, a tradition of readings. This tradition imposes in its turn standards of expectations on the text which are either met or repulsed by it. These attitudes of expectation, however, are necessary since it is only with a particular perspective in view that one can surmise what the textual meaning might be and from this point of view develop the dynamic of reading. On the other hand such perspectives are also capable of distorting the scanning activity which looks for new and appropriate readings.

If Ricoeur's model is to be used with effect in developing a theory of reading pluralism, these observations regarding the conditions of possibility of a particular reading require to be thought out in more detail. Text identity and pluralism of readings must also be seen as elements in a dialectic.

Without further elaboration of these observations at this point we are already confronted with the problem of assessment in the process of reading. When a text permits of, or even encourages a variety of interpretative perspectives the reader must arrive at a decision in the matter of assessment. Such a decision has not got the characteristics of a judgment, it does not possess finality, it is rather a necessary and in each case revisable dimension within the total activity of reading.

(4) Conclusion and Delineation of the Task

Our determination of the concept of 'interpretation' has been advanced decisively by the study of Paul Ricoeur's theory of interpretation. Interpretation is more than mere concern with understanding; now it means to concern oneself with the understanding of texts as complemented and tested through analytical procedures. Here the initiative is derived from two sources, from the text and the interpreter who wishes to understand. However, Ricoeur has not only drawn our attention to the dialectic of understanding and explanation in the theory of interpretation but has also pointed out the dialectical relationship between text and reader. This relationship culminates in the changed self-understanding of the reader which emerges from the 'interplay with the text as partner'.[278]

But how this 'play with the text' is to be conceived of in greater detail Ricoeur has as yet not told us. Moreover, our analysis has demonstrated his distinction between text sense *(Textsinn)* and text reference *(Textbedeutung)* to be problematical. We have tried to show that the sense of a text also constitutes its reference for the reader and that a separation of sense and reference of a *text* degenerates into the idealistic. Furthermore Ricoeur's textual theory lacks critical concern with the opportunities and limits of an interpretative pluralism. Such a critical concern must occupy itself in the first place with the question as to whether and in what manner a plurality of assessments of the same textual sense is legitimate. Our concept of interpretation has accordingly become more precise, even if it is not yet complete.

Hence we are confronted with the following tasks: first of all, Ricoeur's concept of interpretation must be complemented by the dimension of assessment, and secondly, the concept of interpretation thus elaborated must again be measured against the notion of text. This testing is most likely to succeed if it is an effort at describing the process of reading which has as its object the dialectical relationship between text and reader. It is only on the completion of these tasks that we can devote ourselves to the specific problems of a theological theory of text interpretation.

But first we would like to subject to still closer scrutiny the concept of interpretation inspired by Gadamer and Ricoeur and develop it further.

5. Interpretation and Assessment

Application and appropriation for Gadamer and Ricoeur respectively are the concepts at which hermeneutical activity aims. Understanding has its high point, according to Gadamer, in application; interpretation is accomplished, according to Ricoeur, in the appropriation by the reader of what was formerly a foreign text. With due deference to the distinctions just elaborated between Gadamer's claim to a universal concept of understanding exemplified by textual understanding and Ricoeur's theory of text interpretation, both theories have two deficiencies in common.

First of all, both theoreticians fail to explain what their stance might be in the face of possible criticism of the matter under discussion by the understanding person. Is such a criticism of the matter to be understood always to take place subsequent to the act of understanding or does it already play a role, at least implicitly, during the act of understanding?

Secondly, both authors fail to consider sufficiently that the situation of communication in which application and appropriation of texts, in other words reading, is accomplished, can be systematically distorted so that the external conditions of reading distort the disclosure of its contents right from the beginning. Admittedly Gadamer and Ricoeur confronted this observation of Habermas emphatically and in so doing pointed to the general ability of human understanding which, as such, could unmask even such distortions. But they failed to point out the location of this reflection on external distorting factors in the case of a process of understanding which has to be publicly accounted for.

My thesis therefore runs as follows: no concept of understanding can lay claim to adequacy unless it includes right from the start a dimension of criticism regarding both the matter *(Sache)* of the text and the situation in which the interpretation takes place. This is the thesis to be elaborated and defended in the present section.

I again take as my starting point the relevant apories of Gadamer and Ricoeur and, with this in view, introduce the dimension of assessment which completes our model of interpretation. In this way interpretation is determined in a threefold manner: through the dimensions of understanding, explanation and assessment.

a) The Horizon of Understanding and Assessment

(1) Thematic Critique

Gadamer defines the horizon of understanding as 'the range of vision that includes [*umfaßt und umschließt*] everything that can be seen from a particular vantage point'.[279] In the fusion of horizons of the person wishing to understand and of the matter to be understood, both horizons are accordingly transformed. In Gadamer this transformation appears implicitly as positive. He never speaks about a possible narrowing or a negative transformation of the horizons. That is not surprising because for him every authentic conversation is implicitly good and, as a step in the process of learning, progressively fulfils the humanistic ideal of education.[280] This exclusively positive evaluation of the fusion of horizons should, however, give rise to suspicion because it can lead us into moral complications through its lack of elaboration.

If for example, we choose as a text Erich Kästner's quotation from statements said to have been made by Martin Heidegger as Rector of Freiburg University, in November 1933, and if we allow ourselves to be engaged in conversation with this text, in which dialogue the thematic matter of the text is to 'play us', then we become involved in problems of assessment. According to Kästner, Heidegger says: 'Take not as rules for your being, doctrines and "ideas". The Führer himself and alone is the reality of today and tomorrow and he is its law.'[281]

Understanding as fusion of horizons cannot in this case exempt the responsible reader of the text from a concern with the assessment of the textual sense. The communication perspective of this text can, admittedly, be understood even today, but surely distancing begins *during* the process of understanding. My judgment regarding assessment is accordingly not just subsequent, attaching itself later to the act of understanding, rather does it mature in the contemporaneous process of understanding this text itself. Already from the first instant of understanding, the text discloses a reality, even at the stage when the effective historical consciousness introduces its pre-judgments — and especially then — as also when these are brought to play on the matter to be understood. The necessity for assessment cannot be cancelled out even by an extensive intermediary, explanatory phase within the interpretation of this text. The application of the sense of this text is, as a whole, a judgment of assessment, and the application is not without value. Every 'hermeneutics of agreement' comes up against its clear boundary at this stage.[282]

How can we then participate in the meaning of a text? How does hermeneutical dialogue proceed here?

(2) Critique of the Situation

'The text' according to Gadamer,

> brings an object into language but that it achieves this is ultimately the work of the interpreter.[283] The mode of realisation of understanding is interpretation.... All understanding is interpretation, and all interpretation takes place

in the medium of a language which would allow the object to come into words and yet is at the same time the interpreter's own expression.[284] Every interpretation has to adapt itself to the hermeneutical situation to which it belongs.[285]

These observations of Gadamer, especially the last one, highlight the importance of the hermeneutical situation which co-determines the interpretation. Interpretation is accordingly the translation of the text reference — that is to say, the disclosure of the reality of the text in relation to the particular situation in question. This importance of the situation must be critically taken into account. Can the hermeneutical situation attune itself uncritically to all the conversational contents or does it always give rise to a compulsion to seek also the assessment of every movement in the play of hermeneutics? In other words: can the partners in dialogue afford to accept in the first instance all thematic matter without efforts at its assessment — before they have critically reflected on it — or should criticism of the matter to be understood, by the very nature of the case, be always already present in the act of reading itself.

We must further pose the question as to what extent the interpreter must become conscious of his/her hermeneutical situation. This question is also directed at the ethics of the process of interpretation. Ricoeur pointed out — as reported above — that, for example, distorted conditions of understanding also require interpretation in order to be discovered.[286] Though gratefully adopting this insight, we must nevertheless proceed further and require that every interpreter not only be in a position to scrutinise the hermeneutical situation under certain circumstances but also be compelled continually to have a co-thematic awareness of it, in order to do justice as far as possible to the text which has to be understood. As well as thematic critique of the matter, interpretation requires also a critique of the situation if it is to succeed responsibly.[287]

The following example may illustrate the necessity of a critique of the situation: if in the Christian tradition of reading biblical texts the truth of the text must be laid down by the magisterium for readers, before this text is read and re-read, then, in this case, systematic distortions must be diagnosed. The relation between the disclosure of truth in the process of reading and in exchange with other readers on the one hand, and the propositional determination of such truth, as the basis for community, on the other hand, must not in the last analysis be cancelled out in favour of the latter, because in that case the reading of texts would be totally subordinated to ideological purposes and the power of texts to disclose concrete reality would be suppressed.

(3) The Necessity for Assessment

Both critique of content and of situation in interpreting texts call for assessment, something which is not at a later stage subordinated to interpretation but rather constitutes a part of its integrated process. We recognise accordingly three dimensions of interpretation in its totality: understanding, explanation and assessment. The two first named dimensions have already been developed in critical dialogue with Gadamer and Ricoeur. The dimension of assessment requires to be more precisely described at present, after we have once again characterised our model of interpretation in a summary fashion.

b) The Three Dimensions of Interpretation: Understanding —
   Explanation — Assessment

In contradistinction to Ricoeur's model of the *steps* of interpretation, the model of interpretation which we pose here deals with *dimensions.* Ricoeur's clear differentiation of 'understanding — explanation — comprehension' appears to me to be too idealistic and for this reason I find it more appropriate to speak of dimensions of interpretation. It would be truer, it seems to me, to speak of these dimensions as simultaneously coming to pass on different levels of reflection and as being related to each other in a state of mutual tension. Understanding of sense, explanation of textual structure and assessment of textual sense in relation to content and critique of the situation, mutually influence each other. 'Interpretation' is therefore what we from now on call the process in which we engage in the exposition of a text through understanding, explanation and assessment. The purpose of this is that we appropriate the text, feel ourselves addressed by it and, possibly, allow ourselves to undergo a change of self-understanding.

c) The Dimension of Assessment

In the preceding reflections we have globally outlined the tasks of assessment in the process of text interpretation, as material critique and critique of the situation. In so doing we have given an appreciation of critique, not only as a consequence of hermeneutical experience, but as a dimension of interpretation. We have included critique, as such, in the experience of interpretation itself.

The terminology 'assessment-dimension' *(Deutungs-Dimension)* appears to be particularly apt because it is related to meaning *(Bedeutung)*. What a text *means (bedeutet)* for the reader is subjected by him to *assessment (Deutung)*. Assessment is from this point of view always of its nature related to its textual basis. Text and reading are grasped as a dialectical process, not only in understanding and explanation but already and essentially in assessment. Here the determination of the relationship between the text and the reader characterised as an 'understanding' is related to the level of semantic provocation of the text, something which is kept in tension by the expectations of the reader and by the dynamic of reading which emanates from these expectations. The determination of the relationship which is characterised by 'explanation' has to do with the methodological processes which take place between the reader and the text and which aim at illumination of the textual structure. And lastly, the determination of relationship which is characterised by the notion of 'assessment' is related to the tension between the textual sense being disclosed and the reader who discloses, a tension which culminates in the personal responsibility[288] of the reader in relation to the textual sense disclosed by him/her.

The reader's assessment is not an ultimate judgment about the sense of the text but rather a certain achievement of interpretation which, while concerned with a critique of content and situation remains at the same time continually conscious of its hermeneutical limitations.

The hermeneutical limitations become manifest through the fact that a reader can, in principle, read a text repeatedly and in different manners. Admittedly, the same text cannot be read in a totally different way, since every responsible assessment is aware of its obligation to authenticate itself by reference to the text. But the fullness of sense which is the distinction of the text admits of varying assessment.

These abstract reflections require closer study in the next chapter. But even at this point we should keep in mind that the dimension of assessment takes into account not just the fact of an accompanying critique in the process of interpretation but also the provisional nature of this accomplishment to the extent that in the critique the personal relationship of the reader to the text is reflected.

Accordingly on the level of sense, the reflective determination of relationships between the reader and the text happen and they result in the fact that opportunities and limitations of the interpretational act in question can be assessed as well as may be possible. Here the first decisions are made about the thematic matter of the text and these co-determine the further reception of the text in a manner which extends beyond the immediate act of reading.

Assessment is also the level of interpretation on which the interpreter becomes ethically active and that in a twofold manner: to the extent that he/she tries to do justice in the best possible manner to the text, and to the extent that he/she thinks through in a responsible manner, as reader, his/her relationship to the text. In this respect the reader carries a double responsibility: one in relation to the text and the other in relation to her/himself, in the hermeneutical situation.

Here the question surfaces as to how this relationship between 'reading subject' and 'object of reading' is to be determined. But this question can only be intelligently answered when both sides of the relationship so determined have been developed and analysed. But we have concerned ourselves up to the present point almost exclusively with one abstract model of the interpretation of texts. Yet it is only after the reflection on the textuality of texts that we will be in a position to determine more accurately the relationship between text and reader. And with this it has already become evident that it cannot be our task to recognise in an abstract fashion the possible presence of a subjectivism or an objectivism in the process of interpretation.

Rather is it our concern to offer a determination of the relationship between text and reader.

Before we conclude this chapter and devote ourselves in the next one to the task of furnishing the required explanations, we must again briefly at this point take up the question posed by Gadamer regarding the universality of understanding.

d) On the Universality of Interpretation

We recall Gadamer's claim that understanding is a universal act of human existence. 'For man's relation to the world is absolutely and fundamentally linguistic in nature and hence intelligible. Thus hermeneutics is a *universal aspect of philosophy*.'[289]

It is clear from our considerations that Gadamer's claim cannot be maintained in this form. The reason is that his concept of understanding has to be supplemented in several ways in order to withstand criticism and do justice to the text. Accordingly, we can neither speak prematurely about understanding as a universal concept, nor jump to the conclusion of a universal structure of understanding from the basis of textual understanding as a particular form of understanding itself.

But we have at least worked out a foundation, that of textual understanding, from which, in the wake of Ricoeur, philosophical statements about a certain type of human self-understanding are justified. Ricoeur, as we have seen, conceded to the written texts of tradition a general philosophical function: they are to mediate the reader to her/himself and in this manner, to a certain extent, set him/her on the road to an ontology which, however, is not capable of conclusive formulation in the lifetime of the reader.[290]

Interpretation therefore, as a three-dimensional process between the reader and the text, can also lay claim to universality, insofar as it regulates the relationship of the human being to her/his world. This relationship is co-determined by the ongoing critical dialogue, also with her/himself, as externalised in what is scripturally determined. It calls out for understanding, explanation and assessment. One can participate in this dialogue through experience — that is to say, by reading. This experience may be thought of as learning discussion. It is described by Ernst Bloch in the context of general philosophy as follows:

> This learning moves entirely in man's externality, is therein under way *(fahrend)* and so experiencing *(erfahrend)* and so also, with the help of what is outside, experiencing its own interiority. The human being especially is in constant dependence on this constant path into exteriority in order that he can in any manner whatever return to himself and in this manner discover precisely the depth within himself, whose purpose is not to be within itself, without achieving exteriority.[291]

Interpretation is such a path out of oneself and back to oneself, in the company of oneself through the written expression. Text interpretation is accordingly man's 'way out' of her/himself in the learning critical dialogue *(Aus-ein-ander-setzung)* with the world, from which both understanding and self-understanding can be gleaned. Such understanding, however, continually and of its nature calls out for explanation and assessment, if it is to be received in a responsible manner.

How this complex process of interpretation can be made publicly accountable and how one can do justice to the texts which are to be interpreted will be discussed in the next chapter.

CHAPTER II

Text as Category of Theological Thinking

1. Introduction

With the development of a three-dimensional concept of interpretation, we have now covered the first section of our journey towards a theory of theological text interpretation. 'Understanding', 'explanation' and 'assessment' were our titles for the three levels of the process of interpretation, levels which develop simultaneously and exercise reciprocal influence. In so doing we — like Gadamer and Ricoeur — have tacitly presumed the givenness of the notion of 'text'. Such a presupposition is however uncritical and dangerous, since it is the text which sparks off its interpretation and the absence of a concept of 'text' can accordingly contribute to distorted theories of interpretation.

Every theory of interpretation postulates a theory of text. A theological theory of text interpretation can therefore take exception neither to the idea of participation in the contemporary controversy regarding adequate theories of interpretation nor to the concern regarding the acquisition of an adequate theory of textuality. Otherwise such a theological theory would leave the reflection upon its foundations exclusively to other disciplines, for example to literary and linguistic theory, and would by so doing refuse to allow its own special textual and exegetical experiences to be included in the foundational discussion of general hermeneutics.

In this chapter an effort will be made to outline a theologically adequate theory of textuality. A theory of textuality can however only be conceived in connection with a theory of reading since texts become real for us only when we read them. Unread texts remain no more than pure possibilities.

These considerations lead to the following division of the present chapter: we take as our point of departure a reflection on the textual basis of theological thinking, which will highlight the necessity for theology of a theory of text and of reading. This is followed then by projected outlines of a theory of text and of reading. Finally, having discussed the problem of the pluralism of reading and the responsibility of the reader, we shall introduce some reflections on a possible ethic of theological reading.

2. Theology: Science of the Sentence or of the Text?

There is no doubt that one of the first objects of theological thinking is the texts of the Hebrew Scriptures and of the New Testament, which provoke a particularly theological interpretation of human experience. To that extent, theology is, from its beginnings, also a science of the text. But this fact continually falls into oblivion in the course of the centuries; single verses are separated out from the texts and, decontextualised in this manner, are elevated to the status of witnesses to certain versions of the truth.[1] Dogmatic assertions are to prestructure one's handling of biblical texts.[2] The analysis of minimal components of theological texts dominate exegetical work to the disadvantage of the larger textual units.

Such an exercise of theology through the use of atomistic analysis of language runs parallel to a particular scientific style of the past and present century, in which quite often the objectivity of the analytical explanation of content has become the sole guarantee of scientific standard. Not all efforts at theological reflection are, however, encompassed by this description. History has repeatedly produced theologians of the calibre of Rudolf Bultmann, theologians who have developed the totality of theological thought on the basis of the *text* and refused to subscribe to the theory of the verse as the unit of truth of biblical quotations. Neither have they subscribed to the theory that the individual sentence or proposition is the unit of theological truth.[3] Even such theologians, however, have been incapable of halting the progress of the unfortunate distinction between biblical exegesis and systematic theology. This distinction has dominated the organisation of university theology in the modern era and contributed to the misunderstanding that theology is concerned in the last analysis with propositional definitions of truth which are prepared by the historical-critical analysis of the text and carried out by dogmatic theologians. Such a division of labour leads to a situation where the dialectical relationship between the text and its interpretations within the framework of theology is dissolved and the categories of 'text' and 'interpretation', reciprocally related by reason of their origin, now become alienated. They thus fall victim to the separation of the dynamics of biblical exegesis and systematic theology. Texts accordingly become the object of exegesis and their interpretation becomes the object of systematic theology.[4]

The demand for a reassessment of all efforts at theological reflection with their original relation to the text in view as well as the necessity for interpretation of texts, is always accompanied by the demand for a new distribution of theological work as a whole. This latter demand can only be intelligently entertained by us once the underlying demand for a new formulation of the relationship between text and interpretation has been met.

The broadening of the theological perspective on interpretation from the single biblical or dogmatic assertion to the text as a whole requires, however, in the first instance, a calling to mind of that which constitutes a text. Theological understanding of the text requires a concept of 'text'.[5]

In the last two centuries a similar change of perspective has taken place in linguistics and this change has given rise to the research discipline of 'text linguistics'.[6] We wish to occupy ourselves now with this discipline and its object in order to advance our attempt at defining the nature of a text.

3. Reflections on Text Linguistics

a) Text Linguistics and the Theory of Interpretation

As opposed to conventional efforts to derive descriptions of language from the single word and the single sentence, text linguistics in general is concerned with proposing the 'text' as the basic linguistic unit. This extension of the perspective of linguistics is a consequence of the double dissatisfaction with the grammars of the word and of the sentence which were common up to the present. While permitting several useful insights into human linguistic processes, these grammars were nevertheless of no use when it came to generating information about the comprehensive constitution of individual meaning (*Bedeutung*) on the one hand and about sense (*Sinn*) as the linguistic totality of meaning on the other hand.[7] The individual meaning of linguistic expressions is not determined solely by the choice of words or the manner in which the sentence is structured but also by the context in which an expression is embedded. This embedding comes about through the linguistic context on the one hand and, on the other, through the situation of communication which is also constitutive of meaning. And furthermore, the composition of a linguistic context in a particular situation of communication conditions the disclosure of the fullness of its meanings (*Bedeutungsfülle*), in other words of the sense of the coherent totality of expressions.

These insights into the linguistic process call for a comprehensively scientific linguistic approach, which does justice not only to the linguistic aspects but also to the aspects of the communicative situation.

The important role played by the communicative situation for the constitution of meaning and its transparency has already been highlighted in John L. Austin's and John R. Searle's pragmatist studies.[8] This external relatedness of linguistic acts and its internal linguistic organisation compel us to treat as foundational for linguistic studies that unit which can best do justice to those two relational characteristics of linguistic expressions: the text.

The area of linguistics which concerns itself exclusively with the questions concerning 'text' and the textuality of linguistic expressions is usually designated as 'text linguistics'. But confusion reigns here because very diverse linguistic considerations with an interest in the text pose as text linguistics. This is not surprising since in all these considerations 'the description of regular patterns of text formation stands in the foreground'.[9]

It is possible, however, to distinguish between two mainstreams of text linguistic investigation, 'which result from the different definition of the research area called "text" ':[10]
a) text-linguistics as 'transphrastic' analysis, whose task it is to think through the transition from the sentence to the text and by

so doing apply to the text the insights gleaned from the grammar of the sentence; the unit to be defined by transphrastic linguistics is accordingly the concept of text; and b) text-linguistics as practico-theoretical *(handlungstheoretisch)* description of language. This description builds on the insight that 'linguistic operations are constructed only in integral unity with concrete processes of communication in a society, because language as an instrument of communication only comes into being and is relevant as essentially social'.[11] Accordingly for this type of text linguistics, the concept of text is the unit which serves as point of departure and in reference to which all other linguistic elements are described.

Eugenio Coseriu confines the designation 'text linguistics properly so-called' to the second of these streams because it is only in this case that texts, on an autonomous linguistic level, constitute a research object prior to every diversification introduced by particular (historical) languages. As against that he calls the first stream 'grammar of the text' or 'transphrastic grammar'. Finally he rejects as 'inauthentic text linguistics' that form of text linguistics which has as its task to define the functions of individual languages exclusively in reference to the functions of the text. This approach to the subject, which identifies text linguistics with linguistics as such, is rejected as mistaken by Coseriu.[12] The textual function cannot, according to him, be simply identified with a linguistic function, even if grammatical description of a particular language always has to take its origin from texts.[13]

Text linguistics properly so called investigates, then, as its object the text taken as universal phenomenon, which, transcending as it does both idiom and culture, is indeed an 'autonomous level of the linguistic'.[14]

Elisabeth Gülich and Wolfgang Raible are, however, correct in pointing out that the complex phenomenon of the text can be adequately described neither by an approach which takes its orientation from 'extra-textual criteria' of the communicative situation nor purely from 'intra-textual criteria' of a text grammatical nature. Rather is it the case that both approaches are complementary: 'accordingly a text would be, from the intra-textual standpoint, a complex linguistic sign which is composed according to the rules of the linguistic system *(langue)*. From the extra-textual point of view, a text would then have the meaning: "act of communication". That is to say, "text" and "act of communication" exercise reciprocal determination . . .'.[15]

This complementary manner of studying the matter underlines the fact that 'the text in each case is constituted solely in the act of communication, that is to say only through or in the course of its reception does it develop its textuality'.[16] This point of view also gets rid of the illusion according to which a text is capable of complete description and explanation objectively or viewed from the outside.[17] Rather is it the case that texts are always constituted, as such, to the extent that their grammatically arranged semantic potential *(Sinnpotential)* is expressed and received in the situation of communication. This holds in the same way for both oral and written texts with the reservation that in the case of written texts the expression is subject to constant 're-creation' by the receiver.[18]

Text linguistics in the proper sense is therefore concerned neither with writing textual grammars of individual languages nor with assessing everything linguistic in a 'textual' perspective, a procedure which would be tantamount to text ideology. It is rather our intention to understand under the term 'text linguistics' the description of linguistic acts as configurations capable of making sense.

We can in the first instance agree with Coseriu, for whom such text linguistics is nothing other than hermeneutics, 'and the theory of this text linguistics is nothing other than the theory of hermeneutics — in other words of interpretation'.[19] Text linguistics and text hermeneutics are then in the last analysis two expressions for the same thing. We must, however, introduce a qualification in regard to Coseriu, namely that both expressions refer to the same object from different points of view. It is the aim of text hermeneutics to interpret texts in relation to their sense *(Sinn)* whereas text linguistics aims at understanding and explaining texts as structured semantic potentials. To this extent one can distinguish, but precisely not separate, the two concerns.[20]

It is surprising that several theologians and literary experts harbour an antipathy against text linguistic matters even to the present day. The reasons for this antipathy are many and might be enumerated more or less as follows: contemporary text linguistics is impossible to grasp as a whole, or it has gone astray, or it is simply irrelevant for questions of a literary and theoretical nature. For instance, Manfred Frank came to the conclusion not very long ago that structural analysis and with it 'especially its fruitfulness from the point of view of literary science, considerably surpasses the projected outlines of contemporary text linguistics which are punctilious and over formalised and more or less confined to what is fundamental and elementary'.[21] Frank does not however state precisely what he understands under 'contemporary textlinguistics'. But precision is called for here, since it would make clear that contemporary text linguistics not only operates in opposition to structuralist or formalist methodologies and lines of questioning but that it owes some of its inspiration to these methods. And it also surpasses them, as I wish to show.

b) The Dynamic Structure of the Text

(1) On Sense and Meaning in the Text

Text linguistics aims to describe how human acts of communication succeed in linguistically mediating sense. This communication of sense through texts can, however, be adequately described only to the extent that one examines the whole communicative act in which the written text functions, that is to say text production and text reception. This is so because all relations of meaning which are ordered in the text remain pure possibilities until such time as they are received and thus actualised. The relations of meanings in the text have accordingly the character of directives *(Anweisungen)* which can in each case be implemented by the recipient.[22]

Following Siegfried Schmidt we can think of the 'text' as *'an ordered quantity of directives* to the partners in communication. The partners in communication implement the quantity of directives of a text, that is to say its meaning, only in communicative acts of interplay. An isolated text *has* no meaning, it rather *receives* it in the interplay of communication.'[23] In order to distinguish these two levels Schmidt introduces the terms 'text sense' and 'text directive'. 'Text sense' designates the potential communicative role of texts as manifold of directives, and 'text directive' signifies the realised, informative, communicative relevance of the text as implemented by the communicating partners, in the interplay of communicative acts.[24] Schmidt distinguishes thus between the potential and the realised quantity of directives. It is however only the first quantity, the potential one, which he calls text *sense* (Text*sinn*).[25]

Paul Ricoeur adopts a similar mode of expression. A text has, also for him, as we have seen above, an ideal sense and a realised meaning (*référence*) which is to be distinguished from the former.[26]

The fundamental distinction between potential semantic and finally actualised text directive is convincing, not however the restriction of 'sense' exclusively to the potential level and of 'meaning' to the realised level of the text. I suggest therefore that we might more aptly distinguish between 'possible' and 'realised' sense of a text. The possible sense consists accordingly in a number of meanings out of which the reader in the act of reading constructs a real text sense. The quantity of meaning of a text is however to be received only through acts of reading, and never independently of them.

In order to avoid the lack of precision just mentioned in the cases of Schmidt and Ricoeur it seems appropriate to formulate, with Coseriu, the following new definitions, resulting in an expansion of the notion of the linguistic concept of sign beyond Ferdinand de Saussure's distinction between *signifiant* (= the material part) and *signifié* (= the immaterial part):

> The totality of functions of language as such, of discourse in general — that is to say, the totality of functions, which refer to the designation of objects and states of affairs in the 'world', can be seen as a kind of linguistic content.

Coseriu calls this kind of content 'designation' *(Bezeichnung)*.

> The totality of that which is expressed by a particular language as such, the totality of that which is understood only through language, a particular language, can again be seen as a particular kind of linguistic content.

He calls this type of content 'meaning' *(Bedeutung)*.

> And finally the totality of text functions, the totality of that

which is understood through the text and only through the text, the totality of contents which are only given as contents of the text,

this is called *'sense'* (*Sinn*) by Coseriu.[27]
'Everything that happens in a text, everything which is described as process, has a "sense" which as a rule is not immediately identical with that which has been described but rather is such that one must discover it.'[28] Coseriu differentiates accordingly between two 'semiotic levels' and here it is possible that a reader, on the first semiotic level, understands everything 'without understanding anything whatever on the second semiotic level'.[29] In other words: It is possible that a person reading the text remains on the level of designation and meaning without advancing to the level of sense.

This phenomenon of the second semiotic level, the phenomenon of the textuality of texts, that which transforms parts of an expression into texts showing a surplus of meaning over and above the sum total of the meanings of individual utterances, is now to be considered in greater detail.

(2) On the Textuality of Texts

Texts are carriers of sense. As against that, words and sentences or single utterances function for the most part as carriers of single meanings and in this way constitute stages in relation to textual sense.[30] The text sense is accordingly always more than the sum of single meanings. A text does not exist through the fact that we know the relationships of its single expressions. Rather is it the case that we recognise the interlinking relationships between individual expressions because of our proven recognition of the linguistic unit 'text'; we confer textual status, as parts of a greater totality, on such single expressions. 'We can proceed even further and say: this greater totality, the text, which we presuppose, *forces* the ordering of the sentences into the text. This is evidenced by the fact that we always try to construe as a text, configurations which contain several sentences.'[31] Our anticipation of the continuance of the linguistic act and the coherence of its parts are already part of our recognition of the text.[32]

Examples from the corpus of biblical texts force themselves

upon us: *The Book of Proverbs* is acknowledged by us to be a large coherent totality and not just a series of single texts, and that for at least two reasons: (i) We approach all biblical 'books' with the expectation of contextuality, and (ii) this expectation in regard to the *Book of Proverbs* is strengthened by the fact that these texts are exteriorly printed together and interiorly deal with a thematically unified area, as the introductory verses suggest:

> The proverbs of Solomon son of David, king of Israel: for learning what wisdom and discipline are, for understanding words of deep meaning, for acquiring an enlightened attitude of mind — virtue, justice and fair dealing; for teaching sound judgment to the ignorant, and knowledge and sense to the young; for perceiving the meaning of proverbs and obscure sayings, the sayings of the sages and their riddles. Let the wise listen and he will learn yet more, and the man of discernment will acquire the art of guidance. The fear of Yahweh is the beginning of knowledge; fools spurn wisdom and discipline.[33]

Even the collection of psalms does not have such an introduction and nevertheless we anticipate in it a coherent text because as a biblical book it fulfils structurally and thematically our expectation of coherence.

Similarly with the texts of the Gospels. They all, with the exception of Mark, provide explicit forewords through which the thematic unity, namely the coherent communication about Jesus Christ, is maintained. Mark's Gospel has only one introductory saying ('the beginning of the Gospel of Jesus Christ the Son of God')[34] which however fulfils the same function as the extended prefaces of the other Gospels, namely to present a perspective of its thematic context.

With the help of these examples, we recognise, as well as the importance of the situation of communication of the context, a complex textuality of texts: an inner linguistic coherence of the individual expressions and a thematic coherence of the utterances in the text. Both the inner and outer coherences condition each other to the extent that the internal material coherence (*signifiant*) makes possible the outer thematic coherence (*signifié*). The coherence of the meanings in the text constitutes its potential sense. This is actualised in reading in a situation of communication characterised by attitudes of expectation.

What is important is the fact that we do not produce the sense subsequent to the reading but rather co-constitute it *during* the reading.[35] In so doing it is certainly possible to conclude too hastily that the sense of a text is identical with the sum total of individual meanings. In that case we would remain back on the level which was described by Coseriu as the first semiotic level. Or we would resolve the text into its individual parts (for example, bible verses), which we would then interpret independently of each other. In this case too we would be remaining on the first semiotic level. On the other hand in order to penetrate the second semiotic level of a text, that is to say the area where the text as a whole signifies something — i.e. sets sense free — our reading must constantly take place on both semiotic levels together throughout the text.

Accordingly, text and sense are not at one's disposition in a static grasp but rather in the dynamic of the recipient's linguistic activity of reading. The identity of a text is not static but dynamic.

In order to underline the fact that the dynamic text structure is accessible to us only through the process of reading, we wish to deal with all further observations regarding this dynamic textual structure from the perspective of reading.

c) The Dynamic Structure of Text and Reading

(1) Text and Reading in the Model of Communication

Text composition and text reception stand to each other in a correlative relationship of communication. Text composition is the procedure which forms a text as a semantic potential, and reading is the procedure which realises a written text as a form of sense. Text composition and reading — in other words, text production and text reception — are both guided by communicative intentions, in other words by that which the text has to say.

Such communicative intentions are simultaneously construed as syntactic, semantic and pragmatic in the composition and are reconstructed as such in its reception. Texts consist in semantic unities which are syntactically connected with each other and thematically combined in order to form a totality of expression which 'with reference to the situation of utterance can be pragmatically delimited. Texts are accordingly delimited units of communication which are recognisable through clear interruptions.'[36]

Such basic linguistic phenomena as the process of naming, the generation of meaning and signs of meaning cannot be further investigated here. We can, however, following Coseriu, lay as foundation for our observations a corrected version of Bühler's model of communication, which distinguishes between speaker, hearer, sign and reference *(Referenz)*. Here meaning *(Bedeutung)* is seen as something which belongs to the sign, to a certain extent as its innter function.[37] 'What is actually important in Bühler's model — and also in Jakobson's extended model, even allowing for all its shortcomings — is the basic idea that the contributions of the linguistic sign are given through and in the form of certain relations.' Coseriu concludes from these considerations, 'that the specific content of texts, the sense, is derived from the relations through which the sign functions in the act of discourse'.[38]

Coseriu arrives finally at the following concept of sense: 'The sense results from the combination of Bühler's functions (that is to say: presentation, annunciation and appeal) with that of evocation.' Under the notion 'evocation' he understands the 'totality of these functions which are not directly reducible to the function of presentation'.[39]

Coseriu's concept of text sense is plausible, but only up to a point. The concept lacks the dynamic proper to texts. It also lacks a more precise description of the dynamic composition of the relations within a text in the situations of production and reception.

We wish to pursue these relations here in order to seek out the generative force in them which brings about the text. In so doing we distinguish between *relations* which are *internal to the text* and those which are of a *contextual* nature. We designate as internal textual relations all directly linguistic strategies for text production; under the notion of contextual relations we understand all possible semantic relationships of a text to realities which happen to be outside of itself (also to other texts).

These contextual relationships will be considered in more detail in what follows when it will be our task to describe the directive mechanisms of the act of reading.[40] We devote our attention at first, however, to the internal relations of the structures of the composition, not forgetting, naturally, that these relations in the last analysis can only be judged in a fully adequate manner in the interplay of all textual relations.

(2) The Theme-Rheme Structure in the Text

The Prague School of Linguistics has shown that the internal textual relations are ordered through a 'communicative perspective'[41] and that they constitute the linguistic identity of the text in this order. The communicative process identity of the text is achieved by the 'thematic progression' which we can, according to František Daneš, observe in every text:

> By this term we mean the choice and ordering of utterance themes, their mutual concatenation and hierarchy, as well as their relationship to the hyperthemes of the superior text units (such as the paragraph, chapter, . . .), to the whole text, and to the situation. Thematic progression might be viewed as the skeleton of the plot.[42]

In order to determine the thematic progression and its various types one distinguishes in the theory of 'functional sentence perspective' between two parts of a speech act in the text: the *theme* (the starting point, the given) and the *rheme* (the new element in what is being communicated). The thematic part of the utterances introduces the object of the assertion concerning which, in the rhematic part, a statement is formulated. The rhematic part of the expression contains accordingly the determination of the thematic part of the expression.[43]

To enter into a more detailed discussion of this theory is impossible at this stage. Even without such a discussion we can already at this point formulate the following thesis: the theme-rheme structure yields a continual dynamic in the textual process, which impels the reader to move forward incessantly in the semantic constitution of the text. This happens to the extent that the dynamic in each case represents anew as themes the results of the reader's reading activity and, building on those, elicits new achievements in the activity of reading. Luise Lutz evaluates the theme-rheme structure as 'the actual scaffolding of every text: it produces the coherence of the text, it makes the understanding of the text possible'.[44] For her

86 *Text and Theological Thinking*

> the theme-rheme structure is equivalent to a pattern, which lies at the basis of all our perceptual activity: the figure-ground-differentiation. Just as, when perceiving an object on which our attention is trained, we recognise it as a figure against the background of other objects, in the same way, when speaking, we place a concept as 'figure' in the foreground and turn it into a 'theme', in order then to specify it — through the rest of the statement.[45]

It is important to note that 'theme' and 'rheme' are not syntactic concepts. What is to be considered as theme and rheme is a question which is not decided on the level of the sentence but rather on the level of text and context.[46] The reason is that it is only on this level that the thematic progression can be observed.

Daneš distinguishes three main types of thematic progression: i) the simple linear thematic one: every rheme of an utterance becomes the theme of the following utterance; ii) the thematic progression with a theme which runs through each stage: the same theme appears in a series of utterances (not always using the same words), to which different rhemes take up a relationship and iii) the thematic progression with themes which are derived from a hyper-theme and around which different rhemes assemble.[47]

The different types of thematic progression almost always occur, however, in a mixed form.[48] We can nevertheless, even at this stage, derive from each of these three models of thematic progression, a model of dynamic text formation:

First Model. From the standpoint of a particular communicative perspective, a (complex) theme is developed and this happens in a dynamic progression. The dynamic of this process has as its foundation the tension between thematic anticipations (*Vorgaben*) and rhematic determinations, which not only enhance, determine and explain the original thematic anticipation but even change it, so that theme and rheme together fuse into a new thematic point of departure for the further development of the text. This dialectical principle of thematic and rhematic utterance references constitutes a coherent perspectival tension curve in the text: every utterance makes a new contribution towards advancing the communicative contents of the text.

Second Model. In this model of thematic progression different rhemes determine a theme. These rhemes can again be connected among themselves. This model derives its text-constituting dynamic from the accumulation of rhematic utterances which develops into a theme or a thematic area. The coherence of the text results here from thematic constancy.

Third Model. This model is similar to the foregoing with the important difference that the theme is subdivided into several sub-themes, which in their turn together constitute the coherence of the text.

The controlling principle of these text models and of their possible combinations is the communicative perspective. It determines the theme and decides in each case on its development relative to the contribution of information by the rhemes. Thematic selection and rhematic commentary — that is to say, the development of individual units of meaning — owe their existence to the communicative perspective. It is this which makes the choice and combination out of the abundance of linguistic possibilities of designation. To this extent one can describe the communicative perspective as a phenomenon of style:[49] it chooses the various forms which a textual composition can take.[50]

Jan Firbas has introduced the concept of the 'communicative dynamic' of a sentence, a dynamic which is organised by the theme-rheme structure.[51] If we extend this term 'communicative dynamic' to the text, then we may say that the theme-rheme structure of a text, guided by the communicative perspective, now organises its communicative dynamic to the extent that it guarantees a continual increase of the information value of a text.

Furthermore, we must also recognise that even the headings or titles of a text can be organised according to the theme-rheme structure.[52] Either we find in the headings and titles of the text, indications or even precise explanations of the theme as for example, 'The Revelation of John' and the 'Acts of the Apostles', or it can even happen that in connection with a rheme a full theme-rheme structure is present as, for example, in the first verse of the Gospel according to Mark: 'The beginning of the Good News about Jesus Christ, the Son of God.'

This insight into the nature of the theme-rheme structure and the description of thematic progression in the text permit us to evaluate the text and its reception as fluctuating identities. They make it possible for us to get rid once and for all of the fiction that a text is a static figure. Metaphorically speaking, the text is rather in the nature of a path to be trodden by the reader. We are dealing here with a dominant perspective, a central direction. This dominant perspective, however, only becomes clear when considering several subsidiary perspectives in the width of the vista, and then only when the path is followed at all — that is to say, through reading the text.

3. The Complexity of the Text

In what has been said up to the present, the dynamic of textual composition and the dynamic of reading postulated by it have been schematically presented with the help of relations internal to the text. In so doing it became evident that a text consists of several levels which have to be experienced together if the reading is to succeed. The levels of meaning and sense stand here in a dialectical relationship to each other. With the level of meaning as a starting point, a level of sense is continually constructed and meanings are continually disclosed on the basis of this semantic level. It is precisely this dialectic which characterises the text as text. For in reading a single sentence, an accompaniment of a semantic level (*Sinnebene*) or of a level of semantic anticipations (*Sinnerwartungsebene*) does not occur. On the other hand, when it is a question of the text, the production and disclosure of individual meaning (*Einzelbedeutung*) and the production and disclosure of the sense of the whole, always proceed as one and the same process.

The theme-rheme structure has brought schematically before our eyes the process nature of texts. In what we have said we have desisted from discussing the individual linguistic methods of sentence combinations such as the substitutions of pronouns[53] and the functions of conjunctions.[54] The reason is that in this chapter what concerns us are the universally valid characteristics of texts, which of course can be realised in different ways in each individual language.

Before we devote our attention, however, to the relations which are external to the text, that is to say to the communicative conditions of textual reception, we wish to reflect further on the web of relations which is internal to the text. This is constituted not alone by the communicative dynamic of theme-rheme structure but also by the referential functions in the text. And these become organised and dynamic through the theme-rheme structure.

Let us call to mind once more our sign model, according to which every word can function as a designation for an extra linguistic object or state of affairs if it is embedded in the linguistic context of an individual language and there receives semantic qualities. Single, isolated words of natural languages do not on the whole as yet exercise a particular reference function, and therefore have no unambiguous sign character either.[55] This characteristic of an as yet unspecified reference, i.e. polysemy of words, is cancelled out in the text in favour of a monosemification *(Monosemierung)*. 'Monosemification is brought about through the reciprocal semantic determination of lexemes relating to each other in a mutually supportive manner *(solidarisch)*; that is, of lexemes which have in common certain referential characteristics, notwithstanding all their variety in other respects.'[56] Accordingly it is never individual lexemes, but rather associations of lexemes which constitute the referential form of a text.

Lexeme associations of a text, which ground both the text's projection of reality together with their own specific ordering, owe their existence to the recurrence of a certain feature. For it is only the repeated appearance of the same or mutually and uniformly related lexemes which produces the semantic coherence of the text. In our text models we have already presented three variations of such thematic recurrence,[57] which naturally could be multiplied at will.

Algirdas Greimas has coined the notion of 'isotopic' level. With this Greimas wishes to clarify 'that texts, even though they are assembled from heterogeneous units, are nevertheless situated on homogeneous semantic levels (i.e. isotopic levels) and so constitute a totality of meaning.'[58] Such an isotopic level is composed then of at least two lexemes.

Hence, the concept of isotopic level can show that lexemes are grouped together in a text to form lexeme associations. But how this grouping is organised, that is to say the dynamic of lexeme composition in a text, this is not explained with the help of Greimas's model.

Neither is the text dynamic sufficiently illuminated through the theory of 'textphoric' (*Textphorik*).⁵⁹ It is certainly possible to distinguish in the text elements which point backwards (anaphoric) and elements which point forward (cataphoric). In the case of individual languages such forms of indication can be organised in different ways — for example, through the formation of pronouns and through certain usage of the article. Their co-ordination can however be precisely determined only through the theme-rheme structure.

To sum up then, we may say that a text is a complex configuration which is organised in a dynamic structure of communication through mutually supportive lexeme associations and provokes an equally dynamic reception of the references (*Referenzen*) and of their coordination.

d) Theological Disclosure of the Sense of Texts

Our reflection on text linguistics has led us to evaluate the textuality of texts as a dynamic process which only yields up its fullness of sense in a reception equally dynamic, that is to say when the reader enters into the text as process and, simultaneously with the reading of the individual parts of the text, constructs the totality of textual coherence. We have seen the internal relations in the text which contribute to its form and with whose help the reader can enter into the textual process. With the consideration of the internal relations and their pattern of references in the text and going from this to the reality presented, the discussion of the concept of 'text' is, however, not exhausted. For we have not yet concerned ourselves with the influences of the communicative situation on the recognition of the text. The following questions suggest themselves: how are texts pragmatically delimited? Are reading attitudes to the text guided rather by the text itself than by the situation of reception? Do all texts exercise, in the same manner, guiding influences on reading or do these differ according to the genre of text in question? We intend to illustrate these questions with the help of textual examples of a theological nature and we wish to try to offer an answer out of the appropriate praxis.

In determining the external range of a text we have, up to the present, drawn attention only to the pragmatic limitations.⁶⁰

This observation requires to be given greater precision in the light of the corpus of biblical texts. For not only in the Hebrew Scriptures but also in the writings of the New Testament, widely differing forms of textual coherence can, from the pragmatic point of view, be shown to exist.

(1) Textual Determination Exemplified by the Book of Genesis

The *Book of Genesis* can be looked upon as a complete text in which the divine origin of the world and God's activity in it can be distinguished as the communicative perspective. But *Genesis* can also be seen as the first of the five books of Moses which together constitute the Jewish Law, the Torah, the central communicative perspective of which is the legal determination of the relationship between man and God. Furthermore, *Genesis* can be evaluated as a constitutive text in the totality of the Hebrew Scriptures, the central communicative perspective of which is as follows: God's dealings with Israel and Israel's relationship with God. Finally *Genesis* can be designated as one of the seventy-two books of the Bible of both Testaments which has as communicative perspective God's dealing with God's humankind, seen as a totality, a dealing which reaches its high point in God's revelation in Jesus Christ.

Alongside these possibilities of seeing *Genesis* as an independent text and as a constitutive text, the *First Book of Moses* can also be seen as being itself a collection of constitutive texts. The two accounts of creation, the story of the fall, the story of Noah, the story of the Patriarchs and the story of Joseph can in each case be shown to be complete texts within the *Book of Genesis*. And within these texts still further complete texts with their own communicative perspective can be brought to light as has been clearly evidenced by the investigations of form criticism and redaction criticism.

But common to all of these textual differentiations is the fact that for each text a unified communicative perspective can be pointed out which organises the text and makes it coherent through the theme-rheme structure.

Now it is evident that communicative perspectives can be distinguished which are subordinated to others — that is to say, they stand to one another in a hierarchical relationship. The communicative value of a text can be either subordinated to that of another text or superior to it.

(2) The Significance of the Reading Situation for Reception: The New Testament Canon as an Example

These possibilities of establishing hierarchies within the text are nevertheless insufficient to justify the existence of both biblical canons. For how is it possible otherwise to account for the exclusion of the so-called apocryphal texts, which certainly, from the point of view of their perspectives of communication could, to some extent at least, be assimilated by the canons of biblical writings? In the process of canonisation of the biblical texts it is rather the case that still other hierarchical factors, external to the texts, played a significant role.

The assimilation of the biblical texts to both canons does not rest entirely on the thematic compatibility of individual texts but rather represents a decision to select from thematically compatible texts. This decision is rooted in certain interpretative attitudes to such texts as might be considered suitable for inclusion in the canons.

In relation to the New Testament we can clarify for ourselves this process in the following manner. The formation of the canon was guided by interests outside the text, for example by the endeavour to create a norm with the help of which the existence of Christians in this world could be interpreted and formed in opposition to the Gnostic, especially the Marcionite challenges.[61] The individual texts of the New Testament canon which were brought together in this manner turn out to be themselves interpretations — that is, Christological interpretations — of the Jesus event which go back to certain community traditions.[62] In the early Church these interpretations were, on the one hand, further interpreted whilst on the other hand they became elevated to the status of a practical norm for the interpretation of Christian writings and Christian existence. This norm is however, as text, very manifold in itself, so that it is continually in need of new and thorough interpretation, if it is to supply the principal criteria for the interpretation of individual texts. Nor can the necessity of renewed interpretation be banished from the world by pointing to the divinely inspired nature of the canonical writings.[63]

The Church Fathers who were responsible for the elevation of the twenty-seven texts to the status of New Testament canon have taken a wise step, insofar as it was necessary from this point onwards that all individual interpretations be continually assessed in relation to the interpretation of the total perspective of this canon. It follows that both the interpretation of the New Testament understood as a whole in its pluralistic nature and the interpretation of the twenty-seven individual texts, which again consist partly of a plurality of texts, are related to each other in dialectical dependence.

Thus, precisely because of the formation of the canon, no enduring uniformity of biblical interpretation as a whole was possible. Although it is true that every interpretation of a part of a text depended on that of the text as a whole, this does not of itself exclude the possibility of a further plurality of interpretations. The reason is that every reading of a text takes place in its own individual situation which also influences the disclosure of the sense of the text; the situation must be part of the process. How else can the individual meanings in the text be understood in a situation of reception which is alien to the text's situation of origin — how else other than through readers in their historical situations of reception, specific as these are to them alone?

This acknowledgment of the necessity of individual participation in the textual process, by the reader, has tended to get ambivalent treatment in the long tradition of reading New Testament texts. On the one hand the necessity of text interpretation was of course maintained through the very process of the formation of the canon itself. On the other hand, in the course of reading history, it happened continually that certain, sometimes quite individual, reading perspectives were posited absolutely, through which further readers were prevented from achieving an authentic reading experience, because they were denied the right to read for themselves.[64] Orthodoxy and heterodoxy were quite often distinguished not by reference to the text but solely by reference to a particular reading perspective.

Whenever on the other hand reading perspectives are projected independently of the text or whenever certain readership groups dogmatically arrogate to themselves alone the right to read adequately, there is the danger that here the question is not one of the disclosure of the sense of texts but rather of interest and perspectives alien to the texts.

From this point of view we are faced with the following two questions of a more general nature: how can the relationship between text and reading be more accurately grasped in relation to the individual personal activity of the reader in the process of reading? And to what extent do the different text genres co-determine the respective reading genres? It is only when these two questions are adequately answered that we can return to the special problems of theological and ecclesiastical text interpretation, as also to that of the claim of a special interpretative competence.

4. Text and Text Genres

The aim of the present section is to investigate the role of individual influence in the *formation of texts*. Accordingly for the moment we are bracketing out the aspect of reading as part of the textual process in order to focus on the interplay between individual and universal aspects in the process of text formation which is a characteristic of all texts. For it is only when the text formation as a phenomenon is described that the provocation of reading acts which emanate from such formation can be adequately comprehended. Our distinction between text and text genres on the one hand, and between reading and reading genres on the other hand, was made accordingly for purely methodological reasons. In the next section of this chapter this division will again be cancelled out when the dependencies of reading from the text are analysed, as well as the individual influence of the reader and his/her reading situation on the act of reading.

a) Reflections on the Style of a Text

In all known languages one finds procedures for the composition of texts, so that one may with precaution call the text, as level of the structuring of individual languages, an 'empirical universal'.[65] This empirically universal possibility of textual generation is realised in the different languages as an individual act. The principle of individuation in the production of texts is the *style*.

Schleiermacher has already defined a work of written discourse through the characteristics: 'structure' (*Strukturiertheit*), 'adherence to genre' *(Gattungszugehörigkeit)* and 'style'.[66] Ricoeur follows these categories[67] and speaks of 'composition', 'genre' and 'style' as the three dimensions of discourse. He defines 'style':

> This word designates the aspect of the work that makes it a unique configuration. The style of a work lets the hearer or reader *identify* it as an individual. . . . This third category is the decisive one, if Aristotle is correct when he says that man contemplates universals, but produces individuals.[68]

The manner in which these three dimensions of discourse are, however, related to each other remains unexplained in Schleiermacher and Ricoeur to the extent that both fail to work out the original power of style which regulates the entire process of textual generation through structuring and choice of genre.

Following Eroms, therefore, I would like to define 'style' in general as a phenomenon of selection: 'Particular linguistic variants are chosen from those which are in paradigmatic opposition, so that they contextually (syntagmatically) produce a certain effect.'[69] The formation of a text is then a stylistic action; and the style is the principle of responsibility for text composition for it is its own proper style which is responsible for the identity of every individual text as a consequence of an individual choice of language in a particular communicative perspective. Hence style as a principle of text composition must be described with 'categories of linguistic activity'. For here, according to Barbara Sandig, 'the alternative, "content" on the one hand and form or style on the other disappears. "Content" is then to be seen as determining the type of the linguistic act (with illocution and propositional content) and "style" is to be seen as the manner in which the linguistic act is carried out.'[70]

Sandig's differentiations are a further help to us, to the extent that they throw new light on the problem of the text.[71]

> In the case of simple speech acts, the stylistic aspect is constituted by the connection between the type of speech act and the type of utterance: the formulation. In the case of complex speech acts, which are accomplished as a succession of speech acts, the stylistic aspect is constituted by the connection between the selected partial acts and their sequence with the types of utterances. In the case of indivi-

dual texts I call this connection the manner of formulation and I call it the pattern of formulation in the case of conventional types of texts.[72]

A twofold element constitutes accordingly the essence of style: on the one hand the formulation (formation) of the individual utterances and on the other hand the manner of formulation (the manner of formation) of a text. In other words: both the individual succession of theme and rheme of an utterance and the thematic progression as a whole in the unity of the text are stylistic formations. The formation of a text as coherent entity, as a totality of meaning which is ordered through a communicative perspective is the result of stylistic endeavour. This endeavour is facilitated in so far as the community of speakers and the tradition of formulation provide patterns of formation which are at the disposal of the individual process of text production.

Style as an act of selection presupposes paradigms. The stylistic decisions never take place in a stylistic vacuum. Such vacuums do not exist. Every instance of text production is essentially related to patterns of style formation which are already at hand and have been handed down. In all observable communities of speakers certain stylistic acts achieve a normative character, that is to say they regulate expectations which are superimposed on new style formations. But transgressions of such stylistic norms are also 'stylistic', that is to say they are evidence of an individual intention of style formation which, depending on its communicative success, is itself either accepted as constitutive of a new norm or is totally or partly rejected.

Certain manners of formulation, certain stylistic actions, have proved to be particularly resilient and capable of constituting new norms, because they were particularly suited to meeting certain communicative needs. From the point of view of style we may speak of 'types of presentation', from the point of view of textual theory we may speak of 'strategies of textualisation'.[73] These conventions can acquire such constancy that we may speak of the common 'text genres'.[74]

Style must then be described as a characteristic of textuality,[75] so that text acts now become manifest in a new complexity: they are integrated actions composed of conventional and individual types of speech acts (= stylistic genres).[76] Sandig characterises both components of style in the following manner:

By conventional (common) styles are understood the historically and socially conditioned clusters of action and utterance types, which are carried out in a predictable manner, in the form of greater action clusters, that is to say in text patterns or their parts. Correspondingly, it follows that individual styles are to be described as unconventional clusters of action and utterance types carried out in complex actions.[77]

Since, however, stylistic conventions contribute to less problematic communication, it is in the interest of the individual who produces a text to pay at least some regard to these conventions in order to regulate in this way the reading of her/his text. A text act always receives its individual character in the first place from interplay with the conventional styles which are at hand.[78]

We may summarise as follows: texts are units of communication, which consist in thematic and rhematic speech acts, units which are composed within a particular communicative perspective and thus find their specific style. The conditions for the realisation of the communication in question require a type of textualisation which is in each case specific to the communication, a type which must pay due regard both to general stylistic habits (conventions) and to the individual communicative perspective. The free decision in favour of a particular linguistic paradigm, among many, which we call style, characterises the written text as an individual work. This individual character of a text moves continually between norm application and norm denial. It remains therefore in each case related to norms of presentation, that is to say, it remains continually subject to norm exposure.

b) Text Genres

(1) Essence and Function of Text Genres

'Text genres' are, according to our study, conventional patterns of formulation, which are used as a central structure of their text by individual authors and are formed in each case in line with the individual communicative perspective. It follows from this that text genres in the strict sense are never capable of being identically realised. They are capable merely of showing certain common characteristics as they are realised, which are connected with the exemplarity of their communicative function.

For example, 'a newspaper-advertisement-spot' can be identified as text genre to the extent that slogans can be continually published in newspapers which have in common the communicative function 'to persuade the reader to buy a product'.

Text genres are thus distinguishable according to their main function in the process of communication. But they never appear in a pure form. Rather do they always take on further subordinate functions whose particular stylistic combination marks the character of the individual text.

The text is a universal category of human activity. Text genres on the other hand are patterns for individual text acts. However, they play as such a significant role in human communication, especially in linguistic communication through writing. The original distanciation is indeed to some extent compensated for by text genres. For these offer the reader a semantic framework genres. For these offer the reader a semantic framework grounded in conventions and thus predictable.[79] This framework consists in the exemplification of the major communicative function of a text (for example, political information, act of prayer, love song).[80] The major function of a text can be announced through different strategies: — by the heading (title); — by the manner of presentation; — by being embedded in a larger context of action.

Attention has already been briefly drawn to the significance of the *heading* or *title* for the composition and reading of the text.[81] Headings can hint at text genres by reference to particular contents. This can be exemplified by the analysis of two headings from Karl Rahner's *Foundations of Christian Faith*.

Rahner uses thematising headings like 'On the Pauline Theology of the Church'[82] and rhematising headings like 'The Church of Jesus Christ must be One'.[83] The first heading leads us to suspect a scientific analysis; the second, a paranetic exposition.[84]

But titles can also give rise to a false impression. In Ionesco's play *The Bald Prima Donna* no such character appears.[85] The recipient of the play is not prepared by its title for the absurd action, so that he/she is all the more struck by the plot itself.

The *presentation-types* (or strategies of textualisation) are the 'primary principles of textualisation'.[86] Eroms distinguishes four main strategies: to narrate, to argue, to describe, to instruct.[87] These main strategies can also be combined with one another. They only constitute rough strategies, however, in addition to which in each case variations are conceivable.[88]

'Narrating' serves the purpose of communicating information, and for the most part takes the form of a past tense.[89] 'Arguing' serves the purpose of convincing the reader of the text and usually takes the form of the present tense. 'Instructing' serves the purpose of determining the action of someone receiving an order and is mostly realised in imperative or future mode. 'Describing' serves the purpose of a timeless presentation of objects or states of affairs. Because of the danger of monotony, descriptive functions are occasionally realised also through other strategies of textualisation.

The choice of tense and the degree of direct address of the reader, together with the exposition of the theme contribute, as a rule, reliable indications regarding the text genre that can be expected and regulate accordingly the basic reading attitude. Such regulation can also be achieved through *the embedding of a text in a greater context of action.* In this case it can be a question of an embedding text-corpus or of the situation in which the text is read. Only certain text genres can emerge from each of these two conditioning factors.

Denzinger's[90] collection of dogmas can, for example, function as embedding text-corpus for the individual dogmatic texts which are contained in the collection. Every reader of this book expects only a particular text genre, which in addition co-regulates the reading activity through its special combination of 'instructing' and 'arguing'. It goes without saying that we find such an embedding of individual texts also in the *Bible.* Whenever we read in the Gospels concerning Jesus, 'and he told them the following parable', the text genre 'parables of Jesus' awakes in us certain reading expectations.

All institutions which have given expression to typical text genres may be thought of as reading situations specific to these text genres: the law court, the school, the church, the parliament, committees, etc. Here the connection between institution and

(2) The Hierarchy of Functions in the Text

Various textual functions are conceivable, whose centre of gravity is plumbed by reference to the communicative perspective. Such functions are: informative, meditative, aesthetic, documentary, confessional, entertaining, didactic, etc.[91] These distinctive characteristics help us also in the differentiation between literary and non-literary texts. In the case of literary text genres the aesthetic function stands in the foreground and locates the other text functions relative to the central one.[92] Within literary text genres we then may further distinguish between specific text genres, according to the combination of the main aesthetic function and the subordinate functions connected with it, so that we achieve a hierarchy of literary functions.

The appropriate application and transformation of text genres in the process of textual composition gives a clue to the degree of 'stylistic competence' of the author. He/she confers on his/her productions an individual character on the basis of the convention which is in each case dominant. The assessment of such competence is linked to the perception of the norm which prevails in the society in question and accordingly is never absolute.[93] This observation concerning the reading of texts must suffice at the moment, for we are still concerned with the various possibilities of textual composition.

c) Theological Text Genres

The problem of text genres is not new for theology. Since the emergence of historical-critical exegesis, theologians tend to be concerned to investigate texts from the point of view of form and genre as well as from that of *Sitz im Leben*. Accordingly genre research as intended by Hermann Gunkel takes as its point of departure

> that forms of discourse and literary genre were more clearly determined in antiquity than is the case today, that they

follow a certain schema in their composition, that they exhibit more or less constant motifs and possess a particular *'Sitz im Leben'* as place of origin. Depending on opportunity and occasion, the narrator or poet selected his genre and having done so was then, however, restricted to its schema, so that, on the one hand, personal freedom to introduce variations was limited, whilst on the other hand, the conventional and typical were decisive.'[94]

The history of genres, in the course of its development, turned into the history of forms which rests on the sifting of literary critical forms and leads finally to research into the history of transmission *(Überlieferungsgeschichte)*. Such research not only examines the textual units as to the manner in which their final form came about, but also takes as its aim the reconstruction of the whole process in which the units came into being.'[95] The interest in forms and schemata, with the help of which one would wish to approach Old and New Testament texts, often distinguishes therefore between form/style and content and does not treat the texts as communicative units. In addition, the Biblical introductory sciences lack for the most part a reliable methodology.[96]

David Hellholm has convincingly drawn attention to this lack of theory. He elaborated a transphrastic text-grammar theory, which he applies to an ancient ecclesiastical text. His theoretical work is not, however, an unqualified help to us here, for we are in search of models for the description of texts, models which transcend all idioms, in the sense of the 'authentic text linguistics' described above. Firstly such models are to enable us, in a general way, to make statements regarding 'text' as category of action; and secondly such models should make accessible to us ideal types of theological textuality, viewed in the light of criteria for the communicative perspective.[97] Finally these categories, 'text' and 'text typology' should help us in the working out of our theological concept of interpretation. Our endeavour to elaborate a typology has, accordingly, as its aim to list only such types of text acts as, transcending all idioms, can ground every written theological text act, that is to say every linguistic projection of sense.

In the first section of this chapter we identified theology as a textual science. We reflected on the essence of text as potential for sense and on its stylistic vacillation between the norm of textualisation and the will to impose an individual Gestalt, determined by the communicative perspective. Now we aim at drawing conclusions regarding the role of the text in theology.

All theological reflection on texts is interpretative thought. This insight does not, however, isolate a pattern of action specific to theology, since all texts are text acts which interpret reality. We must therefore direct our attention to the specific object, and the communicative perspective of theological text acts which is connected with this object. The object of all theological text acts is the manifestation of God in the world of humankind and the conditions of understanding proper to such manifestation. This manifestation is neither 'immediately' nor 'directly' intelligible but rather requires linguistic formulation and therefore textual acts. In the course of history many such text acts get handed down. Christian theology has developed a special attitude towards certain text acts which have been handed down in written form. This attitude has elevated such texts to norms of Christian thinking: the canon of the writings of the New and Old Covenants.

These texts present us then with the primary object constituted as norm by the community and, accordingly, the provocation of theological interpretation. In the interpretative struggle with these texts, new texts are constituted. We wish to distinguish, then, in general two essential groups of theological text types: i) biblical texts and ii) interpretations of biblical texts and of other texts, with the help of biblical texts.

We have already drawn attention to the fact that biblical texts are not in themselves unitary, that is to say that they themselves, in their turn, permit of distinction into different interpretative text genres. For biblical texts are of course themselves interpretations of the process of divine manifestation. This circumstance will be of still more detailed interest to us in the following section about reading. Here, however, we are concerned with possible theological text genres and we discern that the interpretation of the divine manifestations is the main communicative perspective of all theological text acts — on two different levels of interpretation, however. We distinguish in Christianity 'primary theological acts of interpretation' (biblical texts) and 'secondary theological acts of interpretation'. The central communicative perspective of the primary text acts in the New Testament is the original acknowledgment on the part of humankind that Jesus is the Christ and that in him God is revealed. This communicative perspective is the decisive inner textual principle[98] of the composition of the canon of the New Covenant. The communicative perspective of the secondary text acts is the interpretation — i.e., the understanding, explanation and assessment — of these texts from the standpoint of historical and cultural distance and in the light of the particular existential horizon of the interpreter. This horizon must naturally already and continually co-reflect the effective history of the biblical texts.

Within this secondary type of text act, different text genres have again conventionally proved themselves. These are at the disposal of the author of theological texts: (i) commentaries on biblical writings; (ii) interpretations of certain partial texts (i.e. tracts, sermons, monographs); (iii) short confessional formulae, confessions of faith, dogmas; (iv) interpretations of the situation of reception, that is to say of the world in which Christians, by interpreting, organise their lives.

The corresponding functions of these text genres with reference to the communicative perspectives are: (i) philosophical-historical pedagogy, assessment and apologetics; (ii) elaboration and elucidation of a biblical text within a new context; (iii) recapitulation of a common confession; (iv) coming to awareness of the situation of communication.

Teaching, elucidating, summing up and reflecting are accordingly the essential principles of composition of the secondary theological text acts just mentioned.

For the primary type of text act, i.e. the biblical texts, all the general strategies of textualisation highlighted by Eroms (narrating, arguing, describing, instructing) can be shown to be present. These function in corresponding text genres with a particular communicative perspective.[99]

Finally we may summarise as follows: in theology we distinguish two fundamental groups of text genres: the biblical interpretations of an event — of the Jesus event in the New Testament — and the text acts which interpret the Bible and the world.

5. Reading and Reading Genres

One cannot responsibly deal with texts without at the same time considering that they are to be read. The artificial separation of our reflections thus far into those concerning a potential and those concerning a realised text dimension was justified only for reasons of analysis. For it was our aim to investigate texts as potentials for sense, but only as in each case realised by the reader in the act of reading. Accordingly it was clear from the start that a text has an identity which, from the point of view of its design, is never purely, univocally and objectively comprehensible but is rather in constant need of an individual reading act in order to be able to present itself. One and the same text finds in every new reading act a new and in each case individually justified semantic form (*Sinngestalt*). This semantic form is, however, always provoked and co-organised by the text and to this extent never arbitrary.

The semantic form of the text disclosed in reading is never to be conceived of as static. Reading can never be compared with a jig-saw puzzle where the individual parts require only to be correctly assembled in order to present a picture composed by the producer which then remains constant. The reading of a text is, rather, a dynamic process which remains in principle open-ended because every reader can only disclose the sense of a text in a process and as an individual. This signifies in its turn that reading is in each case more than the deciphering of the signs printed on paper. Reading is always also a projection of a new image of reality, as this is co-initiated by the text and achieved by the reader in the relationship with the text in the act of reading.

The questions which will be investigated in this section have to do with the relationship between reader and text: how far does the text determine the process of reading, how far is it determined by the reader? To put the question in another way: to what extent are the identity and variability of the disclosure of textual sense grounded in the text, to what extent in the reader? In order, however, to describe with greater accuracy the contributions of the reader, it is necessary not only to have a theory of individual reading but also to investigate the influence of the social conditions in which reading takes place: how far is the reader influenced by reading norms and conventions and to what extent does his/her reading exhibit individual characteristics? Parallel to our distinction between text style and text genres in the composition of a text, we can speak here about reading style and reading genres in the reception of the text.

We wish, then, in the first place to discuss certain aspects of a reading theory, in order to go on to the problems of specifically theological reading, after some general reflections on the nature of reading genres.

a) Aspects of a Theory of Reading

It is above all literary critics who have in recent times earned appreciation in the matter of elaboration of reading theories. On both sides of the Atlantic there has developed a 'reader oriented literary criticism'. Under this generic term lie hidden the most widely differing strands. Susan Suleiman, for example, distinguishes six main streams of this 'audience-oriented criticism': the rhetorical, the semiotic/structuralist, the phenomenological, the subjective-psycho-analytical, the sociological-historical and the hermeneutical approach.[100] Each of these approaches contributes important impulses but entails also considerable difficulties. It is impossible to have a full discussion here either of all the approaches mentioned or of further possible approaches. We shall try, rather, to observe convergences in these strands insofar as all these theories assign to the reader of a text an irreplaceable role in the disclosure of the sense of the text and they elucidate this necessary co-operation from different points of view.

Since it is our aim to trace the possibilities and limits of a 'reading-pluralism', we need not immerse ourselves in the details of such a special reading theory. We must rather discover the characteristics of a general theory of reading. Because however all of the existing outlines have to do with the reception of literary texts, we must also investigate the question of whether it is possible to derive from such investigations, coherent generalisations for the reception of written texts as such, or whether on the contrary the reception is always specific to the text genres. But we must first consider to what extent the reader on the one hand, and her/his text on the other, regulate the reception.

Already in the last section of the text we have *de facto* excluded the extreme answers to this question, namely that either the text alone or the reader totally determines the reading. A conception like that, on the one hand, of E.D. Hirsch,[101] according to which the text is always the same and remains so, or on the other hand of the deconstructionists for whom textual sense is totally undetermined,[102] is of no great use to us in the particular discussion of the dialectic between text and reader. On the other hand the debate regarding the extent of the respective regulation holds a promise of an advance in insight. We select from this debate the contributions of Wolfgang Iser and Stanley Fish. Iser is inclined to concede to the text the greater regulative contribution whereas Fish expects to find the main source of regulation in the social reading conventions.

(1) Wolfgang Iser's Theory of Reading

Iser investigates the act of reading from the point of view of the effect of the text and not from that of the reader's assessment of the text. 'A theory of response has its roots in the text; a theory of reception arises from a history of readers' judgements.'[103] The text is 'a potential effect that is realized in the reading process'.[104] To the extent that Iser places the emphasis of his investigation on the effect of the text, he feels obliged to direct his criticisms against 'explanations' of the text:

> The effectiveness of the work depends on the participation of the reader, but explanations arise from (and also lead to) detachment; they will therefore dull the effect, for they relate the given text to a given frame of reference, thus flattening out the new reality brought into being by the fictional text. In view of the irreconcilability of effect and explanation, the traditional expository style of interpretation has clearly had its day.[105]

Although one must agree with Iser that it cannot be the point of reading to look for hidden meanings behind the text, but rather to disclose the text itself, nevertheless his global denigration of explanation comes as a surprise to us, since in the course of his discussions Iser himself *explains* to us with the help of literary examples how the effect of a text comes about.

Reading is a process of communication,[106] which according to Iser is kept in motion essentially through 'elements of indeterminacy'[107] present in the text. An 'implied reader'[108] is anticipated in the text. 'He embodies all those predispositions necessary for a literary work to exercise its effect.'[109] The living reader requires, then, nothing other than to adopt the role assigned to him/her by the text and that happens mainly through taking over the point of view pre-given to him/her by the text. However, Iser immediately admits that the offer of a role made by the text can never be realised other than selectively.[110] No reading process can therefore do full justice to the text. 'The fact that the reader's role can be fulfilled in different ways, according to historical or individual circumstances, is an indication that the structure of the text *allows* for different ways of fulfilment.'[111]

In the reading of the text the reader finds him/herself faced with a text repertoire which, out of known conventions, prepares the situation of the text. Within this framework the text strategies which constitute the specific character of the text are actualised.[112] This results in a foreground-background-relationship[113] as elementary organisation of the conditions of comprehension of the text. Iser speaks also of 'theme-horizon structure' and reminds us with this of the theme-rheme structure, which we have already characterised as the basic dynamic of the text.[114] This structure of theme and horizon 'bridges the gap between text and reader for the reason that it is at the same time a structure of text perspectives and a structure of the activity of consciousness'.[115]

Iser places the greatest possible emphasis on the activity of the reader's consciousness in the process of reading. 'Textual structures and structured acts of comprehension are ... the two poles in the act of communication, whose success will depend on the degree in which the text establishes itself as a correlative in the reader's consciousness.'[116] The mission of the text is thus realised in the consciousness of the reader, an observation which also entails 'that these acts, though set in motion by the text, defy total control by the text itself, and, indeed, it is the very lack of control that forms the basis of the creative side of reading'.[117] The reader's consciousness is accordingly creatively engaged in the disclosure of the sense of the text. Where are the opportunities and limitations of this creativity to be found according to Iser?

Although Iser does not enter into the discussion concerning the communicative dynamic in the text, his phenomenological intuition bears a resemblance to the results of our investigation of the theme-rheme structure: 'Each sentence correlate contains what one might call a hollow section, which looks forward to the next correlate, and a retrospective section, which answers the expectations of the preceding sentence (now part of the remembered background).'[118] This inner textual dynamic regulates the reading act and gives rise to the perspectives of the reader as well as their transformations. Iser speaks of a 'wandering viewpoint' as constituting the manner through which the reader is present in the text.[119] He conceives the relationship between the text and the reader in a dialectical fashion, as 'a continual modification of memory and an increasing complexity of expectation'.[120] But the notion 'dialectic' appears to me to be out of place at this point. For the relationship between text and reader is for Iser, not a relationship of reciprocity between equals but, rather, as we have seen, a process of regulatory mechanisms on the part of the text, in the course of which the reader admittedly creates contents of consciousness, which, however, are always measured against the textual process and in certain cases corrected by it. This impression is corroborated also in what Iser has to say on the manner in which the text finds its Gestalt in the process of interpretation:

> The 'consistent interpretation', or gestalt, is a product of the interaction between text and reader, and so cannot be exclusively traced back either to the written text or to the disposition of the reader.[121]

> The reader's part in the gestalt consists in identifying the connection between the signs; the 'autocorrelation' will prevent him from projecting an arbitrary meaning on the text, but at the same time the gestalt can only be formed as an identified equivalence through the hermeneutic schema of anticipation and fulfilment in relation to the connections perceived between the signs.[122]

> Consistency-building is the indispensable basis for all acts of comprehension, and this in its turn is dependent upon processes of selection. This basic structure is exploited by literary texts in such a way that the reader's imagination can be manipulated and even reoriented.[123]

'Through gestalt-forming, we actually participate in the text, and this means that we are caught up in the very thing we are producing.'[124] There can thus be no question of a dialectical relationship between text and reader, rather is the reader 'entangled' in the text.[125] As a result of this, she/he both forgoes the freedom to choose a point of view[126] and exposes her/his personal identity to the fusion process of the constitution of textual sense in the reader's consciousness, only to receive this identity anew in the achieving of textual sense.[127]

After this acknowledgment of the existential unity of disclosure of sense through reading, and through the reader becoming her/himself, we find Iser's splitting up of textual sense and textual reference strange: Iser, following Ricoeur, warns us to observe the distinction between sense (*Sinn*) and reference (*Bedeutung*). 'Sense is the totality of references implied in the multi-faceted nature of the text. It must be constituted through reading. Reference is the adoption of the sense by the reader into his existence.' And in order to complete the confusion this is immediately followed by: 'Sense and reference together guarantee, then, in the first place the actualising of an experience which consists in the fact that I myself am constituted in a particular manner in constituting an unfamiliar reality.'[128] For Iser again concedes with this statement that it is incorrect to distinguish between the sense and reference of a text in the act of reading.

The importance of regulative mechanisms of the text becomes evident with the help of the positive structures and also with that of the blanks or 'elements of indeterminacy' within the text.

> Blanks and negations both control the process of communication in their own different ways: the blanks leave open the connections between perspectives in the text, and so spur the reader into coordinating these perspectives — in other words, they induce the reader to perform basic operations *within* the text. The various types of negation invoke familiar or determinate elements only to cancel them out.[129]

The concept of the blank as a text element which furthers communication lends emphasis to the fact that Iser attributes to the layout of the text the decisive function for its reading and so acknowledges that the participation of the reader in the realisation of textual process is controlled by the text.[130] A multiplicity of interpretation does not arise from the structuring of the blanks, 'but rather from the conceptual contents of those positions which, within this structure, find their way into the interplay between theme and horizon'.[131] What Iser understands more precisely, however, by these 'conceptual contents', he does not tell us. Only at the end of his expositions does he again draw attention to the fact that there is no such thing as one sole sense for a fictional text and precisely this lack is 'the productive matrix which enables the text to be meaningful in a variety of different contexts'.[132]

To sum up, we may assess Iser's position as follows: the text is developed in the act of reading as a process of regulative mechanisms, which involve the reader in a Gestalt formation of the notions evoked by the text and are combined by him/her in accordance with his/her reading competence into realities of consciousness. This process of Gestalt formation is subject, however, not only to the initial regulations, but also to controls which go out from the text. The freedom of the reader in the process of reading lies therefore, according to what we conclude from Iser, mainly in the fact that he/she is capable of achieving possible secondary acts of completion with the help of the primary representational acts called up and controlled by the text.[133] But the proper achievement of the reader is confined to ensuring that correspondence with the text in all its exigencies is maintained.

Iser has not a single word to say about the criticism which might take place during the process of reading. This is all the more worrying because, in his text concept, a text is so powerful in its repercussions that one may fear that both the textual configuration taking place in the consciousness of the reader and the new formulation of reader identity may turn into a slavery to the text.

(2) Stanley Fish's Theory of Reading

While Iser identifies the text as the primary regulative agency in the process of reading, Fish[134] sees in the reader her/himself the major regulative role in the reading process. Neither text nor reader is an individual reality independent of the other. Rather, each is under the influence of the norms and conventions proper to the respective interpretation community in which writing and reading take place.

> Indeed, the text as an entity independent of interpretation and (ideally) responsible for its career drops out and is replaced by the texts that emerge as the consequence of our interpretive activities.... The relationship between interpretation and text is thus reversed: interpretive strategies are not put into execution after reading; they are the shape of reading, and because they are the shape of reading, they give texts their shape, making them rather than, as is usually assumed, arising from them.[135]

Fish does not intend to completely dismiss the text as possessing its own essence. His aim is rather to show the configuration strategies of the text as being themselves products of the interpretive community to which it belongs. For 'it is interpretive communities, rather than either the text or the reader, that produce meanings and are responsible for the emergence of formal features'.[136]

It follows for Fish from these fundamental considerations that, when dealing with a theory about the attitudes of readers, it cannot be a question of distinguishing between 'correct' and 'incorrect' reading of a text but rather of acknowledging the possible perspectives from which each reading may arise.[137] Interpretation is thus the central category under which text and reading meet, since both are products of the interpretive community.

Fish's desire to put an end to objectivist text interpretations and to establish persuasion rather than demonstration as the basic model of textual criticism, has been developed mainly with reference to problems of literary criticism. His aim is, in the last analysis, to show conclusively that literature is a product of the reader and not the reverse.[138] Literature 'is the product of a way of reading, of a community agreement about what will count as literature, which leads the members of the community to pay a certain kind of attention and thereby to *create* literature'.[139] With this he shows every typology of text genres to be a characteristic of the community and rejects the existence of conclusively valid aesthetic categories. Text genres, their typology and arrangement in aesthetic value scales, are historical processes and must be taken seriously as such.[140] Finally Fish's thoughts become philosophical when he points out, 'that what we know is not the world but stories about the world, that no use of language matches reality but that all uses of language are interpretations of reality'.[141]

Fish totally objects to all forms of the endeavour to find eternally valid criteria in texts and their interpretations. This makes, on the one hand, all reading communities free for ever new reading creations and text productions, but excludes, on the other hand, every possibility, at least when it is a question of communication in written texts, of seeing similar provocations of reading behaviour. Accordingly one can no longer speak about a pluralism of reading genres in the sense that such a pluralism would be enkindled by the text. One may speak, rather, at most of a limitless pluralism of reading communities, whose reading criteria may undertake unpredictable activity with the text. With this, texts become victims of the reading communities and every possibility that texts might change readers and reading communities is denied. It also follows from Fish's analysis that the otherness of a text which stems from long past tradition is no longer of any interest other than that it makes it possible for the contemporary reading community to have access from its already given horizon of understanding. The struggle for a horizon of interpretation, not yet at hand, vanishes. From this point of view Fish's positivistic praise of interpretive communities leads to a simplistic notion of historical process. 'The interpretation constrains the facts rather than the other way around and also constrains the kinds of meaning that one can assign to those facts.'[142] Is Fish's interpretational positivism really the only alternative to the fiction of an objectivistic theory of the independence of the text from the process of reading, or to Iser's theory of the effect of the text on the reader in the reading process?

We nevertheless owe to Fish the insight that the reading community exercises an important influence on the reading of texts. We reject, however, Fish's theory of the total influence of the community since it does not fully take into account either the text's potential for criticism or its effect on the reading process, and also because it gives rise to the impression that text reception is subject exclusively to community norms. It is true that Fish declares his disagreement with an indifferent pluralism of interpretation where everything goes.[143] But he does not, on the other hand, make it clear where criticism may penetrate in the process of reading: textual criticism and criticism of those interpretational conventions which prevail just at this moment in time. One must admittedly agree with Fish that every text is read in some situation,[144] but one would wish to know whether and how such situations may be transformed. For when Fish defends himself against the accusation of relativism with the argument that he is, of course, under an obligation to community conventions,[145] in so doing he is in the last analysis, only substituting a communitary relativism for an individual one. In that case, where is the convincing difference?

(3) Criticism and Plurality of Readings

Our dissatisfaction with Iser's and Fish's reading theories should not, however, lead us to ignore the fact that both theories offer important insights for our outline of an alternative reading theory. Iser compels us to assess the effect of the text on the reader, Fish highlights the effect of the reader on the text. We must now investigate whether and how these two effect potentials can be more precisely assessed.

Earlier, towards the end of Chapter I, we pointed out the relationship of tension between text and reader, which in the reader is preserved productively in the endeavour to understand, to explain and to assess. In so doing, it was, however, emphasised that the reader enables the text to influence his/her situation and that this influence should not remain unreflected, if reading is to take place in a responsible manner. It was the responsibility of the dimension of assessment to deal with the text in a critical manner, regarding both content and situation.[146]

Now, once again, the consideration of the text and its reception has driven us to this threshold of criticism. The insistence on the possibility of criticism in the process of reading signifies here, however, no new denigration of the text but rather the endeavour to allow the text in the best possible manner to speak and for this purpose, to orient the individual reader and the reading community in relation to self-criticism and criticism of content.[147]

Self-criticism, that is to say the criticism of the pre-understandings which guide the reading and which Gadamer and Fish have in turn pointed out, is necessary. Otherwise there is either no openness whatever or no adequate openness to the claim of a text in a particular situation, or, alternatively, uncontrolled influences of the situation of reception prevent the text from coming into its own other than in a distorted form. Criticism of content is also necessary, since otherwise lasting effectiveness would be conceded to every claim of a text, without allowing a critical consciousness on the part of the interpreter to become effective, already in the course of reading itself. Reading interest and potential for text effectiveness should not remain beyond criticism, if reading is to take place in a responsible manner relative to the text, the reader and the reading community. It is only this twofold criticism which protects the text against arbitrariness on the part of the reader and protects the reader against arbitrariness on the part of textual effectiveness. Neither does such criticism interfere with a possible pluralism of reading. Rather is it concerned right from the beginning with promoting a possible pluralism on the part of the text and with warding off every instance of monistic reader domination.

How can one describe the pluralism of reading more closely, in the context of a theory of text reception?

b) Reading as Style-Related Activity

'The text gives expression to something, but the fact that it does so is in the last analysis the contribution of the interpreter.'[148] We have already seen that texts are perspectivally constructed and are regulated through a central communicative perspective. Something similar suggested itself also for the act of reading. Gadamer's description of the role of prejudices in the act of understanding may be verified also in the case of the text: if the reader wishes to understand the text he/she must select a perspective which can involve him/her in the textual process,[149] but in such a way as to be her/himself, in turn, modified by that textual process.

Corresponding, then, with the particular selection of a communicative perspective and with its textualisation — which we have characterised as a phenomenon of style — is to be found on the side of reading its own selection of perspective, which in its turn is a phenomenon of style. For several reading paradigms are conceivable, which allow a text to give expression to its subject matter. Reading also is a style-related activity. It becomes evident that the reader, in his/her style-relatedness, individually selects from the reading types available to him/her in a traditional conventional manner that particular reading type which appears appropriate to her/him both from the standpoint of the text and from that of her/his reading interest. But simultaneously, a limitation of reading appears again through this style-relatedness: every reading is condemned to the necessity of, on the one hand, choosing between the different reading genres which appear appropriate and, on the other hand, acknowledging a central perspective among the different thematic perspectives which the text develops, in order to arrive at a disclosure of sense from the text. Here the choice of a particular reading genre determines from the start which perspectives of the text come into the range of vision of the reader's image world and which remain far from his/her reading focus. Thus, the extra-textual context with all its relationships becomes effective. Reading takes place always within some particular cognitional approach to reality which can bear the impression of widely varying influences (economical, cultural, religious, climatic influences etc.). Reading finds itself therefore in the tension between social norms and the transformational applications of these norms made by the individual.[150] The most widely varying reading genres result from this and from the differing textual requirements. These reading genres are at the service of the reader for textual reception even if the choice of one option always means, at least for the moment, rejection of others.

Reading genres are accordingly conditioned by the text to be read, by the cultural, social, religious and political image context of the reader, by reading norms in part acquired through education, as well as by specific reading interests. These norms and interests, which are to occupy our attention in the next section, constitute the framework in which every reader develops his/her reading style.

c) Reading Genres

One of the fundamental norms which influence the act of reading is the impression that in the reading of texts one is capable of disclosing semantic relationships (*Sinnbezüge*) — i.e. the assumption that reading can be meaningful. On this basis two possibilities are conceivable: on the one hand that reading opens and assesses the sense of a text and on the other that reading inserts a sense into the text. We have expressly excluded the latter possibility from our theory because it does not recognise texts as identities. The former possibility of meaningful reading leads to a variety of reading genres which in each case are specified by determined functional interests and always come about in a social system of norms. So, according to Jan Mukařovský there is, for example, for the aesthetic reading function 'a contiguity and a concurrence of very many parallel aesthetic norms', which are again in their turn conditioned by time and generation.[151] 'In all of this the relationship between the aesthetic and the social hierarchy is undeniable. Every social rank and indeed many environmental areas (for example state-city) have their own aesthetic canon, which is one of their characteristic signs.'[152] From this point of view Mukařovský suggests a sociology of aesthetic norms, but emphasises at the same time that these always occur in the immediate vicinity of other norms.

> It is for example characteristic of their mutual proximity that one aesthetic norm can develop into another and conversely. Accordingly the ethical norm which in a novel is realised as opposition between the good and the evil hero — as component of the poetic structure — becomes transformed into an aesthetic norm and in due course is totally changed into a cliché, which has absolutely nothing more to do with the living moral value and can even be experienced as comical.[153]

This example shows that norms are changeable and can be transformed precisely through the process of reading. Accordingly what we have elaborated in relation to text genres holds also for reading norms: both conventions indicate the starting point of the respective activities (text production and text reception). The individual activities are, however, not totally subordinated to the norms which have been handed down but rather combine their personal style with the conventions which have accrued to them. From this stems the character of the text or of the reading act respectively. It follows further from these considerations that there can be, in principle, an endless number of reading genres which all take the text seriously and approximate to it in critical dialogue with the reading traditions available.

As well as the norms, the functions of the reading act play an important role. We may again follow Mukařovský and apply his reflections to our problem. He speaks of a 'hierarchy of functions'.[154] In this hierarchy a particular function dominates in each case which, in textual process, gets expressed in the communicative perspective and in the process of reading, becoming manifest in the reading perspective. Mukařovský discusses as an example the functional breadth of the religious cult:

> It is acknowledged that the religious cult as a rule contains a considerable number of aesthetic elements; in the case of several religions the process of making the cult aesthetic goes so far that art is often the integrating element of the cult (cf. for example, Catholic and Orthodox ecclesiastical art). The cult is often so permeated by the aesthetic function that the theoreticians do not hesitate to declare it to be art, especially in times in which the properly religious aspect of the cult is weakened (. . .). Meanwhile, for the Church, the prevalent element of cult is always the religious function.[155]

Applied to reading in general, Mukařovský's observations signify the following: we can read a text with different interests, i.e. we can place it in a particular functional framework. When, for example, a letter of St Paul is sent by post to a community, it is in the first place the function of communication which stands in the foreground. If, on the other hand, one reads out the same text at a liturgical service, what stands in the foreground is the religious teaching character. The same text can again be studied as a document of its time, its documentary function is accentuated in this case. All of these functions can of course be co-thematic. Nevertheless they are always in a hierarchical arrangement.

Norm and function in their historical contingency are accordingly co-ordinates of reading. At the same time they also

118 *Text and Theological Thinking*

determine the possible assessment of a text in the process of reading. It follows, however, immediately from what we have said that such assessments can never be absolute. Textual configurations (*Textgestaltungen*) and reading are subject rather to the specific variables of time, place and language. And nevertheless it is possible to formulate a general statement about texts, the aim of which is to distinguish those texts with a greater potential for sense from those with a lesser. The criterion here is the communicative dynamic of a text. Texts with a weak dynamic are soon, i.e., after only few endeavours at reading, automatised.[156] As against that there are works which even through a long reading tradition do not become automatic or lose their dynamic. One could name such texts 'classical'.[157] Their potential for sense does not become exhausted.

Evidently in addition to certain literary texts, biblical and other works of the Christian tradition can be numbered among the group of 'classical texts', since their potential for sense has not allowed itself to become automatised, but provokes, on the contrary, ever new disclosures of sense. 'New' does not signify here 'original' but rather indicates the fact that through all the semantic disclosures of a text, the same text in each case gets expressed, but in a new style.

d) Theological Reading Genres

Corresponding to our investigation of theological text genres we here pose the question of theological reading genres. What is the dominant characteristic of the theological reading of texts? What norms and functions play a role in theological reading?

Theological reading aims at theological disclosure of the sense of those texts which mediate testimony of God's manifestation in the world. Such texts are firstly, our primary theological text-genres: the biblical writings; and then our secondary theological text-genres: the interpretations of the biblical writings and of other texts with the help of these biblical writings. We have already seen that the norm of secondary text acts in theology, the biblical canon, is itself a collection of interpretations, namely the interpretations of particular events and experiences. There is accordingly no direct access to the norm of theological interpretative acts which would be free of interpretation, and as a result there is no uniformity of exposition but rather always a plurality of possible reading genres simultaneously. The norm of theological reading is then, already from the outset, itself pluralistic.[158] Neither is this normative text exposed to the arbitrariness of reading genres since — as already shown — every text indicates a determinate framework of sense. Its identity is its special communicative perspective. This can, however, only be taken into account on the basis of a decision regarding function: as confession, as document, as aesthetic thematic, as founding document of a community etc.

In the totality of theological disciplines several such functional reading genres are to be found, although they all find their origin and framework in the one pluralistic norm, namely the canon of scripture. If then the norm of secondary theological interpretations has already itself a pluralistic essence and from this point of view provokes a plurality of readings, how much more do the secondary theological interpretations provoke such a plurality of readings!

Every disclosure of the sense of divine reality in the theological process of interpretation is an individually authenticated selection out of the fullness of possible projections of sense to be gleaned from the transmitted texts. Because of this double indirectness no interpretation can achieve the fullness of divine manifestation of sense. The texts which bear testimony to God's fullness of sense have therefore a simultaneous character of disclosure and of concealing the sense.[159] This paradox again postulates the presence of the theological community of interpreters or respectively the Christian reading community for an additional reason: this community confesses its belief in a pluralistic norm of scripture and understands itself as on the way to an always new interpretation of life by reference to the divine logos becoming manifest in the texts. In this process it is never a single reading genre which is in question but rather always a new creative synthesis of traditional reading genres and the individual-communitary activity of faith.[160] This process of communal plurality hosts the unitary dynamic of the Christian quest for truth.

6. Reading Pluralism and Reader Responsibility: Criteria for an Ethic of Theological Interpretation

In this second chapter of our study it has been our aim to supply the theory of interpretation elaborated in the first one with an adequate text theory, making it possible for us to work out a critical theory of theological interpretation. Our reflections on text theory have obliged us on the one hand — intratextually — to assess the dynamic process characteristic of the coming to be of the text and on the other hand — extratextually — to consider all the influences which constitute the involvement of the reader in the textual process. In this matter it was, lastly, a question of studying to what degree the reader regulates the text reception and to what degree this is done by the text. The discussion of the contributions of Iser and Fish, dealing with literary theory, helped us to acknowledge that the text presses its claims to effectuality on the imagination of the reader, while the reader, in his/her world of images, through which he/she perceives these claims, is always already co-determined through her/his interpretation community and its tradition. This means that there is no such thing as a neutral, innocent, a-historical reading. Rather, every reader already makes a selection — whether consciously or unconsciously — between possible reading attitudes, which he/she then applies to the text. These attitudes are predetermined by the reading community so that we are justified in speaking about 'reading genres', which are then individually applied by the reader. This is why we may speak here of 'reading style'. The choice of reading genre and the elaboration of the reading style must, however, be appropriate to the text, that is to the text genre and text style. They must do justice to this text. We have established, however, in this connection that reading can be co-determined by a variety of functions, from which it follows that, in different reading contexts, different reading genres may quite definitely in their own way do justice to one and the same text. This takes place when the function which happens to be the guiding one, for example the historiographical, co-reflects or at least does not exclude the other functions, for example the aesthetic, the religious, the economical, etc.

Every reading act finds itself then under the simultaneous

claim of the text and of the reading function. The question regarding the pluralism of readings addresses itself therefore both to the different functions of the reading context — extratextual — and to the different elaborations of the respective reading style — intratextual — at the same time.

A consideration of various criteria of an ethic of theological reading must therefore devote attention to both textual claim and individual realisation on the one hand and on the other to the claim made by theological reading functions. In what follows we wish in the first place to describe more precisely text interpretation as a basic Christian activity. Then we wish to contemplate possible reading functions of biblical texts in order to penetrate from this vantage point the complex responsibility of theological text interpretation.

a) Text Interpretation as Basic Christian Activity

The community of Christians, that is to say of those human beings who acknowledge in Jesus of Nazareth (in his life, his death and his resurrection) the Christ, God's Messiah, is characterised from its beginnings by missionary self-understanding.[161] The message of Jesus Christ has been communicated as Gospel, as good news, 'so that you may believe that Jesus is the Messiah, the Son of God and so have life through belief in his name' (Jn 20: 31). Christians are made aware of the mystery of their salvation through this Gospel (1 Cor 15: 2). It is handed on by witnesses (Lk 1: 1-4; 1 Cor 15: 3), who give an account of all that 'which Jesus has done and taught up to that day on which he was taken up (to Heaven)' (Acts 1: 1-2), so that potential believers may become authentic followers of Jesus Christ. Hence, text interpretation is already anchored fundamentally in this self-understanding; the Christian testimony is transmitted in the first instance in text genres of rather an oral nature which then become more and more scriptural (Gospel sections, letters, pseudo letters). These are to be read either by those who are already believers as a strengthening of their faith (Lk 1: 4) or those who are not yet or not fully believers as inducement to faith (Rom 1: 15). The theological character of these texts goes without saying — it is a question of 'the Gospel of God' (Rom 1: 1) or of 'the Gospel of Jesus Christ, the Son of God' (Mk 1: 1) —

and this theological character is reinforced through the connection with the Hebrew Scriptures which have as their theme the relationship between God and his people, a connection which is evident in all New Testament writings. All in all it is not difficult to find justification for the assertion that text interpretation is and must be a basic Christian activity.

Admittedly text interpretation is not the total essence of Christianity. It is, however, a fundamental activity of Christian self-understanding, because in such interpretation the fundamental discussion with the Christian tradition must repeatedly start anew. From this point of view it is not only the method and the result of theological text interpretation which is significant for Christianity but already the activity of interpreting itself, without which there cannot be continuity of the Christian claim for tradition. In the acknowledgment of an uninterrupted reading of these fundamental Christian texts, the Christian community however has already by that same fact also undertaken to allow these texts to repeatedly speak anew. It has undertaken to devote its attention to their specific claim, to allow itself to be provoked by this claim and possibly to allow itself to be moved to a new and responsible self-understanding.

Such a strong adherence to the text must however lead to a certain ambiguity which becomes dangerous for the Christian texts: on the one hand they are acknowledged in their uninterrupted ability to speak in order to give impulses to continuous reading, on the other hand precisely this appreciation can repeatedly lead to a sanctification of the texts which threatens to withdraw them from the interpretative claim of the reader in order then to reserve 'correct' reading for special agencies of interpretation.[162]

Against such unbiblical exclusiveness in interpretation, the textual claim already quoted can however be always asserted, the claim to be good news for everybody. This is a claim in relation to which all the reading functions which are to help towards developing the textual claim must be subordinate. The claim of the biblical texts to universal listening/reading is incontrovertible. But such reading/listening can be undertaken in the most varied functions, whose characteristic quality and indebtedness to the text are now to be investigated more precisely, taking as our example the reading of biblical texts.

b) Possible Functions of Reading Biblical Texts

'Only because the text calls for it, does interpretation take place and only in the way called for.'[163] We have shown Gadamer's thesis, which attributes all regulatory power to the text, to be inadequate. On the one hand, it fails to consider the complex reading situations which influence reading by predetermining the reading genre of the reader in a conventional manner, according to reading function. It is inadequate on the other hand because it overlooks the delimiting of a text by a more comprehensive textual complex and by its being embedded in such a context.

(1) The Problem of Cemented Selection

Both shortcomings of Gadamer's theory are of particular moment in the reading of biblical texts and by an exemplary reading of the Johannine Prologue this can be shown conclusively. The two questions which present themselves in relation to the reading of John's Prologue as an excerpt are as follows: (1) Is the Prologue itself a text or can it be read only in the context of the whole Gospel text and (2) What reading genres are appropriate to the Prologue?

Both questions clearly call attention to an urgent issue in biblical reading: can one responsibly, in view of the canonical character of the Bible, treat individual texts and even parts of such individual texts — forewords for example — as independent texts which outside of their context in the work can lay their own claim to textuality? Has sufficient account been taken of the Johannine Prologue when it forfeits its character — from the point of view of textual composition — as theological foreword, to receive its own textual character and so to advance to the status of being the basis of important theological speculations, speculations which then in their turn lay claim to be biblically founded, even though they rest on a cleverly selected extract from a greater text? Added to this is the accompanying predetermination of reading attitudes in relation to the Prologue, whose Logos Christology was very often turned into a horizon for the reading of all other biblical texts. One could assert that for several periods of Christian thought, this partial text had the validity of a guiding text for scriptural reading, that in other words, it was itself turned into a canonical authority within the biblical canon.[164]

The price for this promotion of the Prologue to the status of key text for biblical christological thinking is the loss of its context, that is to say of the rest of the Gospel, as well as the subordination of other biblical partial texts to the authority of this one. Such a price, and this we dare not forget, must be paid, provisionally, every time we read a partial text of the biblical canon, since in such cases the passage to be read is the focus of attention and from this as centre, light or shadow falls on the remaining textual complex. This methodical necessity to concentrate in passing on a selected passage cannot, however, be meaningfully encountered by declaring apriori that the textual passage in question is the guiding passage as such. Rather one can do justice to a textual complex as comprehensive as the biblical one only through in each case new and different selections of reading, so that a partial text is read within its own text (the Prologue for example in the context of the Gospel of St John) and a canonical text is read in the context of the other canonical texts. Every cementing of a canon within the canon undermines the claim of the canonical text collection as a whole to proclaim the news of salvation and as such to be the *norma normans non normata* of Christian self-understanding.

(2) The Problem of Assessment

As we have seen in the first chapter of this book the phrase 'to be involved in a textual process through reading' does not mean the blind acceptance of the matter being communicated and the phrase 'to live in an interpretation tradition' does not signify the uncritical further elaboration of its pattern of selection. Rather did we recognise 'assessment' as an integrated dimension of interpretation in which the individual decisions relating to text content and the situation of understanding are made and vindicated.[165]

In the light of our reflections on text theory we are now in a position to grasp more precisely the dimension of assessment: it comprises all the aspects of reading which are stylistically relevant, that is to say the aspects which in the particular selection involved in reading are based on a reading situation which is already predetermined in several ways. Understanding and explanation are only possible in the context of an individual style, i.e. of a selection and modification of available reading genres. For without reading genres no reader style, without reader style no horizon, without horizon no understanding and no explanation. Assessment then is the activity in which the reader endeavours to behave in a responsible manner relative to the text and to make his/her selections *(Answahlentscheidungen)* accordingly. In assessment the reader accepts or rejects, therefore, certain reading functions as responsible or irresponsible.

What this means for the reading of biblical texts may be illustrated by the reading of Lk 2: 1-20. This partial text of Luke's Gospel describes the circumstances of the birth of Jesus. Separated from its context, that is to say seen as an autonomous text, this text contains several perspectives which impose themselves upon the reader who, without any reading prejudice connected with Christmas, endeavours to discover the claim of the text. In the order of their appearance the text releases the following possible perspectives:

Story: The birth of Jesus	v.1:	Announcement of Roman political history
	v.2:	Geographical historical announcement
	v.3:	Demographical-tourist announcement
	v.4f.:	Personal announcement concerning a certain Joseph from the Tribe of David
	v.5-7:	Gynaecological announcement
Assessment of and reaction to the birth of Jesus	v.8:	Pastoral announcement
	v.9-14	Angelic announcement with theological message
	v.15-17:	Reaction of the shepherds: turning towards the crib

v.18-19:	Reaction of the conversation partners of the shepherds and of Mary
v.20:	Return of the shepherds: Religious announcement

Up to verse 11 the text lacks any theological perspective. This is only introduced with the angelic exposition of the event reported in v. 1-7. When, thus, a contemporary reader, ignorant of the biblical context, reads this text from the standpoint of the text, that reader is presented immediately with the following reading genres: From v.1 histocial account; from v.4 biographical narration (concerning Joseph of Nazareth and the person to whom he is engaged); from v.6 nativity story (of a nameless son). None of these reading genres does justice however to the part of the text which now follows. Rather does the angelic explanation require from the reader a drastic change of perspective. The reader discovers in v.11f. that this nameless baby is the Messiah, something which is then underlined by the reaction of the shepherds. From this change of perspective a compulsion to re-adjust the perspective rebounds onto the preceding part of the text. The reading style 'biographical narration' shows itself to be inadequate. A new reading genre is required which takes into account the turning-point in the text. Whoever on the other hand refuses to accept this requirement of the text and continues to read, on the assumption that the text offers a plain 'biographical narration' acts irresponsibly. The question at issue here is not whether someone agrees with the theological turning-point of the communicative perspective of this text but rather whether he/she recognises and reads accordingly the theological turning-point in the claim of the text.

In the first instance there can as yet be no question here of a plurality of reading genres since this text does not permit of a purely political, historical, biographical or tourist reading genre because its communicative perspective is a theological one. Indeed the other perspectives are at hand, but they are not central. Whoever expounds this text as purely tourist or purely sociological can claim for it no possible reading pluralism but quite simply misses the theological claim of the text. The plurality of assessments can only become effective after acknowledgment of the communicative perspective of the text. For our text that signifies: reading pluralism can be expounded only within a theological reading and never apart from that.

It must now be admitted that for the sake of the exposition we have operated with a text which does not exist autonomously since our text is indeed just part of a greater text, namely Luke's Gospel which in its turn is a part of the New Testament canon. But what holds for our model of analysis may also be affirmed of all the biblical texts: only a theological reading does justice to them in the last analysis although several subordinate perspectives allow other partial expositions to come under consideration.[166]

A non-theological reading of biblical texts is indeed possible from the point of view of the technique of reading. But it may not then lay claim to finally do justice to the texts. Nevertheless no theological reading type may overlook the subordinate perspectives of the text, it must rather deal with them precisely in its own theological manner. 'Theological' means here not that the reader her/himself must believe in God or Christ in order to responsibly read the text but means rather that every reader whether a believer or not allows the text to validate its claim which is, finally a theological claim.

There is, however, a plurality within theological reading. Biblical texts may accordingly be read with the expectation that they contain information about the belief of certain groups of the Palestinian population in God. Or they may be read with the expectation of experiencing God's offer of salvation in Jesus Christ today. Or they may be read with an interest in making statements about the Judaeo-Christian God etc. All of these are theological reading genres, which do justice to certain theological reading functions and are compatible with the claim of the text.[167]

Assessment of biblical texts consists accordingly in exposing their main claim which we have acknowledged to be theological and, corresponding with a reading genre and a reading function compatible with this claim, in doing justice individually[168] and as far as possible to the text in all its dimensions. In this way a response to the text is vindicated in a responsible and personal manner.

c) The Responsibility of Theological Text Interpretation

No reading is ethically neutral, since every reading represents an answer to a textual claim, an answer which may be responsible or irresponsible.[169] In the first chapter of this book we have developed responsible interaction as a three-dimensional interaction with the text. In this second chapter we have discussed this interaction with the help of a theory which would pursue the dialectical relationship between reader and text. Thus we saw that the reading of texts always begins through individually formed reading genres and reading functions, both of which, however, must receive their legitimation from the text, if they are to do justice to the text. We have illustrated these thoughts with the help of textual examples from the Bible and defined the biblical communicative perspective as 'theological', which accordingly calls for theological reading genres and reading functions. But we have not as yet discussed what 'theological' signifies. This discussion is the object of the third and last chapter of this work: What constitutes a responsible 'theological' interpretation and what does it mean to think 'theologically' about texts in a responsible manner?

CHAPTER III

Text and Interpretation as Categories of Theological Thinking

1. Introduction

The object of the investigations in the two preceding chapters was the interpretation of written texts. Even though we have, on several occasions in the course of our study, taken up theological problems in order to throw light on its progress, it is, in the last analysis, mainly philosophical and philological reflections which we have set in train. This appeared necessary because theology as a science of the text must do justice precisely to the exigencies of philosophy and philology and as a result may not abstain from discussion of theories relevant to such requirements. For it is only on this basis that the elaboration of hermeneutical criteria for theologians is a means to an end, a means towards making theological text interpretation transparent, public and responsible.

In this chapter, then, we return to the significance of such a theory of interpretation for specifically theological thinking. We seek to discover the essential claim of the texts which motivate theological thought and look for thought models capable of doing justice to such a textual claim.

As a basis for discussion we choose David Tracy's contributions to a theological theory of interpretation. This choice is justified for the following three reasons: first of all, the projected theological theory of interpretation which Tracy offers is novel in recent Christian theology and, secondly, as well as that, it endeavours to critically re-elaborate and further pursue the outlines of such theories already in existence; finally, Tracy acknowledges his debt to the philosophical hermeneutics of Gadamer and Ricoeur which are also discussed in our work. Since we have the task of examining to what extent the diagnosed strengths and weaknesses of these theories are traceable also in Tracy's interpretation theory, our study may perhaps make its own modest contribution to the more recent effective history of Gadamer and Ricoeur.

2. From Hermeneutical Theology to Theological Hermeneutics: David Tracy's Theological Theory of Interpretation

In his two works, *Blessed Rage for Order*[1] and *The Analogical Imagination*[2], David Tracy is concerned to discover a defensible methodology for Christian theology.[3] He determines the locus of such methodical discussion as *'fundamental theology'*.[4] This discussion of the basics of theological activity serves the purpose of achieving publicly justifiable research into universal human experience and language, as well as into religious experiences and their linguistic expression. The results of such investigations are then to be balanced against each other in a mutually critical correlation. In the course of this consideration varying theories of truth may be actualised but they must in each case be explicitly defended. The contemporary horizon of understanding and the contemporary interpretation of the text of religious tradition may not be played off against each other, but are on the contrary, already by their nature, mutually correlated principal sources of theological thinking. There is, however, no direct access to these main sources, which would be objective or of a once and for all character; what is required is rather a continuing phenomenological analysis of contemporary interpretation and a decisive theory of interpretational praxis, so that the task of laying the foundations of a critical theological hermeneutics constitutes an abiding and unavoidable challenge to theological thinking.[5]

From this theological discussion of fundamental principles the concern with concrete theological interpretation receives its orientation. Tracy describes the ever new interpretation of the text of Christian tradition for the respective situation as the main task of *'systematic theology'*.[6] If fundamental theology in general concerned itself with the discovery of the religious dimensions of human existence and with a general and public discussion of the experience of God, systematic theology on the other hand is concerned with the specifically Christian confession of faith in the God of Jesus Christ, a profession which has become expressed in the texts, symbols, formulae and prayers of the Christian tradition. This activity is thus hermeneutical throughout. The interpretation of the Christian texts contributes to a disclosure of the truth present in these texts.[7]

The aim of *'practical theology'*[8] is, then, to reflect on the practical application of this disclosed theological truth which can lead to a transformation of individual and communitary life.[9] In this matter it is not a question of setting up an opposition between theory and praxis; the aim is rather to emphasise precisely the inseparable correlation of these two categories: no justifiable praxis without critical theory; without practical realisation, no completion of theory.[10]

This threefold delineation of the theological task, which, though distinguishable, may not be separated into parts and the threefold determination of the areas of operation of theologians as Academy, Church and Society,[11] constitutes the frame of reference for Tracy's theological discussion of method. This expression of task delineation, Tracy emphasises,

> ... does not entail a lesser role for 'historical theology' but rather insists on the intrinsically historical (as hermeneutical) theological character of all three disciplines in theology: fundamental, systematic and practical. Exegesis and church history are, on this reading, also theological, ordinarily as systematic or practical theology. The present division of the three sub-disciplines (all hermeneutical to different degrees) should highlight the necessary character of 'historical theology' for all theology.[12]

In what follows we wish to investigate more closely the extent of the role of hermeneutics in this understanding of theology and how Tracy proceeds from the call for theology's hermeneutical self-understanding to the formulation of a hermeneutical claim which theological thinking can make in the pluralistic society of today.

a) The Hermeneutical Character of Theology

'Theology is the attempt to develop mutually critical correlations in both theory and praxis between an interpretation of the Christian tradition and an interpretation of the contemporary situation.'[13] Interpretation is therefore the business of theology. This self-understanding of theology includes the awareness that the interpreters 'are not subject-less, context-less, history-less interpreters', that they strive not for certainty but for understanding. 'And we pursue that understanding with the knowledge that our interpretations, too, will prove inadequate, for *all* is interpretation.'[14]

The insight that interpretation constitutes our only access to reality and the acknowledgment of the historicity of every endeavour to understand, force the interpreter to present his/her interpretational criteria in a public manner, so that her/his interpretational aims and the contents of such interpretation may, in public discussion, be confirmed, criticised or rejected. For no interpreter can by virtue of her/his historical, social and personal contingency[15] validate a claim to absolute truth for her/his interpretation.

Tracy understands this model of interpretation as a universal heuristic model, which can 'guide the concrete programmes of concrete and particular differing theologies'.[16] The interpretation model is not, accordingly, itself theological interpretation but rather the theory of such an undertaking.

The task of developing concrete interpretations is primarily that of the systematic theologians who, of course, according to Tracy's concept of theological division of labour, have to understand and mediate their particular religious tradition.

> They seek, therefore, to retrieve, interpret, translate, mediate the resources — the questions and answers, form and content, the subject matter — of the classic events of understanding of those fundamental religious questions embedded in the classic events, images, persons, rituals, texts, and symbols of a tradition.[17]

When Tracy accordingly formulates: 'All contemporary systematic theology can be understood as fundamentally hermeneutical'[18] that is not tantamount to saying that theology exhausts itself in mere interpretation but, rather that every theological systematics already of its nature builds up, on the basis of interpretations of such classical forms of expression of a religious tradition. These forms require to be rendered publicly justifiable. The constructive function of systematic theology may accordingly never relinquish its hermeneutical basis, if such systematic theology is to take place in a responsible manner.[19]

Our question is now: which texts of the Christian tradition according to Tracy are of particular interest to theology and how does he propose to do them justice?

b) Claim and Interpretation of Classic Texts

(1) Tracy's Concept of the Classic

Every interpreter of the manifestations of cultural or religious expression — such as texts, works of art, symbols, rites, etc. — who allows her/himself to be engaged in an authentic conversation with these manifestations, a conversation in which the prevailing consideration is not her/his interests but those of the object to be understood, encounters continually expressions which communicate to her/him in a particularly poignant fashion an experience of insight into truth. Such manifestations Tracy calls 'classics'. He makes a sharp distinction in this matter between classicist norm and the phenomenon of the classic expression.

> My thesis is that what we mean in naming certain texts, events, images, rituals, symbols and persons 'classics' is that here we recognize nothing less than the disclosure of a reality we cannot but name truth.[20]

This definition owes its origin to the insight described by Gadamer according to which, in the experience of art, there is at work an authentic experience which does not leave unchanged the person who has this experience.[21]

Tracy now distinguishes between 'classic' and 'period piece'.[22] All sorts of expressions of human experience claim our attention; not all however claim it in such a fundamental manner that we can say:

> ... we sense ourselves recognizing something both important and true, some claim to our attention we cannot easily shirk, some reality which lures us into civilized discourse, some question which demands conversation. In experiencing a classic in any discipline, we recognize that some disclosive and transformative truth seems to be at stake.[23]

Tracy's phenomenology of the classic is grounded accordingly in the special claim which a classic expression makes in relation to the recipient:

> ... a claim that transcends any context from my preunderstanding that I try to impose upon it, a claim that can shock me with the insight into my finitude as finitude, a claim that will interpret me even as I struggle to interpret it. I cannot control the experience, however practiced I am in techniques of manipulation. It happens, it demands, it provokes.[24]

This claim is based therefore on the power of the expression to disclose a paradigmatic sense which Tracy calls 'truth' and on the ability of the expression to ethically transform the personal, social and historical existence of human beings.[25] The claim is made possible through the intensity of the disclosed experience of an author. This disclosure takes shape by means of a genre, which for its part is realised through the style of the author.[26]

How Tracy envisages the conversation called for by him with such classics is now to be expounded, in order to provide the basis for a critical appreciation of his theory of interpretation. It is only through a critical analysis of his interpretation theory that we proceed to a critique of the concept of the classic and of the concept of truth implied by this, since the qualification 'classic' is itself, of its nature, always the result of interpretation.[27]

2) Tracy's Theory of Interpretation[28]

Tracy's theory of the interpretation of classic texts owes its origin essentially to the inspiration of Gadamer and Ricoeur. The emphasis on conversation as hermeneutical paradigm[29] stems from Gadamer, and the insight that understanding and explanation are to be seen not as opposites but rather as allies comes from Ricoeur.[30] With both fathers of contemporary hermeneutics Tracy emphasises the autonomy of the text and the historical intersubjective communitary framework within which every interpreter moves and also the necessity to abandon oneself to the 'play' with the text, according to the rules.[31] The rules of this conversation with the text require that the reader enable the text to validate its claim so that the world of the text may open itself to her/him. The reader however participates always, of her/his nature, in a community of capable readers, in which it should be possible to critically discuss every interpretation: 'The larger dialogue with the entire community of capable readers is a major need for any claim to relative adequacy in interpretation.'[32]

Tracy is concerned in his theory, which takes its orientation from the reader, to allow justice to be done to the text. With regard to the text therefore, he clearly distinguishes his position from the anarchical models of Barth, Derrida and other theoreticians.[33] But to do justice to the text does not entail that one must exclude a pluralism of readings. In fact, precisely the opposite is the case: we require a reading pluralism in order, as far as possible, to do justice to the text,[34] something which a single reading perspective of itself can never guarantee. It is only an alleged reading pluralism which, having no proper interest in the claim of the text, is excluded, since in this case the claim of the text could not be developed.[35]

Text and reader stand in a dialectical relationship to each other; their realities have the character of process and are never static.[36] It is to this dialectical relationship that the reader also owes the possibility of being himself changed through the event of reading, especially by the reading of classic texts:

> When we read any classic ... we find that our present horizon is always provoked, sometimes confronted, always transformed by the power exerted by that classic's claim.[37]
>
> Then the classic becomes a classic provoking a genuine (as different) interpretation. And the reader becomes a genuine reader of the classic, provoked into a new self-understanding.[38]

In what does the contribution of this theory of interpretation consist and where do the difficulties lie?

(3) Critical Appreciation of Tracy's Theory of Interpretation

In line with Ricoeur, Tracy further develops in a critical fashion the interpretation theory of Gadamer. Gadamer's short-sightedness in relation to the possibility of systematically distorted communication and his precipitate ontological claim are exposed and methodically re-elaborated.[39] Although Ricoeur's theory of interpretation plays the role of godfather, its own problems are also present.

I see four problematic areas in Tracy's theory of interpretation:

the absence of an explicit theory of text and reading, the conceptual distinctions between sense and reference of a text as known from Ricoeur and criticised by us, the absence of a clear statement regarding the ethical problem of interpretation, and the lack of an explicit assessment dimension of every interpretation. As this list shows it is not a question here of insoluble problems or of contradictions but rather for the most part of deficiencies which may be supplied so that Tracy's theory can retain a solid foundation. For this reason the following reflection is intended as a constructive proposal for the further development of Tracy's approach in the light of our theory of text and interpretation as presented in Chapters I and II.

Tracy's theory of interpretation is both text conscious and reading conscious. He speaks of style and genre in the matter of text reception[40] and of 'reader's response' as focus of his reception theory.[41] But he fails to further develop either his concept of the 'text' or a theory of reading derived from this. Style and genre remain accordingly nothing other than production categories and are not acknowledged as being also reception categories (reading style and pluralism of genres of reading). Furthermore it remains unclear how a text introduces and develops its subject-matter, so that the experience of the dialectical relationship between text and reader can only be shown from the standpoint of the reader and not also as an insight demanded from the reader by the very construction of the text. Neither does the relationship between text genre on the one hand, and reading function as the foundation of a possible pluralism on the other hand, come into sight. Nevertheless Tracy's approach is not closed off against these additional considerations regarding textual and interpretational process. Tracy emphasises rather the openness of his conversational model for later additions of a text-linguistic nature, provided these do not intend in an a-historical manner to confer the independence of their technical character on their own exclusive interpretational model.[42]

In line with Ricoeur, Tracy distinguishes between textual sense to be disclosed in reading and its reference for the disclosure of the world.

> On the present model... the referent of the text will be a

referent *in front of* the text, not behind it . . . the referent will exist in front of the text even for those self-referential texts whose very referent is *to the sense*.⁴³

Tracy's question, which these quotations answer, ran as follows: 'whether the sense of the text in the structures and signs, or even in the endless abyss of indeterminacy, does or does not also disclose a referent, a world'.⁴⁴ It becomes clear from this question that 'referent' and 'world' of the text are identical for Tracy and that they are disclosed by textual sense through structure and sign, or even through elements of indeterminacy.⁴⁵ That is confusing: for is it not rather the text, which through structure, sign and elements of indeterminacy discloses its sense? This conceptual confusion and the comment that the world of some texts is their sense may be avoided — as already shown for Ricoeur⁴⁶ — when the possible sense of the text is present for the reader through her/his focus; but then the actual textual sense is the reference of the possible textual sense for the reader in question.

Tracy's determination of the ethical dimension in the matter of interpretation is unclear. He requires an additional research community which devotes itself to the ethical task, i.e. the reflection upon the reading contributions which have been made by the community of interpreters.

> To understand all is not, after all, to excuse all. . . . This additional ethical task of discrimination and adjudication of conflicting views is necessary. It is, however, a distinct task from the ethical tasks of attention to the interpreter's original experience and understanding of the claim exerted by the classic as a genuine possibility for existence, of attention to the text (its structures and forms) demanded by formalist analyses of the text, of attention to the world of the text as a possible one for existence and, finally, of attention, in justice, to a responsible pluralism of readings. The task of discriminating and adjudicating possible worlds impels the interpreter, therefore, into further conversation with ethicians, philosophers and theologians. That same conversation is always already operative in every great critic . . .⁴⁷

In another place Tracy formulates the matter in the following fashion: 'There is, of course, an ethical task to literary criticism itself, but this should not be confused with rendering ethical judgments on the vision or world of the work as part of the interpretation of the work.' And he continues: 'Ethical judgments seem far more hermeneutically appropriate *after* the interpretation of the 'world' of the work as a *possible*-mode-of-being-in-the-world.'⁴⁸

Tracy distinguishes, accordingly, between interpretation and adjudication of what has been interpreted and further between the ethical implication of participation in the conversation with the text (attention is due to the claim of the text) and the adjudication of the textual claim being validated in this manner. At the same time, he asserts, however, that such ethical adjudication of world disclosure and disclosure of the text, subsequent to interpretation, an adjudication which takes place in reading, is already at work 'in every great critic'. This assertion is surprising because it implies that good reading always of its nature also includes criticism, even of the text.

Criticism of content must also be exercised relative to tradition:

> The fact that every tradition is ambiguous need not become the occasion to reject the reality of tradition as enriching. Rather the need is to find modes of interpretation that can retrieve the genuine meaning and truth of the tradition ('hermeneutics of retrieval') as well as modes of interpretation that can uncover the errors and distortions in the tradition ('hermeneutics of critique and suspicion').⁴⁹

It is therefore equally valid for text and tradition that criticism of content, as mediated by both of them, must be exercised. But it remains unclear when such criticism of content ought to start. Tracy gives the impression of tending to want this criticism of content to chronologically follow the process of interpretation. This order would, however, have serious consequences: In the first place, the process of interpretation would appear to be reduced to what one might call a value-free, innocent activity which is then to be followed by an activity for which values are a relevant issue. But the assumption, that value-free zones of thought exist, contradicts Tracy's concept of interpretation: 'Interpretation, properly understood, does involve critical reflection by the interpreter from the beginning of the provocation to that reflection by the text itself until the final (and critical) fusion of horizons.'[50] And: 'What is worthy of the free mind is *critical* conversation with all the classics in all the disciplines.'[51]

'Critical conversation' cannot then aim solely at an ideological critique of the conduct of conversation[52] but must also intend critical acknowledgement of the textual sense which is being disclosed in interpretation. Therefore an explicitly ethical approach to interpretation includes criticism of both content and procedure right from the start.

Tracy's opinion is naturally buttressed by the absence of a theory of text and reading: for as soon as the theme-rheme structure in the text is acknowledged to be the source of the reading dynamic, appropriate attention is also paid to the claim of the particular textual perspectives which constitute the central communicative perspective. When accordingly a theme-rheme sequence introduces a partial thought, then its claim must already be of ethical significance and call forth from the corresponding reader can escape remaining unreflected. Contrary to his theoretition, which as a matter of course are always open to renewed discussion in the course of further reading. It is only in this manner that the progressive effect of text formation on the reader, can escape remaining unreflected. Contrary to his theoretical protestations, however, Tracy still treats the text as static unity which the reader reproduces by interpretation before going on to assess it. But the effect of a text is developed dynamically and for this reason requires also a dynamic criticism of the reading content and of the act of reading itself. This criticism does not of course exclude a critical assessment of the text after it has been read, but rather makes this really possible.[53]

Therefore interpretation cannot be confined to the dimensions of understanding and explanation. The introduction of an explicit decision dimension, namely the assessment of textual effectivity, into Tracy's interpretation theory thus proves necessary for us. Critical interpretation becomes critical interpretation only when all its dimensions are adequately tested and as far as possible brought into awareness. It is only then that we may, with Tracy, speak of a "form of authentically shareable, public discourse"[54] which does not take place in an illusory, not-yet-ethical framework but rather is already clear about its responsibility to text and interpretation, namely that the claim of the text must be acknowledged but in the form of a critical realisation. Otherwise a continuing effectiveness would be conceded to the textual claim which, controlling the process of interpretation, could have manipulated the possible perspectives of Tracy's appended ethical dialogue. It is for this reason that the text theory which we developed in our second chapter, endeavouring, as it does, to do justice to the dynamic of textual process, requires right from the start that criticism co-determine the formation of reading style and the selection of the reading genre and in this way also enable the correct function of the reading act to progressively appear during the reading as adequate or inadequate to the text.

(4) Reflections on the Nature of the Classic

Tracy's description of the classic is itself grounded in hermeneutical experience. We are only in a position to acknowledge the transforming power of a text when we read it. To this extent the category of the classic is a category of reception.

Tracy attributes to the classical expression normative status,[55] that is to say he acknowledges in the reception of the classic its power to transcend any simple everyday experience of reading as well as to have a provocative effect over a longer period. Even more: classics defend themselvs against any definitive interpretation.[56] We may remind ourselves here of Mukařovksý's theory according to which certain texts escape the fate of becoming automatised in the process of reading.[57]

The normative character of a classical expression stems, thus, not from an interpretational authority which has somehow been instituted, but is founded rather on the experience of readers with this text.

According to Tracy a classic expression discloses paradigmatic knowledge, even truth, even in fact transformative truth, that is to say the kind of truth which changes the human being with whom it comes into contact.[58] This definition shows that Tracy is concerned with a concept of truth which is phenomenologically based, which owes its origin to specifically hermeneutical experience. Objective truth, premature ontologisation and positivistic theories of truth are accordingly excluded.

The norm relating to the classic stems, then, from experience with specific forms of expression. Tracy releases the concept of the classical from the fetters which it still has in Gadamer, who requires of us an entering into the process of transmission[59] within which the expressive dynamic of the classic's power of expression is mediated. Tracy on the contrary, at least implicitly, calls for a hermeneutical examination which allows the classic to become recognisable as classic and from this point of view concedes to it normative power. He thus rescues the category of the classic from Gadamer's idealistic premises and transfers it to the status of hermeneutical activity, which is in principle open to criticism.

However, there is one danger which, in spite of this rescue of the concept, is not yet excluded: is an expression classic because it has paradigmatic character in all the dimensions of its composition? Can a classic possess normative authority even when parts of its formulation no longer really produce a provocative effect? Is a text still a classic when parts of its composition have actually disappeared through criticism?[60]

When we for example classify the *First Letter to the Corinthians* as a 'classic' because its reading even to the present day communicates to us messages which are worthy of disclosure about the manner in which an early Christian community functioned and about Paul's theology of the community, at the same time the question must be posed concerning the disclosure value of the partly anti-feminist statements in Chapters 11 and 14. Should we not rather speak of a 'period piece' with reference to these chapters? If we accordingly call the letter as such a 'classic' because its thematic as a whole resists automatisation of reading surely this does not exclude a criticism, during the reading, of Paul's relationship to the role of women in the Christian community.[61]

We learn from this example that classic texts are not 'classics' because all their parts have to be classic but rather because in them paradigmatic perspectives are exposed which even to the present day are capable of provoking our thought and action. Now there is no thought or action which is devoid of value and this means that even the interpretation of so called classic texts must always be alert to the question as to which effects appear in a positive manner during the reading, and which appear negatively.

Again, the absence of a theory of textual and reading dynamic appears to lead Tracy to still another uncritical assumption, namely that certain texts are, as a whole, more worthy of disclosure than others. This approach overlooks their special and occasionally quite strong ties to a particular time. Certainly the normative character of classics is founded on the fact that they mediate paradigmatic perspectives and here one must agree with Tracy. But should one not, then, be more careful and speak about 'classic perspectives' which are provoked by certain texts, even though the same texts simultaneously reveal all kinds of 'unclassic perspectives'. Thus, for example, no one would assert that *all* sections of Plato's *Republic* are classic, one need only reflect on the exclusion of poets. Nevertheless Tracy can include Plato's texts under the classics[62] since even to the present day paradigmatic thought and action perspectives may be gleaned from these texts.

Tracy's theory of classic texts is a theory of reception. It should, accordingly, also do justice to the required criticism of content and of the situation in which the act of reading takes place, since it could otherwise transpire that the normativity of classics is the product of reading genres which are ideological, unhistorical, or totalitarian. Classics are not to be excluded from criticism, their normative claim to disclose truth and to transform the world of the reader and his/her behaviour must also be responsibly assessed by the community of interpreters. Otherwise ideology slips stealthily in — through the back door, so to speak — and we are back with Gadamer's notion of entering into tradition without knowing what repercussions are there to come upon us. We should not be silently overcome by the vast effectiveness of classic texts, rather must this be the occasion of change resulting from criticism of content and situation.[63] It is only then that Tracy's dictum regains its validity: "What is worthy of the free mind is *critical* conversation with all the classics in all the disciplines."[64]

c) Interpretational Theology as Revisionist Theology

Tracy defines the interpretational task of Christian theology from two points of view: in the first place, every theology must risk, in a general and fundamental manner, the interpretation of the meaning and truth of those classical texts, events, persons, pictures and images 'whose world discloses the reality of religion, whose effective history forms the horizon of our own efforts to understand and appropriate, to retrieve and criticize the reality of the religious dimension of the culture'.[65] This religious dimension points to the 'whole of reality' which reveals itself as such, of itself, in our world but not of our making.[66] Secondly, it is the concern of every Christian theology to interpret in a systematic and particular manner the event of God in Jesus Christ, which is mediated by tradition and unfolds in the concrete situation.[67] Tracy devotes the main part of his discussions in *The Analogical Imagination* to these two obligations of interpretation. We are now interested in investigating which reading perspectives serve Tracy's purpose in developing his fundamental and systematic projects and whether these perspectives do justice to the textual process which is to be interpreted.

(1) Tracy's Religious Interpretation Perspectives

Tracy emphasises the claim of religious perspectives not to be concerned with sectors of the human experience but rather with the endeavour to reach a total statement about the human condition.

> Unlike the classics of art, morality, science and politics, explicitly religious classic expressions will involve a claim to truth as the event of a disclosure-concealment of the whole of reality *by the power of the whole* — as, in some sense, a radical and finally gracious mystery.[68]

Every religious communicative perspective, and thus every religious reading perspective, finds itself in the tension associated with the fact that it is in a better position to announce its object than to fully state it. For the revelation of the whole of reality never takes place other than textually and that means perspectively only, i.e., not comprehensively. This is the case for the simple reason that linguistic perspectives are of their nature restrictive. For this reason, the expression 'religious perspective' already implicitly contains for us all the restriction that is necessarily involved in what Tracy calls the 'disclosure-concealment' experience.[69] In the light of this conceptual definition one can more accurately appreciate why Tracy opts, even in the case of the interpretation of religious classics, for a disclosive and transformational model of truth.

The experience of religious classics takes place in basically the same manner as the experience of any other classic expression,[70] so that one may also say of the religious classic: '... the classic by definition incarnates a notion of truth that is neither mere adequation nor correspondence, neither verification nor falsification. Rather truth here becomes a manifestation that lets whatever shows itself to be in its showing and its hiddenness.'[71]

'Truth' is here understood as the linguistically mediated revelation of reality which intrudes itself upon us and is self-restricting, receiving from this point of view its authoritative claim to be able to elucidate human existence.[72] 'Truth' is not the product of interpretation in the strict sense of the word, but on the other hand it is not to be achieved without interpretational activity.[73]

> To enter the conversation of religious classic through real interpretation, therefore, is to enter a disclosure of a world of meaning and truth offering no certainty but promising some realized experience of the whole by the power of the whole. That world affords no technically controlled comprehensibility yet it does release the self to the uncontrollable incomprehensibility of an experience of radical mystery.[74]

The perspective applied by Tracy in the critical discussion with such texts, which bring to light reality as such — even if the light is dimmed — is called by him religious. Certain texts call for such a religious reading perspective.

This general reading perspective, which is grasped from the point of view of fundamental theology and which endeavours to do justice to all religious classics is now particularised by Tracy from the standpoint of systematic theology for the reading of Christian classics. The classic texts of Christian tradition do not communicate an abstract view of the 'reality of the whole' presented by them but rather 'a loving and jealous, living, acting, covenanting God, a God who discloses who God is, who we are, what history and nature, reality itself ultimately are'.[75] Which perspectives of interpretation will do justice to these texts?

(2) Tracy's Christian Interpretation Perspectives

Tracy designates the event and the person of Jesus Christ as the classical dimension of Christianity as such,[76] more precisely: 'The only fully appropriate, fully adequate expression of that event is the event itself — the event of God in Jesus Christ'.[77] There is however for contemporary human beings no immediate access to this event, so that they are dependent on the only relatively adequate forms of expression of the Christ event which, as canonical writings, are normative for the self-understanding of the contemporary Christian: 'as that set of inspirations, controls and correctives upon all later expressions, all later classical texts, persons, images, symbols, doctrines, events that claim appropriateness to the classic witnesses to that event'.[78]

The great variety manifested by these writings is to be welcomed as enriching.[79] In this variety of textual witnesses Tracy sees a twofold unity: on the one hand the uniform reference of the texts to the event and on the other hand the formal dimension according to which all texts of the New Testament are a particular response to the event, which took place in particular situations and was perceived in them. It is also to these particular situations that the different linguistic forms of expression (genres) such as proclamation, narration, symbol, image, theological reflection, owe their origin.[80]

What holds for the 'situation-event-response' structure of these texts, holds in principle also for the contemporary interpreter of these texts: he/she interprets the text event in his/her particular situation and thus permits that the situation comes into contact with the textual disclosure of the classic event, and may be transformed by this disclosure.

Tracy endeavours continually to allow the full variety of these textual witnesses to come into its own. He is very well aware that the reader needs to employ particular reading perspectives. Even though he avoids the expression 'perspective' up to almost the end of *The Analogical Imagination*[81] he nevertheless speaks of 'focal meaning'[82] or alternatively 'scope'[83] of Christian forms of expression. Thus he acknowledges the fundamentally perspectival nature of text and interpretation.[84] The central focus, the central 'scope' or the central communicative perspective of the New Testament texts is for Tracy the event and the person of

Jesus Christ, to which, however, none of the many production perspectives (New Testament texts) nor any of the many reading perspectives (theological interpretations) can fully do justice.[85] Tracy concedes therefore that for the theological interpreter of the foundational texts of Christianity it is inevitable that he/she adopt a certain central perspective of interpretation, whilst remaining conscious of the historical and situational restriction which becomes evident in so doing.[86]

> Through such developments does the search for relative adequacy occur: a choice of some focal meaning, the development of ordered relationships of God-self-world by means of the focal meaning; the continuous transformation of relationships and focus alike as the fuller reality of the symbols and the fuller demands of the situation are critically responded to in every systematic theology.[87]

Tracy now describes three main perspectives which are intended as an aid to the textual formation of the central perspective of the interpreter (the communication of the Jesus Christ event: 'The always-ready, not-yet event/gift/grace of Jesus Christ').[88] These are: manifestation, proclamation and praxis. He emphasises however that none of these perspectives of interpretation should behave in an exclusive manner relative to the others.

Rather must they in each case co-reflect the two other perspectives in order to be able to present an at least somewhat adequate response to the text provocation.[89]

The status which Tracy here attributes to theological praxis calls for criticism, however. For in this order, 'praxis' appears as 'historical action', i.e. as one of the Christian responses which, alongside manifestation and proclamation, are possible in the contemporary situation. In this way praxis is on the one hand distinguished from proclamation and manifestation, and on the other hand reduced to an 'actionism' which follows on hermeneutical activity. The distinction between sense and reference, that is to say, between objectifiable textual sense and its, in each case, individual reference on the one hand, and, on the other, the corresponding differentiation into systematic and practical theology — this distinction favours this alienating and unfortunate reduction of praxis as one of the possible applications which spring from the hermeneutical activity.[90]

The aim of all hermeneutical endeavours of Christian systematic theology remains, however, 'the transformation of both questions and the responses in the situation by the classic, paradigmatic, disclosive and transformative power of the event'.[91] Our interpretational situation is therefore in each case just as much the object of interpretation as the texts themselves through which it is again to come into view.[92] The method suggested by Tracy for this double interpretational venture is a dynamic, frontally open method which is to guide the theological development of thought without dominating it.[93] Tracy's fundamental understanding of theology is in the last analysis therefore open to unplanned interpretational results, to unsuspected changes of the interpretative perspective and with this of the situation of interpretation itself.

In order to do justice to this openness Tracy calls for a self-understanding of theology as 'revisionist theology'.[94] We wish to devote our attention now to this new self-understanding of theology and its theocentric central perspective in order to arrive at a more comprehensive appreciation of Tracy's approach.

(3) Tracy's Concept of Revisionist Theology

Tracy's understanding of theological thinking is grounded in the mutually critical correlation between the situation in which this thinking lives and the textually transmitted Christian touchstone experiences provoking this thinking and its particular situation. Theology is — as we have seen[95] — always, of its very nature, related to interpretation: to the interpretation of texts in the situation and to the interpretation of the situation through the texts.[96] This dialectical and dynamic interpretational foundation of theological thinking excludes static one-sidedness according to which either the situation or the Christian textual message remains uninterpreted or else they may repress one another.[97]

But neither may theological interpretation of the situation exclude apriori any other interpretation of the situation. It must rather join in the conversation with all interpretations of the contemporary situation — if it is to remain responsible in relation to this situation — in order to discover, together with other participants in the conversation, the state of the situation and in order to trace illusions, recognise and eliminate distortions and outline projects of life for the present and for the future. In this conversation theology makes its specific interpretational contribution, one which develops particular Christian projects for human life in a situation which has thus been reelaborated and developed out of the testimonies of Christian tradition. Theological thinking itself is always of its nature a dimension of the situation and therefore is burdened with the questions and the perspectives of the situation. Tracy's demand for a double set of criteria becomes obvious: theology thus understood requires criteria of adequacy for the description of the situation, and criteria of appropriateness for the interpretation of the Christian texts.[98] The phenomenological method provides Tracy with criteria of adequacy, and criteria of appropriateness are provided by the hermeneutical method which is here discussed. Both methods require from theology an openness towards research results and their critical correlation so that it must be required of every adequate theology that it hold itself open to new experiences and whenever necessary revise its prevailing thought perspectives. Theology must remain open to revision.[99] The insistence on openness does not, however, signify an insistence on absence of perspectives but rather on the possibility of a change of perspective.[100] But the change of perspective does not refer to the basic perspective which leads theology to its thought, 'the perspective of the reality of God'.

Tracy understands theology, talking about God, as radically theocentric:

> Whatever else it is, any Christian theology is finally and radically theocentric.... Christianity, when true to its heritage, cannot but recognise that its fundamental faith, its most radical thrust and loyalty, is to the all-pervasive reality of the God of love and power disclosed in Jesus Christ.[101]

And Tracy is correct in emphasising that several interpretational perspectives are possible in the interpretation of Christian texts, but that every instance of theological thinking ceases to be 'theological' when a perspective other than the theo-logical gains the upper hand.[102]

Revisionist theology is concerned therefore in the last analysis always with the mystery of God, the contours of which in the analysis of the situation are invariably intimated as the mystical and achieve Gestalt in the interpretation of Christian texts, without ever giving up the mystery itself.[103]

d) The Hermeneutical Claim of Theological Thinking

The main inspiration of Tracy's thought stems from the assumption that we human beings are in a position to render an account, in a public conversation, of our life projects and their perspectives. Nobody lives without some sort of perspective. We understand the most widely varying thought and action perspectives on the basis of analogies in our personal life situations.[104] Tracy's thought becomes theological through the decision to adopt a central perspective which is theological. This decision is made possible by the provocation of texts and by their manifold interpretations which mediate experiences of the reality of God in Jesus Christ: New Testament texts and other texts of Christianity.[105] Two authorites keep Tracy's theological thought in motion, the New Testament as classic expression of Christianity and the historical situation of the interpreter. The New Testament is here, however, the norm,[106] whilst the situation is only the object of interpretation with the help of this norm which, in turn, must be interpreted in the situation. Since every interpretation requires a perspective, the interpreter of these normative texts must necessarily opt for a certain selection from them — Tracy calls this selection the 'working canon',[107] — in order to grasp from this standpoint the plurality of textual forms, in all of which, however, he/she must remain aware of the limited nature of this one point of view and remain open for corrections through, in principle, all possible other appropriate interpretation perspectives.

In this complex interpretation of Christian texts in situations and in the interpretation of situations through Christian texts, contours of a religious truth are set free which are only to be grasped through the concept of the understanding of God's reality, offered by the texts themselves. The texts impose accordingly the theo-logical interpretation perspective as central perspective or they confirm it. From this theological point of view new light then falls on the situation. New concepts of life and projects of life appear and inspire the transformation of the existential presence of the interpreter. These transformational possibilities and the theo-logical perspectives through which they are disclosed, must be introduced into a public conversation with other interpretations in the particular situation. It is only then that from the hermeneutical constitution of theology, possibly a theological constitution of universal hermeneutical thought may develop.

Theological hermeneutics as a possibility of hermeneutical theology is thus introduced into the conversations between the interpretations of reality. But does this mean that all theological thought is hermeneutical, or alternatively that adequate theology as 'hermeneutical theology' must be distinguished and brought into relief over against what are, in its view, other, less adequate theological approaches?

3 Hermeneutics and Theology: Retrospective and Prospective

The investigation of David Tracy's contribution towards a responsible interpretation theory of Christian theology has again made us aware of the fundamental hermeneutical affinity of Christian theological thinking. The person and event of Jesus Christ are only accessible through the statements of witnesses which by reason of their textual form call for an interpretational dialogue with them. We believe in the God of Jesus Christ, not in the Bible; but we believe in this God and the divine revelation in Jesus Christ through the biblical texts and the texts of Christian tradition because only through the textual witnesses can we have access to the event and the person of Jesus Christ. Even so-called immediate experience of Christ must be identifiable on the basis of these witness statements, if such experience wishes to be acknowledged publicly as Christian experience of God.

The God of Jesus Christ is not to be known by us human beings in a non-verbal fashion, rather are we always challenged to experience God in our linguistically constituted humanity. The Christian texts offer the occasion of such provocation. They do this, however, not in innocent naïvety but rather in the ambiguity which is proper to all human instances of becoming language. In these texts a reality imposes itself upon us which shatters our self-understanding. In them appear paradigmatic elucidations of our human situation which direct us towards the God who wishes to change our lives if we say Yes to this proffered change. In the texts, God appears, however, not in a neutral or propositional form of language but rather in the narrative, praising, arguing and instructing genres, all of which have to be interpreted by us.

But interpretation does not mean repetition of the texts, parroting of their truth. Rather does interpretation signify the new creation of the truth of these texts in the always different situation of the interpreter and his/her social environment.[108] Interpretation entails a risk, uncertainty, requires the giving up of cemented judgmental approaches and freedom from such, as also from constituted and prescribed regulations of language. Interpretation does not mean that all the various linguistic forms must be reduced to a common denominator. Appropriate interpertation entails rather the courage to acknowledge difference, radical otherness of experiences.

Theological thinking does not find itself accordingly under the compulsion to harmony but rather under the obligation to justify publicly the appropriation of occasionally very old and sometimes particularly different experiences of human beings, whose horizons have become foreign to us. Can we nevertheless learn from these experiences? This is possible if we do not overlook the historical difference of experience but rather take it seriously. This is the source of our hermeneutical energy, of our search for ever new understanding. But this search on the other hand, is only set in motion through our pre-informed, already awakened interests and prespectives. Gadamer, Ricoeur and Tracy have shown us the significance of these perspectives, which motivate us on the one hand to the reading of our classic texts but which on the other hand must always, even during this reading, be themselves ready for change. Our perspectives can only change if we are willing to expose them to such change.

Our discussion of the dynamic textuality of texts and of the process nature of reading texts has made it clear to us that the processes of text production and of text reception are regulated both by conventional and individual dimensions:[109] genre and style determine text and reading. Text genres and text styles provoke reading genres and reading styles. A responsible pluralism of interpretations rests, then, not on arbitrariness of reading genres but rather on the selection and stylistic imprinting of reading genres which are appropriate to the text. The occasion of every reading and of every selection of reading genres and reading styles is, however, always a particular function of communication. It constitutes the horizon of this formation of perspectives.

Tracy's manner of dealing with biblical texts as 'classics' is, as we have seen, an indication of the unexhausted potential for reception of these texts which for almost the past two thousand years have provoked reading perspectives and have changed reading attitudes. Our study wishes to invite the reader to this process of interpretational discussion with the texts, bearing witness to the manifold human experiences of the God of Abraham, of Isaac, of Moses, of the Prophets and of Jesus Christ. The discussion with these texts must, as we have seen however, include a discussion of the interpreter with her/himself. Therefore, the invitation to discussion with the texts of the Judaeo-Christian tradition of experience and thought is at the same time an invitation to freedom, namely to the freedom of saying No to interpretation perspectives which have been handed down, when the text requires this, and to find one's way or return to other perspectives as these are made possible by the text.

Texts are dynamic potentials, which call for dynamic discussion. Theological thinking is not exhausted in the reading of texts but is based on such reading and on this basis can renew itself. The Christian theology of today is grounded on the debate with biblical texts and the texts of the Judaeo-Christian tradition of interpretation and thought. Our insight is reinforced in reflection on the conditions of interpretation, in hermeneutics; an insight into the finitude of interpretation and into the whole community relatedness and the essential reference to tradition of our thinking, but also into the freedom for new experience precisely with old texts and the freedom to further constitute ever new perspectives of thought and action within this framework.

Theology, accordingly, is not exhausted solely through discussion of the technique of understanding old texts or through the historical-critical resurrecting of textual origins. Rather, on the basis of such preparatory labours, theology must also enter into conversation with the texts themselves, that is to say with what the texts represent.[110] The texts of the Christian tradition point at the same time forwards and backwards. They refer to their time, their individual circumstances, and, through these concrete situations, to our time with its concrete data. And precisely because they are always capable of further reference, we call them 'classical'. But they can only refer to us if we read them. Their sense is disclosed only for those who, through interpretation, enable reference to themselves to take place.

Critical interpretation is the soul of theology: it opens itself to the Word of God, which speaks through the text; it opens itself to changes of the horizon of intepretation through the Word of God; but it also remains aware of the preliminary nature and finally of the inadequacy which is always an inherent property of human interpretation, even of the most 'adequate'. In this consciousness of its restricted nature is founded, however, the freedom to ever new and responsible interpretation of God's action and God's presence in our history.

Notes

Introduction, pp. xv–xix

1. In recent times, under the catch phrase 'narrative theology', a tendency of theological thinking has developed which aims at articulating theological thoughts, not in an analytic-discursive form but rather in a narrative-synthetic mould. Such narrative communication forms, which take their orientation from the discourses of Jesus in the Gospels, are certainly meaningful in particular areas of communication — as for example in catechetics; if theology, however, is to do justice to its commission to think in an analytic and critical manner, it cannot confine itself exclusively to narrative forms of discourse. It is worth noting that even narrative forms of speech always include argumentative characteristics. The call for a greater degree of narration in theology may therefore be assessed as a criticism of the tendency of theological discourse to have an all too discursive style, rather than implying that all argumentative thought and speech acts be given up. For narrative forms of discourse no more lack reception — and that is to say at the same time, interpretation — than all other forms of human discourse. This is not to deny that 'narrative theology' has developed a sensitivity for greater linguistic unities, something which theology requires. Concerning narrative theology see especially the following works: Bernd Wacker, *Narrative Theologie?* (Munich: Kósel, 1977); Josef Meyer zu Schlochtern, 'Erzahlung als Paradigma einer alternativen theologischen Denkform: Ansätze zu einer "Narrativen Theologie"', in *Theologische Berichte* 8, ed. Franz Furger (Einsiedeln: Benziger, 1979), 35–70; Dietrich Ritschl and Hugh O. Jones, *'Story' als Rohmaterial der Theologie* (Munich: Kaiser, 1976); 'The Crisis of Religious Language', *Concilium* 85 (1973); Sallie McFague, *Speaking in Parables: Study in Metaphor and Theology* (Philadelphia: Fortress, 1975) and *Metaphorical Theology: Models of God in Religious Language* (London: SCM 1983).
2. Cf. Peter Eicher, *Theologie: Eine Einführung in das Studium* (Munich: Kösel, 1980), 205.
3. It is the aim of the present study to develop a theory of interpretation of written texts. Reference is made to the differences between oral and written communication on page 45 below. When accordingly it is not further specified, 'text' signifies here 'written text'.
4. It goes without saying that a general theory of textual understanding can be illustrated with the help of the most widely differing text exemplars. Laying the foundations of a general theory of interpretation serves here, however, the purpose of reflection on the method of theological thinking.

156 *Interpretation and Theological Thinking*

For this reason in our case theological text exemplars recommend themselves right from the start.

5. Martin Heidegger's question in *Being and Time*, tr. Macquarrie and Robinson from the 7th German edn (Oxford: Blackwell, 1962) is 'the question concerning the meaning of being' (p. 19), which is advanced as 'interpretation', as the title of the first part (and the only part) of his study illustrates: 'The interpretation of Dasein in terms of temporality, and the explication of time as the transcendental horizon for the question of Being' (p. 65).

6. Cf. Hans-Georg Gadamer, *Truth and Method* (New York, Seabury, 1975), translation edited by Garret Barden and John Cumming from the second (1965) edition, 153-7. Abbreviated in the following as TM. German edition: *Wahrheit und Methode, Grundzüge einer philosophischen Hermeneutik* (Tübingen: J. C. B. Mohr | Paul Siebeck |, 1975) abbreviated in the following as TM/WM; and Hans-Georg Gadamer and Gottfried Boehm, eds., *Seminar: Philosophische Hermeneutik*, 2nd edn (Frankfurt/M: Suhrkamp, 1979), especially Gadamer's introduction, 7-9.

Chapter I, pp. 1-72

1. Under the expression 'recipient of a text' we understand all those who comprehend this text whether through reading or listening. In this study we will generally deal, however, only with the reader of a text because here it is a question in the first place of reflection on theological work with the help of written texts and not of reflection on the liturgical activities of Christians, even if these activities could themselves become the object of a theological meditation. What is here in question is especially theology itself as the object of methodological reflection. Therefore there is no need to go directly into the peculiarities of the delivery and the audition of texts.
2. See 'Theology' in Karl Rahner and Herbert Vorgrimler, *Kleines Theologisches Wörterbuch*, 8th edn, (Freiburg i.B.: Herder, 1971), 352.
3. Cf. Karl Rahner, *Foundations of Christian Faith: An Introduction to the Idea of Christianity*, tr. William V. Dych (London: Darton Longman & Todd, 1978), xii.
4. This problem is posed in literary criticism in the debate about the relative advantages of text-immanent and historical-critical methods of interpretation.
5. David Tracy calls texts with such an unbroken facility for remaining open to ever new disclosures of meaning 'classics', see his *The Analogical Imagination: Christian Theology and the Culture of Pluralism* (New York: Crossroad, 1981), 108. Cf. also below, 133f.
6. On the definition of 'fundamental theology', cf. among others Tracy, *The Analogical Imagination*, 54-8, and Peter Eicher, *Theologie: Eine Einführung in das Studium*, 165-8. According to Eicher, p. 168, fundamental theology represents not only 'the cognitional conscience of theology as a whole for the Church, but also, through this fact, an eminent critical theory regarding the claim of science as such'. Fundamental theology is accord-

ingly that dimension of theology which reflects on methodology and scientific approach in particular. To this extent the theory of interpretation falls within the scope of fundamental theology.
7. Helmut Peukert, *Science, Action and Fundamental Theology: Toward a Theology of Communicative Action*, tr. James Bohman (Cambridge, Mass./London: MIT Press, 1984), 215. German edition: *Wissenschaftstheorie — Handlungstheorie — Fundamentale Theologie: Analysen zu Ansatz and Status theologischer Theoriebildung* (Dusseldorf: Patmos, 1976).
8. Ibid., 215.   9. Ibid., 312, note 8.   10. Ibid, 228.   11. Ibid., 244f.
12. Cf. my review of Peukert's book in *The Journal of Religion* 61 (1981), 438-40.
13. The hearing of written texts presupposes and depends on reading. The intonation of the person reciting co-determines the listener's reception of the text delivered. The listener thus has access to the delivered text only through the interpretation as this becomes evident in the deliverer in the intonation and style of delivery.
14. Cf. my study of Friedrich Schleiermacher's hermeneutics: 'The Impact of Schleiermacher's Hermeneutics on Contemporary Interpretation Theory' in David Jasper, ed., *The Interpretation of Belief: Coleridge, Schleiermacher and Romanticism*, (London, Macmillan, 1986), 81-96.
15. David Tracy, *Blessed Rage for Order: The New Pluralism in Theology* (New York: Seabury, 1975), 73.
16. It goes without saying that there are several exceptions here. Cf. for example the praiseworthy efforts of David Hellholm to investigate an ancient text, the *Shepherd of Hermas* in terms of its textuality and the tensions and peculiarities which result from it. See Hellholm, *Das Visionenbuch des Hermas als Apokalypse: Formgeschichtliche und texttheoretische Studien zu einer literarischen Gattung I* (Lund: Liber Läromedel, 1980.
17. This objection also touches on the recommendation of the Second Vatican Council, according to which scriptural exegesis must expressly concern itself in the first place with the investigation of the meaning intended by the author of a particular writing, and this before the judgment of the Church comprises within its official teaching the meaning of the text. Cf. *Dei Verbum*, 12, in *Vatican Council II. The Conciliar and Post-Conciliar Documents*, ed. Austin Flannery (Pennsylvania: Scholarly Resources, 1975).
18. Cf. my article 'Biblical Interpretation as Appropriation of Texts: The Need for a Closer Cooperation between Biblical Exegetes and Systematic Theologians', *Proceedings of the Irish Biblical Association* 6 (1982), 1-18.
19. Cf. Josef Blank, *Schriftauslegung in Theorie und Praxis* (Munich: Kösel, 1969), 11, 28 and especially 15: 'The theological relevance of the scientific interpretation of sacred scripture, exegesis, becomes a special problem because of the fact that, in the first place, the tradition which lived with the Bible as the decisive testimony to faith and revelation appears today to be broken and questionable. In the face of a relationship to Christianity, to the Church and to the Bible, which is questionable and no longer, by any

means to be taken for granted, theological work on the Bible requires special justification, even more so if authority is to be in any way based on the Bible.' see also idem., *Verändert Interpretation den Glauben?* (Freiburg i.B.: Herder, 1972), especially 29-79.
20. Eicher, op. cit. 205 (partly emphasised in the original).
21. See Introduction above, 156 note 6.
22. TM, 431.   23. TM, XII.   24. TM, 473.
25. Hans-Georg Gadamer, *Reason in the Age of Science*, tr. Frederick G. Lawrence (Cambridge, Mass.: MIT Press, 1981), 1. This work is abbreviated in the following as RAS.
26. RAS, 20.   27. RAS, 19.   28. RAS, 111f.
29. RAS, 112.   30. RAS, 77.
31. TM, 465: 'Fundamentally I am *not proposing a method*, but I am describing *what is the case*. That it is as I describe it cannot, I think, be seriously questioned.' (Emphasis in the original.)
32. Hans-Georg Gadamer, 'Replik', in *Hermeneutik und Ideologiekritik*, Theorie-Diskussion (Frankfurt/M.: Suhrkamp, 1971), 313f. The collection *Hermeneutik und Ideologiekritik* is abbreviated in the following as HuI, tr. T.W.
33. TM/WM, 520.
34. Hans-Georg Gadamer, *Kleine Schriften I: Philosophie — Hermeneutik*, 2nd edn, (Tübingen: J. C. B. Mohr [Paul Siebeck], 1976), 50. *Kleine Schriften* is abbreviated in the following as KS.
35. See above, 9f.   36. HuI, 300.
37. TM, XI: 'The hermeneutic phenomenon is basically not a problem of method at all.'
38. 'Even allowing for all the differences which exist between the natural and the human sciences, the inherent validity of the critical methodology of the sciences is surely in no way whatever questionable.' (TM/WM 518, tr. T.W.).
39. TM, 146 (emphasis in the original). Cf. also TM, 446-7.
40. TM, 235-341.   41. TM, 359.   42. TM, 260.
43. TM, 260 (emphasis in the original).
44. TM, 331: 'Hence it is more than a metaphor, it is a memory of what originally was the case, to describe the work of hermeneutics as a conversation with the text.'
45. TM, 245.   46. TM, 248.   47. TM, 250f.   48. TM, 255.
49. TM, 258f. (emphasis in the original).
50. TM, 261. Gadamer here refers back to Heidegger's reflections on the hermeneutical circle. Martin Heidegger, *Being and Time*, op. cit. 194f.: 'But if we see this circle as a vicious one and look out for ways of avoiding it, even we just "sense" it as an inevitable imperfection, then the act of understanding has been misunderstood from the ground up ... What is decisive is not to get out of the circle but to come into it in the right way.' (Emphasis in the original).
51. TM, 261.   52. TM, 262f.   53. TM, 265f.   54. TM, 264.
55. TM, 266. On the problem of some safeguard against misunderstandings in Gadamer cf. Heinz Günther Stobbe, *Hermeneutik — ein ökumenisches Problem: Eine Kritik der katholischen Gadamer-Rezeption*, Ökumen-

ische Theologie, vol. 8 (Zurich and Cologne: Benzinger, and Gütersloh: Gerd Mohn, 1981), 30-32.
56. TM, 266.
57. '... that in all understanding, whether we are expressly aware of it or not, the power of this effective history is at work'. TM, 268.
58. TM, 269. 59. TM, 273-4. 60. TM, 276.
61. TM, 273: 'Every encounter with tradition that takes place within historical consciousness involves the experience of the tension between the text and the present.'
62. TM, 273.
63. 'Understanding itself proved to be an event [Geschehen, process], and the task of hermeneutics consists, seen philosophically, in asking what kind of understanding it is, what kind of science it is, which is in itself changed [fortbewegt, advanced] by historical change.' TM, 276. — 'Hermeneutics in the sphere of literary criticism [Philologie, philology] and the historical sciences is not "knowledge as domination", i.e. an appropriation as a "taking possession of", but rather a subordination to the text's claim to dominate our minds.' TM, 278.
64. TM, 142.
65. TM, 274-5 and 289 by way of example.
66. Cf. TM, 274-8. 67. TM, 274. 68. TM, 289.
69. TM, 301 (partly emphasised in the original).
70. TM, 323.
71. Cf. on this point also Gadamer's concept of interpretation in TM, 360.
72. TM, 365f. 73. TM/WM, 508. 74. TM, 301. 75. TM, 258.
76. TM, 310. 77. TM, 319. 78. TM, 321.
79. TM, 321 (emphasis in the original):
80. 'For an historical text to be made the object of interpretation means that it asks a question of the interpreter. Thus interpretation always involves a relation to the question that is asked of the interpreter. To understand a text means to understand this question.' TM, 333.
81. TM, 340. 82. TM, 335. 83. TM, 345-6. 84. TM, 350.
85. On the fusion of horizons as 'the full realisation of conversation' cf. TM, 350.
86. TM, 352. 87. TM, 354.
88. Cf. on this point the discussion of Paul Ricoeur's thoughts, below 44f.
89. TM, 399, (passage underlined in the original).
90. TM, 403, (partly emphasised in the original).
91. TM, 404 (emphasis in the original). Language then signifies for Gadamer always of its nature conversation, cf. especially TM/WM 538. Here he distinguishes himself clearly from Paul Ricoeur, for whom 'language' in the first place signifies only 'speaking'. Cf. below 164, notes 220, 221.
92. TM, 413f.
93. TM, 415.
94. TM, 432 (emphasis in the original).
95. TM, 433 (emphasis in the original).
96. TM, 441 (emphasis in the original).
97. TM, 445.

98. 'In understanding we are drawn into an event of truth and arrive, as it were, too late if we want to know what we ought to believe.' TM, 446.
99. TM, 446.
100. 'The player experiences the game as a reality that surpasses him.' TM, 98.
101. TM, 92.   102. TM, 105.   103. TM, 101.   104. TM, 95.
105. '... *all playing is being played with*. The attraction of a game, the fascination it exerts, consists precisely in the fact that the game tends to master the players.' TM, 95 (emphasis in the original).
106. TM, 92.   107. TM, 446.
108. Jürgen Habermas and Claus von Bormann, otherwise sharp critics of Gadamer, assess this contribution in a positive manner. Habermas welcomes especially Gadamer's analysis and overcoming of the objectivistic illusion of historicism. Cf. Jürgen Habermas, 'Erkenntnis und Interesse', in *Technik und Wissenschaft als 'Ideologie'*, 11th edn (Frankfurt/M.: Suhrkamp, 1981), 146–68, especially 157; idem, *Knowledge and Human Interests*, 2nd edn, tr. Jeremy J. Shapiro (London: Heinemann, 1978), 179 and 341, note 25; also Claus von Bormann, 'Die Zweideutigkeit der hermeneutischen Erfahrung', HuI, 83–119, especially 112.
109. Gadamer expressed this view on the occasion of a conference on Hermeneutics, 9 and 10 November 1979 at the Northwestern University in Evanston, Illinois, U.S.A.
110. Jürgen Habermas, 'Der Universalitätsanspruch der Hermeneutik', HuI, 120–59.
111. HuI, 133.
112. HuI, 134. Examples of such pseudocommunication are repeatedly used in the tradition of the Theatre of the Absurd in order to represent the absurdity of communication and life experience which is communicatively hidden. Cf. for example Eugène Ionesco, *The Bald Prima Donna: An Anti-Play*, tr. Donald Watson, in Eugène Ionesco, *Plays* I (London: John Calder, 1960), 85–119. The play consists exclusively of scenes dealing with pseudocommunication.
113. HuI, 133.
114. HuI, 148.
115. HuI, 150. Cf. Jürgen Habermas, *Theorie des kommunikativen Handelns*, 2 vols. (Frankfurt/M.: Suhrkamp, 1981).
116. HuI, 151 (emphasis in the original).
117. HuI, 154.
118. HuI, 156f.   119. HuI, 154.
120. Hans-Georg Gadamer, 'Replik', HuI, 283–317.
121. HuI, 300 and 309.   122. HuI, 291.   123. HuI, 305.   124. Ibid.
125. Ibid. Cf. HuI, 306: Conversation 'can in no way be forced, but only enabled'.
126. TM/WM, 518 (tr. T.W.).
127. Cf. Gadamer's polemic against the predominance of technology in TM/WM 518f.
128. Thomas McCarthy, in *The Critical Theory of Jürgen Habermas* (London: Hutchinson, 1978), 191f. appropriately summarises Habermas's reservations as follows: 'From a methodological point of view, the principal issue is whether hermeneutic *Sinnverstehen* is or can be the sole and adequate

basis of social inquiry. And this question, Habermas feels, has to be answered in the negative.' And further: 'Whereas Gadamer speaks of "the dialogue that we are," Habermas speaks of the dialogue that is not yet but ought to be. Whereas Gadamer is moved by respect for the superiority (*Überlegenheit*) of tradition, Habermas is motivated by the anticipation of a future state of freedom.'
129. TM, 415 (emphasis in the original).
130. TM, 432 (emphasis in the original).
131. TM, 433.
132. 'Die Natur der Sache und die Sprache der Dinge', in Hans-Georg Gadamer, *Kleine Schriften* I (abbreviated as KSI), 59-69 especially 65. This article is translated as 'The Nature of Things and the Language of Things' tr. David E. Linge, in *Philosophical Hermeneutics* (Berkeley: U.C.P. 1976), 69-*181*.
133. Ph. H, 63.   134. Ph. H, 64, 65.
135. Ph. H, 66.   136. Ph. H, 67.
137. 'The Universality of the Hermeneutical Problem', Ph. H, 3-17.
138. TM, 431.
139. Hans-Georg Gadamer, 'Semantik und Hermeneutik', *Kleine Schriften III: Idee und Sprache: Platon-Husserl-Heidegger* (Tübingen: J. C. B. Mohr [Paul Siebeck], 1972), 251-60, here 258f. i.e. Ph. H, 93.
140. Ph. H, 93f.   141. HuI, 315.
142. Ph. H, 94 (my italics).
143. Formulations like these are often to be found in Gadamer. It is no doubt their aim to emphasise the fact that the person understanding is not the 'maker' of his/her understanding but rather the receiver. Cf. for example KS III, 259f.
144. Stobbe, ibid., 38 (emphasis in the original).
145. TM, 430.   146. ibid.   147. Stobbe, op. cit., 43.   148. TM, 236.
149. TM, 210 (emphasis in the original).
150. TM, 260.   151. Stobbe, op. cit., 59.   152. KSI, 80.
153. TM, 317.   154. Stobbe, op. cit., 91.   155. Gadamer, RAS, 103.
156. TM, 420-25.
157. Cf. on the problematic of Gadamer's text definition also Thomas J. Wilson, *Sein als Text: Vom Textmodell als Martin Heideggers Denkmodell: Eine funktionalistische Interpretation* (Freiburg/Munich: Alber, 1981), 72-9.
158. Similarly Stobbe, op. cit., 112: 'In this manner the result of communication, i.e. the agreement regarding the matter at issue, which constitutes "the aim of all communication and all understanding" coincides with the criterion of the truth of understanding.' Cf., as against that, Gadamer KSIII, 260: 'In this process of endless self-advancement of thinking, in allowing the other to come into his own over against oneself, the power of reason is proved right.'
159. Wolfhart Pannenberg, *Theology and the Philosophy of Science*, tr. Francis McDonagh (London: Darton, Longman & Todd, 1976), 169. Concerning Habermas's frontal opposition to this type of hermeneutical dialogue cf. above 22f.
160. TM/WM, 517 (Epilogue).

161. KSI, 50.
162. Cf. on this point also Horst Turk, 'Wahrheit oder Methode? H.-G. Gadamers "Grundzüge einer philosopischen Hermeneutik"', in Hendrik Birus, ed., *Hermeneutische Positionen: Schleiermacher-Dilthey-Heidegger-Gadamer* (Göttingen: Vandenhoeck & Ruprecht, 1982), 120-50.
163. TM/WM, XIX.
164. Cf. Stobbe, op. cit., 144f.: 'What requires to be done is to unravel the Gordian knot which Gadamer has tied in the "Middle of Language" and to further weave the threads which thus fall apart.'
165. RAS, 79.
166. Ibid.
167. HuI, 88f., Cf. also ibid., 114f. and 116: 'But criticism would, without any doubt, have its place in a theory of concrete experiences: its task would be, following the truth which has been handed down without either exhausting it or generating it, to secure a general level of truth, short of which it would be imprudent to fall.'
168. It is not possible to dismiss the necessity of a critical hermeneutics with a simple request for a 'Hermeneutics of Good Will' such as expressed by John C. Robertson in his 'Hermeneutics of Suspicion *versus* Hermeneutics of Good Will', *Sciences Religeuses/Studies in Religion* 8/4 (1979), 365-77. Robertson does not acknowledge the objections of Habermas against Gadamer's concept of hermeneutics.
169. *Sein und Zeit*, ibid. 41. Heidegger's critique of traditional hermeneutics showed that 'that I. [Interpretation] is a process of exposition, whose hermeneutical implications are discussed by philosophical hermeneutics while the logic of the respective science must ground it as a concept of method and manner of proceeding'. So H. Anton, in his article 'Interpretation', *Historisches Wörterbuch der Philosophie*, ed. J. Ritter and K. Gründer, Vol. 4 (Basel: Schwabe, 1976), columns 514-18, here col. 515.
170. Cf. Anton, ibid., col. 516: 'Universality is one aim among others of I. [Interpretation] and is then characteristic of I.s [Interpretations] when these thematise states of affairs whose significances can be reconstructed and inter-subjectively tested.'
171. Paul Ricoeur, *Hermeneutics and the Human Sciences: Essays on Language, Action and Interpretation*, ed. John B. Thompson (Cambridge, England: Cambridge University Press, and Paris: Editions de la Maison des Sciences de l'Homme, 1981). 59f.: 'With Heidegger's philosophy, we are always engaged in going back to the foundations, but we are left incapable of beginning the movement of return which would lead from the fundamental ontology to the properly epistemological question of the status of the human sciences. Now a philosophy which breaks the dialogue with the sciences is no longer addressed to anything but itself. Moreover, it is only along the return route that we could substantiate the claim that questions of exegesis and, in general, of historical critique are *derivative*. So long as this derivation has not been undertaken, the very movement of transcendence towards questions of foundation remains problematic.' (Emphasis in the original).

Furthermore: 'Gadamer's work marks, in relation to Heidegger, the beginnings of the movement of return from ontology towards epistemological problems.' Gadamer does not, however, progress any further than these initial steps because he — as we have shown above — is capable of recognising only the fusion of horizons, but not the dynamic of the dialectic between distanciation and appropriation which underlies this process. Accordingly he remains tied to an all too sudden ontologising of language and overlooks the methodical problems which are inherent in the dialectic just outlined. — *Hermeneutics and the Human Sciences* is abbreviated in the following as HaHS.

172. Cf. a corresponding assessment in David Pellauer, 'The Significance of the Text in Paul Ricoeur's Hermeneutical Theory, *Studies in the Philosophy of Paul Ricoeur*, ed. Charles E. Reagan (Athens, Ohio: Ohio University Press, 1979), 98.
173. Paul Ricoeur, *Freud and Philosophy: An Essay on Interpretation*, tr. Denis Savage (Yale University Press: 1970), 45. This work is abbreviated in the following as Freud.
174. Freud, 46 (emphasis in the original).
175. Paul Ricoeur, *The Conflict of Interpretations*, ed. Don Ihde (Evanston: N.U.P.: 1974), 17, abbreviated in the following as CI.
176. Freud, 43: 'I am, I think; to exist is for me to think; I exist inasmuch as I think. Since this truth can neither be verified like a fact nor deduced like a conclusion, it has to posit itself in reflection; it's self-positing is reflection; Fichte called this first truth the *thetic judgment*. Such is our philosophical point, philosophically speaking.' (Emphasis in the original).
177. Freud, 47.   178. Freud, 49.
179. Freud, 55.   180. CI, 10.
181. This long path involves several detours, which should lend to the individual stages greater transparency. Cf. Lewis S. Mudge, 'Paul Ricoeur on Biblical Interpretation', in Paul Ricoeur, *Essays on Biblical Interpretation*, ed. with an Introduction by Lewis S. Mudge (Philadelphia: Fortress, 1980), 15.
182. Paul Ricoeur: *Le Conflit des Interprétations: Essais d'Herméneutique* (Paris: Seuil, 1969), 23.
183. CI, 24.   184. TM, 397-447.
185. Paul Ricoeur, *The Symbolism of Evil*, tr. Emerson Buchanan (Boston, Beacon: 1969), 348f. This work is abbreviated in the following as SE.
186. SE, 348.   187. SE, 347-57
188. Freud, 41f.
189. CI, 12 (this passage is emphasised in the original). Cf. on this point the exposition of Patrick L. Bourgeois, 'From Hermeneutics of Symbols to the Interpretation of Texts', in *Studies in the Philosophy of Paul Ricoeur*, op. cit., 86f.
190. Freud, 41. Cf. also Paul Ricoeur, *Interpretation Theory: Discourse and the Surplus of Meaning* (Fort Worth, Texas: Texas Christian University Press, 1976), 45-69. This work is abbreviated in the following as IT.
191. Freud, 42.
192. 'The sole philosophical interest in symbolism is that it reveals by its

structure of double meaning the equivocalness of being. Being speaks in many ways.' CI, 67.
193. CI, 71.   194. CI, 68.
195. See below 94-100 the sections on style (selection) and genre (combination).
196. 'Creativity in Language: Word, Polysemy, Metaphor', in *The Philosophy of Paul Ricoeur: An Anthology of His Work*, eds. Charles E. Reagan and David Stewart (Boston: Beacon, 1978), 125.
197. Ibid., 129f.: '... I shall treat metaphor as a creative use of polysemy and in that way as a specific strategy of language. Instead of reducing or suppressing polysemy, metaphor uses polysemy as a means to preserve polysemy and to make it work in a most effective way.'
198. Ibid., 130ff.   199. IT, 64.
200. Cf. especially: Paul Ricoeur, *The Rule of Metaphor: Multi-disciplinary Studies of the Creation of Meaning* (London: Routledge and Kegan Paul: 1978).
201. 'Creativity in Language', op. cit., 132.
202. 'Metaphor and the main problem of Hermeneutics', in *The Philosophy of Paul Ricoeur*, op. cit., 138, cf. note 196 above.
203. IT, 50f.   204. IT, 51.
205. Concerning the difference between metaphor and symbol cf. IT, 69.
206. David Pellauer, op. cit., 98.
207. 'Metaphor and the Main Problem of Hermeneutics', op. cit., 134 (emphasis in the original).
208. See above 14 and 30f.
209. HaHS, 61 (emphasis in the original).
210. HaHS, 61f. and 90.
211. *Philosophy Today* 17 (1973), 129-41.
212. Under this are to be understood all linguistic faculties which are required by a reader in order to grasp the linguistic form of a text.
213. Ibid., 134.   214. Ibid., 134-9.
215. David Pellauer, op. cit., 107.
216. Cf. Freud and CI.
217. CI, 29-30.
218. CI, 32.
219. CI, 82.
220. CI, 84. Here the difference regarding Gadamer's concept of 'language' becomes particularly clear. For Gadamer language is in the first place 'conversation', for Ricoeur however 'speaking'. Cf. p. 19ff. and note 91 above.
221. CI, 85, the continuation of the quotation is as follows: 'Speaking is the act by which the speaker overcomes the closure of the universe of signs, in the intention of saying something about something to someone; speaking is the act by which language moves beyond itself as sign toward its refernce and toward what it encounters. Language seeks to disappear; it seeks to die as an object'.
222. CI, 86f.
223. After the word and the sentence the next level of the realisation of

language is the text. A text is always more than the sum total of its sentences. It is a cumulative holistic process, which contains an excess of significance which tran'scends its semantic elements. Cf. Paul Ricoeur, 'Metaphor and the Main Problem of Hermeneutics', op. cit., 142. More precisely, one ought to point out here that there are of course such things as 'single word assertions', which can also evoke a totality of significations in a certain situation of communication.
224. Gottlob Frege: 'Über Sinn und Bedeutung', *Zeitschrift für Philosophie und philosophische Kritik*, NF 100 (1892), 25-50. This appeared also in: Gottlob Frege, *Funktion, Begriff, Bedeutung: Fünf logische Studien*, 5th edn, ed. Günther Patzig (Göttingen: Vandenhoeck & Ruprecht, 1980), 40-65. The quotations below follow this edition.
225. CI, 86f.
226. IT, 43 (emphasis in the original).
227. 'The Hermeneutical Function of Distanciation', op. cit., 141 (emphasised in the original).
228. IT, 94.
229. 'Explanation and Understanding: On Some Remarkable Connections Among the Theory of the Text, Theory of Action, and Theory of History', in *The Philosophy of Paul Ricoeur*, op. cit., 150.
230. Cf. Paul Ricoeur, 'Qu'est-ce qu'un Texte? Expliquer et Comprendre', in *Hermeneutik und Dialektik: Aufsätze II* ed. Rüdiger Bubner, Konrad Cramer and Reiner Wiehl (Tübingen: J. C. B. Mohr [Paul Siebeck], 1970), 186f.
231. Ricoeur's reflections have naturally consequences also for Action Theory and Theory of History, though we cannot here enter into a consideration of this matter. Cf. the essay quoted above in note 229.
232. Cf. 'Qu'est-ce qu'un Texte?', op. cit., 192f.
233. Ibid., 192. 234. IT, 85. 235. IT, 74f.
236. IT, 77. 237. IT, 79. 238. IT, 80.
239. IT, 87f. 240. HaHS, 192. 241. Freud, 28.
242. Freud, 33 (emphasis in the original). On the absence of an explicit critique of the object of interpretation in Gadamer and Ricoeur cf. below, 64f.
243. HaHS, 88. 244. HaHS, 90. 245. HaHS, 91.
246. HaHS, 93: 'The *matter* of the text is not what a naive reading of the text reveals, but what the formal arrangement of the text mediates. If that is so, then truth and method do not constitute a disjunction but rather a dialectical process.' (Emphasis in the original).
247. HaHS, 94: 'A hermeneutics of the power-to-be thus turns itself towards a critique of ideology, of which it constitutes the most fundamental possibility. Distanciation, at the same time, emerges at the heart of reference: poetic discourse distances itself from everyday reality, aiming towards being as power-to-be.'
248. Ibid. (emphasis in the original). 249. HaHS, 95f.
250. HaHS, 97 (emphasis in the original).
251. Ibid. 252. HaHS, 100.
253. 'Qu'est-ce qu'un Texte?', op. cit., 182: 'Le texte est un discours fixé par l'écriture.'

166 Interpretation and Theological Thinking

254. Cf. CI, 86f.   255. Cf. note 224 above.
256. Frege, op. cit., 46, note 5.
257. Ibid., 48 (emphasis in the original).
258. Ibid., 49, note 7.   259. Ibid., 50.   260. Ibid., 65.   261. Ibid., 40f.
262. IT, 90.   263. Ibid.   264. IT, 91.
265. CI, 97.
266. Frege op. cit., 48.
267. CI, 87.   268. IT, 94.   269. IT, 87f.
270. John B. Thompson, *Critical Hermeneutics: A Study in the Thought of Paul Ricoeur and Jürgen Habermas* (Cambridge, England: Cambridge University Press, 1981), 191–6.
271. Ibid., 191f.   272. Ibid., 195.   273. HaHS, 185f.
274. HaHS, 193: 'It is because absolute knowledge is impossible that the conflict of interpretations is insurmountable and inescapable.'
275. Cf. Ricoeur's endeavours to make the pluralism of possible methods fruitful for the theory of interpretation in CI, among other works.
276. IT, 92–5.   277. HaHS, 192.
278. HaHS, 185–90: '"Play" as the mode of being of appropriation'.
279. TM, 269.
280. Cf. Gadamer's discussions concerning the guiding humanistic concepts, TM, 5–39.
281. 'Nicht Lehrsätze und "Ideen" seien die Regeln eures Seins. Der Führer selbst und allein ist die heutige und kunftige Wirklichkeit und ihr Gesetz.' — Erich Kästner, 'Schwierigkeiten, ein Held zu sein', in Erich Kästner, *Kästner für Erwachsene*, ed. Rudolf Walter Leonhardt (Frankfurt/M.: Fischer, 1966), 436–9, here 438. The quotation continues: 'I do not know whether the important personality as he spoke the words 'euer Sein' (your being) pronounced the word Sein with an "i" or with a "y". For all I care he may be the greatest philosopher of our glorious century and remain so and I do not mind whether this "be" is written as "sein" or "seyn"! I believe and hope that in the Pantheon someday Socrates and Seneca, Spinoza and Kant will not shake hands with him.'

'Ob der bedeutende Mann, als er, euer Sein sagte, Sein mit i oder mit y ausgesprochen hat, weiß ich nicht. Möge er der größe Philosoph unseres glorreichen Jahrhunderts sein oder seyn und bleiben! Ich glaube und hoffe, daß ihm, eines Tages im Pantheon, Sokrates und Seneca, Spinoza und Kant nicht die Hand geben werden.'

In the meantime Heidegger's 'Rektoratsrede' (inaugural lecture as chancellor) has appeared in print: Martin Heidegger, *Die Selbstbehauptung der Deutschen Universität/Das Rektorat 1933/34* (Frankfurt/M.: Klostermann, 1983). One does not find, however, in this text the quotation given by Kästner. In our choice of a sample text what is at issue is not a judgment of Heidegger but rather the fact that a reader of the Kästner text is forced to assess it. From our sample text it becomes very evident that from time to time further information is necessary in order to arrive at an appropriate assessment.

282. Ernst Fuchs, *Hermeneutik*, 2nd edn (Bad Cannstadt: Müllerschön, 1958), 136: 'All understanding is actually grounded in mutual understanding!'

(emphasis in the original). Cf. on this point Rüdiger Bubner, *Dialektik und Wissenschaft*, 2nd edn (Frankfurt/M.: Suhrkamp, 1974), 97: 'Understanding as grasp of meaning cannot simply be identified with mutual agreement as *practical consensus*.' (Emphasis in the original).
283. TM, 350.   284. TM, ibid.   285. TM, 358.
286. Cf. 54f. above.
287. Franz Schupp, in *Auf dem Weg zu einer kritischen Theologie*, Quaestiones Disputatae 64 (Freiburg i.B.: Herder, 1974), 153, insisted in regard to theological hermeneutics that this requires 'both understanding and critique by necessity'.
288. In the word *Verantwortung* (responsibility) is hidden the word *Antwort* (response). In a reading which is characterised by understanding, explanation and assessment the reader responds to the challenge of the text.
289. TM, 432-3 (emphasis in the original).   290. CI, 24.
291. Ernst Bloch, *Tübinger Einleitung in die Philosophie* I, 6th edn (Frankfurt/M.: Suhrkamp, 1968), 11.

Chapter II, pp. 73-128

1. This holds especially for all fundamentalist Bible exegesis. Cf. James Barr, *Fundamentalism*, 2nd edn (London SCM, 1981), 40-89 and 120-59.
2. Cf. especially ibid., 46: Barr designates as the guiding principle of fundamentalist interpretation "that one must ensure that the Bible is inerrant, without error. Inerrancy is maintained only by constantly altering the mode of interpretation, and in particular by abandoning the literal sense as soon as it would be an embarasment to the view of inerrancy held".
3. Rudolf Bultmann, "Ist voraussetzungslose Exegese möglich?" in his book, *Glauben und Verstehen: Gesammelte Aufsätze*, Vol. 3., 3rd edn (Tübingen: J. C. B. Mohr [Paul Siebeck], 1965), 142-50, especially 143f.
4. Anthony C. Thiselton also pleads for a stronger recognition of the close connection between exegesis and systematic theology, *The Two Horizons: New Testament Hermeneutics and Philosophical Description with Special Reference to Heidegger, Bultmann, Gadamer, and Wittgenstein* (Exeter: Paternoster Press, 1981), 314ff. Thiselton's comprehensive report on contemporary reflections on Biblical Hermeneutics comes to the following conclusion, p.445 (emphasis in the original): "The hermeneutical goal is that of a steady progress towards a fusion of horizons. But this is to be achieved in such a way that the particularity of each horizon is fully taken into account and respected. This means *both* respecting the rights of the text *and* allowing it to speak." Thiselton does not, however, investigate what makes a text to be a text and how the reader allows the text to speak. There is also lacking in this otherwise praiseworthy hermeneutical overview any indication of the necessity of an explicit text theory. — On the relationship of historical-critical exegesis and existential interpretation cf. also Paul Tillich, *A History of Christian Thought*, ed. Carl Braaten (New York: Simon and Schuster, 1972) 244f.

5. Alan Millar and John K. Riches have not as yet gained insight into this point, see "Interpretation: A Theoretical Perspective and Some Applications", *Numen* 28 (1981), 29-53. Cf. especially 33, where "utterance" is introduced without any text-consciousness.
6. Teun A. Van Dijk, in *Textwissenschaft: Eine interdisziplinäre Einführung*, tr. Christoph Sauer (Munich: DTV, 1980), 1-17, emphasises the inter-disciplinary character of text-theoretical thinking and shows its significance for the various disciplines. Strangely enough in this endeavour theology, under the heading *'Textwissenschaft und Anthropologie'*, gets only a scant mention. Cf. especially 14. — Bernhard Sowinski, in *Textlinguistik: Eine Einführung* (Stuttgart: Kohlhammer, 1983), 11, on the contrary emphasises right at the beginning of his presentation theology's interest in the point: "Among textual sciences theology is to be mentioned in the first place, not only because of the priority accorded to it over the centuries but also because theology is to be numbered amongst the oldest of the text-related disciplines."
7. Text linguistics is a young discipline. In a work as recent as Karl-Dieter Bünting, *Einführung in die Linguistik* (Frankfurt/M.: Athenäum Fischer, 1972) it is only mentioned in the Epilogue, and then as a hermeneutical synonym for Pragmatics, cf. 198. With the development of Pragmatics, i.e. the more recent concentration on the application of linguistic signs, a special interest in the text as the natural environment of linguistic signs also develops among the theoreticians of language. — On the History, Definition and Methodology of Textlinguistics see especially "Textlinguistik" in Hadumod Bußmann, *Lexikon der Sprachwissenschaft* (Stuttgart: Kröner, 1983), 538f.; Wolfgang Dressler, *Einführung in die Textlinguistik* (Tübingen: Niemeyer, 1972); W. Kallmeyer et al., *Lektürekolleg zur Textlinguistik*, (Frankfurt/M.: Fischer Athenäum, Vol. 1, 2nd edn 1977; Vol. 2. 1974); Siegfried J. Schmidt, *Texttheorie: Probleme einer Linguistik der sprachlichen Kommunikation* (Munich: Fink, 1976); Harald Weinrich, *Sprache in Texten* (Stuttgart: Kohlhammer, 1976); Hans-Werner Eroms, 'Textlinguistisches Arbeiten aus sprachwissenschaftlicher Sicht', (MS, Regensburg, 1977); Elisabeth Gulich and Wolfgang Raible, *Linguistische Textmodelle: Grundlagen und Möglichkeiten* (Munich: Fink, 1977); Teun A. van Dijk, *Textwissenschaft*, op. cit.; Eugenio Coseriu, *Textlinguistik: Eine Einführung* (Tübingen: Narr, 1980); Bernhard Sowinski, *Textlinguistik*, op. cit.
8. John L. Austin, *How To Do Things With Words*, eds. J. O. Urmson and Marina Sbisa, 2nd edn (Oxford: Oxford University Press, 1976); John R. Searle, *Speech Acts: An Essay in the Philosophy of Language* (London: Cambridge University Press, 1969).
9. Hadumod Bußmann: 'Textlinguistik', op. cit., 538.
10. Ibid.
11. Siegfried Schmidt, op. cit., 39.
12. Eugenio Coseriu, op. cit., 27f.
13. Ibid., 29.   14. Ibid., 35.
15. Elisabeth Gülich and Wolfgang Raible, op. cit., 47.
16. Wolfgang Klein and Ulrich Nassen, 'Textlinguistik und Texthermen-

eutik', in Ulrich Nassen, ed., *Texthermeneutik: Aktualität, Geschichte, Kritik* (Paderborn: Schöningh, 1979), 29.
17. Ibid.
18. Cf. 44-6 above, where in conjunction with Ricoeur the autonomy of the written text and its consequences for interpretation are discussed.
19. Coseriu, op. cit., 35.
20. Klein and Nassen come to a similar conclusion, op. cit., 32 (emphasis in the original): 'Even if it is not possible to arrive at *the* sense of a text, nevertheless an investigation of the textuality of texts could bring more to light on the connection between the constitution of the text and that of the sense and, in so doing, could make a contribution to the relative objectification of hermeneutical understanding. A cooperation between text linguistics and text hermeneutics within this frame of reference would be more than a mere preparation of the results of research of one discipline for the other respectively.' — Kurt Nikolaus, 'Zur Kritik der Textlinguistik', in M. Kohl and J. Lenerz, eds., *Sprache: Formen und Strukturen. Akten des 15. Linguistischen Kolloquiums,* Münster 1980, Vol. 1 (Tübingen: Niemeyer, 1981), 281-91, criticises the fact that traditional text linguistics occupies itself more with 'sentences-in-contexts' (285) than with texts. He sees on the contrary the proper domain of text linguistics 'precisely in the question of problems of cognitive text elaboration and the memory processes involved in it, that is to say in the last analysis, in a theory of the application of language and a theory of human linguistic activity' (289). 'Every text linguistic theory which does not include in its reflections as a matter of course the cognitive processes of the genesis and understanding of texts misses the essence of its subject matter.' (290)
21. Manfred Frank, 'Was heißt "einen Text verstehen"?', in Ulrich Nassen, ed., *Texthermeneutik: Aktualität, Geschichte, Kritik*, op. cit., 66.
22. Cf. Harald Weinrich, *Sprache in Texten*, op. cit., 18.
23. Schmidt, op. cit., 76 (emphasis in the original).
24. Ibid.
25. On this point see also my essay 'The Theological Understanding of Texts and Linguistic Explication', *Modern Theology* 1 (1984), 55-66.
26. IT, 87f. Cf. in this study 44f. above.
27. Coseriu, op. cit., 47ff. Hans-Werner Eroms, *Die dynamische Struktur der Texte* (MS, Passau, 1982), 7f., requires here however and rightly so, 'that we relocate Coseriu's conceptions in a dynamic process-concept.

'We do not pose the question concerning the "sense" of a text after reading the text — we might do that for didactic purposes —, but rather continuously during reading and reflection: it is that which is aimed at, namely the simultaneously presupposed sense of the text. The grasp of the actual meaning of the sentences contained by a text is regulated in the first instance as mere hypothesis, which in the course of the reading is either strengthened or modified. In this way we can truly speak of an interdependent relationship between the actual meaning and the sense, of a cybernetic process.'
28. Coseriu, ibid. 49.   29. Ibid.

30. In exceptional cases of oral and written communication single words or single sentences can form so-called 'one-word-texts' or 'one-sentence-texts' respectively. Cf. on this Hans-Werner Eroms, 'Zur Analyse kompakter Texte', *Sprachwissenschaft* 7 (1982), 333.
31. Hans-Werner Eroms, *Die dynamische Struktur der Texte*, op. cit., 3 (emphasis in the original).
32. Cf. Wolfgang Dressler, *Einführung in die Linguistik*, op. cit., 56.
33. Pr 1:1-7. (Biblical quotations according to *The Jerusalem Bible* (London: Darton, Longman & Todd, 1968).
34. Mk 1:1.   35. Cf. 169, note 27 above.
36. Ingolf U. Dalferth, *Religiöse Rede von Gott* (Munich: Kaiser, 1981), 209.
37. Coseriu, op. cit., 56-68.   38. Ibid., 68.
39. Ibid., 102.   40. Cf. 90ff. below.
41. Our concept of 'communicative perspective' is based on the concept of the 'functional sentence perspective', which was elaborated on in the later Prague School of Linguistics in connection with Vilém Matthesius. We have however enlarged on this concept to the extent that we have transferred it from the level of sentence to that of text. We can of course in so doing continue to positively appreciate the communicative dynamic which reigns within a sentence or utterance, now however from the new perspective of the text. It does not appear to us that through this enlargement we are doing violence to the Prague model; for this model was, as a consequence of its investigations into the communicative dynamic and the thematic progression, open, from the beginning, to textual problems even if it has not as yet explicitly shown interest in the constitution of sense within a text but has rather confined itself to the formal composition of texts. But now in order to emphasise the semantic problematic of a text, we speak here, from the outset, of the communicative perspective of a text.

    For the Prague School of Linguistics and especially for an elaboration of the concept of 'functional sentence perspective' cf. František Daneš, ed., *Papers on Functional Sentence Perspective* (Prague: Academia, and Den Haag/Paris: Mouton, 1974).
42. František Daneš, 'Functional Sentence Perspective and the Organisation of the Text', *Papers on Functional Sentence Perspective*, op. cit., 114.
43. On the development and contemporary state of the discussion of 'Theme-Rheme-Theory' cf. Luise Lutz, *Zum Thema 'Thema': Einführung in die Thema-Rhema-Theorie*, Hamburger Arbeiten zur Linguistik und Texttheorie, 1 (Hamburg: Hamburger Buchagentur, 1981), and Hans-Werner Eroms, *Funktionale Satzperspektive* (Tübingen: Niemeyer, 1986). On the coining of the concepts 'Theme' and 'Rheme' by Hermann Ammann cf. Lutz, op. cit., 11. Cf. also Jean-Marie Zemb, *Métagrammaire: La Proposition* (Paris: OCDL, 1972), 142, where 'Theme' and 'Rheme' are defined as follows: 'Le rhème est ce qui est dit de quelque chose, le thème est ce de quoi l'on parle quand on en dit quelque chose, faire une proposition consiste à dire quelque chose de quelque chose, se prononcer sur la convenance d'un rhème à un thème selon les catégories de la qualité

et de la modalité.' On the discussion of Zemb's theory see Lutz, op. cit., 95-103.
44. Lutz, ibid., 74.   45. Ibid., 38; cf. also 45.
46. Ibid. 67. — Lutz draws attention to the lack of uniformity in the application of the notions 'Theme' and 'Rheme' and the resulting problems, ibid. 78f. But these difficulties are not of any great importance for our area of questioning because our primary concern is with the concept of the dynamic within a text and this concept is supported by all Theme-Rheme definitions.
47. František Daneš, 'Functional Sentence Perspective and the Organisation of the Text', op. cit., 118-23.
48. Cf. Hans-Werner Eroms, 'Komplexitätsmaße bei der Textsortendifferenzierung', in *Textsorten und literarische Gattungen: Dokumentation des Germanistentages in Hamburg vom 1. bis 4. April 1979* (Hamburg: Erich Schmidt, 1983), 133.
49. Concerning the concept of style cf. 94-7 below.
50. Schmidt, op. cit., 161, speaks also of decisions regarding selection in the production of the text but does not recognise the style character of such decisions.
51. Cf. Lutz in this matter, op. cit., 29.   52. Cf. also 98ff. below.
53. On this matter cf. Roland Harweg, *Pronomina und Textkonstitution*, 2nd edn (Munich: Fink, 1979).
54. Cf. on this point Wolfgang Dressler, op. cit., 66-73.
55. Cf. Kallmeyer et al., Vol. 1, op. cit., 113.
56. Ibid. 123f.   57. See 85ff. above.
58. Kallmeyer et al., Vol. 1, op. cit., 147.   59. Ibid. 177-252.
60. See 83f. above.
61. Cf. Helmut Köster, *Einführung in das Neue Testament im Rahmen der Religionsgeschichte und Kulturgeschichte der hellenistischen und römischen Zeit* (Berlin/New York: de Gruyter, 1980), 436-40, and also Hans Freiherr von Campenhausen, 'Die Enstehung des Neuen Testaments', in Ernst Käsemann, ed., *Das Neue Testament als Kanon: Dokumentation und kritische Analyse zur gegenwärtigen Diskussion* (Göttingen: Vandenhoeck & Ruprecht, 1970), 109-23.
62. The significance of texts which were possible candidates for the Canon as it was being constituted rests also in the first place on their use in the various communities, in other words on reading praxis.
63. Köster, op. cit., 439: 'The question of inspiration played no role whatever in the matter of canonisation.' Cf. on this point James Barr, *Holy Scripture: Canon, Authority, Criticism* (Oxford: Clarendon Press, 1983), 23-6.
64. Cf. Barr, ibid. 29f: 'Roman Catholicism emphasized tradition, and against the single-minded emphasis on scripture in popular Protestantism it insisted that scripture came from the church. But within its own internal thinking it was very slow to take advantage of this. Around the end of last century and the beginning of this the Roman church authorities, faced with biblical criticism and the modernist movement, took refuge in a

conservatism of a type very similar to that made familiar at about the same time by Protestant fundamentalism. . . . In this way Roman biblical scholars were being prevented from using the dynamics of tradition, which their church understood so well and upon which it built so much, as the model for the understanding of scripture.'
65. Coseriu, op. cit., 155.
66. Cf. Manfred Frank, *Das individuelle Allgemeine: Textstrukturierung und — interpretation nach Schleiermacher* (Frankfurt/M.: Suhrkamp, 1977), 313-33; idem, 'Was heißt "einen Text Verstehen"?', op. cit., 63f.; idem, *Das Sagbare und das Unsagbare: Studien zur neuesten französischen Hermeneutik und Texttheorie* (Frankfurt/M.: Suhrkamp, 1980), especially the Preface, 7-12, and the first essay "Der Text und sein Stil: Schleiermachers Sprachtheorie', 13-35.
67. Paul Ricoeur, in 'Schleiermacher's Hermeneutics', *The Monist* 60 (1977), 188, pays the following tribute to Schleiermacher: 'He was one of the first to perceive that style is not a matter of ornamentation; it marks the union of thought and language, the union of the common and the singular in an author's project. The style displays a singularity inside the common resources of language, and, above all, in the style the formal aspect of the work's structure is joined to the psychological aspect of the author's intention.'
68. Paul Ricoeur, 'The Hermeneutical Function of Distanciation', op. cit., 136 (emphasis in the original).
69. Hans-Werner Eroms, 'Stilistik', in Margareta Gorschenek and Annamaria Rucktäschel, eds., *Kritische Stichwörter zur Sprachdidaktik* (Munich: Fink, 1983), 235.
70. Barbara Sandig, *Stilistik: Sprachpragmatische Grundlegung der Stilbeschreibung* (Berlin/New York: de Gruyter, 1978), 15.
71. Where Sandig helps us to envisage the phenomenon of style as a text phenomenon I follow her. But I cannot do so in cases where she treats style merely as form, that is to say where she reduces it to nothing more than a formalistic aspect of language. Style is more; style is in the last analysis the principle of individuation and I agree with Manfred Frank when he says in *Das individuelle Allgemeine*, op. cit., 318,: 'To try to deny the singularity of the universal (*Allgemeine*), which is manifest in the style of a discourse, would be tantamount to stating that every instance of understanding exhausts itself in correctly grasping the 'logical content' of language, and that mutual understanding never penetrates as far as the individual (extra-grammatical and extra-generic) 'vivification' (*Beseelung*) of the speech intentions — an abstraction through which one in no way grasps the majority of linguistic speech acts.'
72. Sandig, op. cit., 15. Even though Sandig's investigation confines its interest to 'usual styles' and furthermore to such as 'are neither poetic nor literary' (ibid., 5), we may nevertheless, grant certain precautions, adopt from Sandig important insights which concern text style in general.
73. Cf. Eroms, 'Stilistik' op. cit., 237.
74. The concept of 'text genre' emphasises the textuality of a text, yet does not overemphasise the normative aspect. Certainly style always deals with the

application or rejection of norms. But within this basic involvement with norms there exists the freedom of choice. And this freedom is equally a characteristic of the definition of style. Gadamer would seem to hold a contrary opinion. Cf. TM/WM, 466ff. — Concerning the notion of 'text genre' (*Textsorte*) cf. also Eroms, 'Stilistik', op. cit., 239f.
75. Cf. Sandig, op. cit., 43. And: 'Style is essentially a textual phenomenon, and texts and text patterns are *the* units of linguistic activity.' Ibid., 98 (emphasis in the original).
76. Cf. Sandig, ibid. 166, and Bernhard Sowinski, *Deutsche Stilistik: Beobachtungen zur Sprachverwendung und Sprachgestaltung im Deutschen* (Frankfurt/M.: Fischer, 1978), 31–7.
77. Sandig, ibid., 177f.
78. Sardig, ibid., 5, note 1: 'The concept of style as individual style brings with it endless difficulties in a theory of linguistic style.' These difficulties in describing style are not, however, to be taken as an excuse for no longer concerning oneself with the individualising potentiality of style, something which happens all too often in formalistic descriptions of language.
79. Cf. Eroms, 'Stilistik', op. cit., 240: 'Individual variations, and with these, differences in style, are achieved especially through superimposition of patterns of action. Many stylistic effects result from the fact that communicative intentions are given expression in an indirect manner.' Bernhard Marfurt, 'Textrezeption und Textsorte', *wirkendes wort* 5 (1980), 302, takes 'text genre' (*Textsorte*) in the sense of a pragmatic concept: 'We treat text genres as something which is constituted, not just on the basis of certain structural characteristics of texts (as for example inner structure or particular vocabulary), but rather as something which stands in a dialectical relationship with the process of interaction, which is achieved through the 'use' of the text genre. It is our opinion that the text structure (by which we mean approximately the objectified, inner-linguistic characteristics of text genres) and the textual usage (such characteristics as the text function in the respective situation of application) —that these can only be distinguished analytically from each other and that a determination of text genres for this reason must equally take into account both aspects, the characteristics of text structure and also the process of interaction which is constituted through the application of the text.'
80. Luc Gobyn draws attention to the necessity of paying attention, not only to the structure of a text, but also to its function in the endeavour to differentiate text genres: 'Differenzierungskriterien für Textsorten', in *Sprache: Formen und Strukturen,* op. cit., (cf. 169 above note 20), 278.
81. Cf. 87 above.
82. *Foundations of Christian Faith,* op. cit., 337.
83. Ibid. 348.
84. Generally speaking one may say that such headlines as rhematise have a more provocative effect than those which thematise. They can, however, because of this also preempt the tension which is only to be built up by the development itself of the text and in this way they can reduce the dynamic of the process of reception.

85. Eugene Ionesco, *The Bald Prima Donna: An Anti-Play*, op. cit.
86. Eroms, 'Stilistik', op. cit., 237.   87. Ibid.
88. One may for example think of 'reporting' and 'describing' as variations of 'narrating', while the variant 'discussing' belongs to 'arguing'.
89. Cf. Harald Weinrich, *Tempus: Besprochene und erzählte Welt*, 3rd edn (Stuttgart: Kohlhammer, 1977).
90. Henricus Denzinger and Adolfus Schönmetzer, eds., *Enchiridion Symbolorum: Definitionum Et Declarationum De Rebus Fidei Et Morum*, 36th edn (Freiburg i.B.: Herder, 1976).
91. Cf. Jan Mukařovský, 'The Place of the Aesthetic Function among the Other Functions', in *Structure, Sign, and Function: Selected Essays by Jan Mukařovský*, tr. and eds. John Burbank and Peter Steiner (New Haven/London: Yale University Press, 1978), 31-48. Mukařovský speaks of the basic polyfunctionality of human activity and the basic omnipresence of functions' (37).
92. Cf. Jan Mukařovský, 'Ästhetische Funktion, Norm und ästhetischer Wert als soziale Fakten', in *Kapitel aus der Ästhetik*, tr. Walter Schamschula, 3rd edn (Frankfurt/M.: Suhrkamp, 1978), 7-112, especially 11-34.
93. The concept of 'stylistic competence' should be taken into account in the discussion of 'communicative competence' (Habermas). Cf. 23 above.
94. Georg Fohrer, *Einleitung in das Alte Testament*, 11th edn (Heidelberg: Quelle & Meyer, 1969), 26.
95. Ibid, 29.
96. David Hellholm: *Das Visionenbuch des Hermas als Apokalypse*, op. cit., (cf. 157 above, note 16), 67: 'As distinct from literary theory's theory of genres the history of forms (*Formgeschichte*) has proceeded right from the beginning almost exclusively in a practico-inductive manner and there is an almost complete absence of model formation of a theoretico-deductive type right up to the present . . .'.
97. Hellholm's work is, nevertheless, a welcome new beginning of theological text consciousness. Nor is this contribution diminished by the fact that Hellholm has not as yet produced a general theory of text and text composition of a comprehensive linguistic nature. Such a universal 'text-linguistics of sense' was not the purpose of his investigation since he concentrated on a particular text, the book of *Visions of Hermas*. — Regarding 'text linguistics properly so-called' cf. 76ff. above.
98. On the extra-textual principles of the formation of the canon cf. 92ff. above.
99. Eroms: 'Stilistik', op. cit., 237f. The different strategies of textualisation can, however, be united in a text to make up its composition, as for example in the parable of the Sower in Mt 13: 1-9 and in its assessment 13: 18-23. Narrating: 3b-8; Arguing: 18-23; Describing: 1-3a; Instructing: 9.
100. Susan R. Suleiman, 'Introduction: Varieties of Audience-Oriented Criticism', in Susan R. Suleiman and Inge Crosman, *The Reader in the Text: Essays on Audience and Interpretation* (Princeton: Princeton University Press, 1980), 3-45, especially 6ff.
101. E. D. Hirsch, Jr., *Validity in Interpretation* (New Haven/London: Yale

University Press, 1967), 46: '... a verbal meaning is determinate ... it is an entity which is self-identical ... it is an entity which always remains the same from one moment to the next ... it is changeless. ... Verbal meaning, then, is what it is and not something else, and it is always the same. That is what I mean by determinacy.'
102. Cf. for example Roland Barthes, *The Pleasure of the Text*, tr. Richard Millar (New York: Hill and Wang, 1975), 4: 'The text of pleasure is a sanctioned Babel.' Concerning Jaques Derrida's deconstructionism see Susan R. Suleiman, op. cit., 40ff.
103. Wolfgang Iser, *The Act of Reading: A Theory of Aesthetic Response* (London and Henley: Routledge & Kegan Paul, 1978), x.
104. Ibid., ix.   105. Ibid., 19.
106. Ibid., 22. Cf. here also the German original *Der Akt des Lesens: Theorie ästhetischer Wirkung* (Munich: Fink, 1976), 42.
107. Ibid., 24.
108. Iser introduced the concept of 'implied reader' in his book *The Implied Reader: Patterns of Communication in Prose Fiction from Bunyan to Beckett*. (Baltimore: Johns Hopkins University Press, 1974).
109. *The Act of Reading*, 34.   110. Ibid., 37.
111. Ibid. (original emphasis).
112. ibid., 69.   113. Ibid., 92f.   114. Ibid., 96f. Cf. 85–8 above.
115. *Der Akt des Lesens*, 165. The English version differs here.
116. *The Act of Reading*, 107.   117. Ibid., 108.   118. Ibid., 112.
119. Ibid., 118.   120. Ibid., cf. also 157f.   121. Ibid., 119.
122. Ibid., 120.   123. Ibid., 125.   124. Ibid., 127.
125. Ibid., 131. Here Iser follows the thesis of Wilhelm Schapp, that we only arrive at reality and presence through our entanglement in stories. See Schapp, *In Geschichten verstrickt: Zum Sein von Mensch und Ding*, 2nd edn (Wiesbaden: Heymann, 1976).
126. *The Act of Reading*, 141.   127. Ibid., 150.
128. *Der Akt des Lesens*, 245 (tr. T.W.); cf. *The Act of Reading*, 151.
129. Ibid., 169 (original emphasis).   130. Ibid., 202f.
131. *Der Akt des Lesens*, 312 (tr. T.W.).   132. *The Act of Reading*, 231.
133. Cf. on this point especially *Der Akt des Lesens*, 312.
134. Stanley Fish, *Is There a Text in This Class? The Authority of Interpretive Communities* (Cambridge, Massachusetts/London: Harvard University Press, 1980).
135. Ibid., 13.   136. Ibid., 14.   137. Ibid., 16f.
138. Ibid., 11: '... it is the reader who "makes" literature.'
139. Ibid., 97 (emphasis in the original).
140. Cf. ibid., 98, and 239, 243.
141. Ibid., 243.   142. Ibid., 293.   143. Ibid., 295.
144. Cf. ibid., 318–21.   145. Ibid., 331.   146. Cf. 69ff. above.
147. In Hans Robert Jauß, 'Literaturgeschichte als Provokation der Literaturwissenschaft', in Rainer Warning, ed., *Rezeptionsästhetik: Theorie und Praxis*, 2nd edn (Munich: Fink, 1979), one finds approaches to a theory of reading which is aware of the necessity of critical reflection on the subject-matter and the situation: 'The history of literature is a process of

aesthetic reception and production, which is achieved in the actualising of literacy texts through the receiving reader, the reflecting critic and the writer himself who in turn is again productive.' (129) Cf. also idem., 'Racines und Goethes Iphigenie: Mit einem Nachwort über die Partialität der rezeptionsästhetischen Methode', in *Rezeptionsästhetik*, ibid., especially 380-94.
148. Gadamer, TM, 350.
149. Ricoeur speaks in this connection of a first 'guessing' of the textual meaning. IT, 75. Cf. 51 above.
150. On the significance of the horizon of expectation on the part of the reader cf. Jauß, 'Literaturgeschichte als Provokation der Literaturwissenschaft', op. cit., 132f.
151. Mukarovský, 'Ästhetische Funktion, Norm und ästhetischer Wert als soziale Fakten', op. cit., 55 (emphasis in the original).
152. Ibid., 60.   153. Ibid., 65.   154. Ibid., 19.   155. Ibid., 27.
156. Cf. ibid. 107.
157. David Tracy calls such works 'classics'. Cf. 133f. and 144f. below for our discussion of this concept in connection with Tracy's hermeneutics — A similar concept of the 'classic' was already used by Friedrich Schleiermacher. Cf. his *Hermeneutik*, ed. Heinz Kimmerle, 2nd edn (Heidelberg: Carl Winter, 1974), 79.
158. Cf. on pluralism in the New Testament: Ernst Käsemann, 'Differences and Unity in the New Testament', *Concilium* 171 (1984), 55-61; and also James D. G. Dunn, *Unity and Diversity in the New Testament* (London: SCM, 1977).
159. Cf. Gerhard Ebeling, *Einführung in Theologische Sprachlehre* (Tübingen: J.C.B. Mohr, [Paul Siebeck], 1971), 256.
160. Ibid. 40 (emphasis in the original): 'One *can* often express the same thing in a totally different way without restricting the identity of the sense. One *must* often express it in a quite different manner to preserve the identity of the sense under changed circumstances of understanding. Though all of this holds not only for theology it does hold also for theology. Theology shares the lot of language in general.'
161. Ernst Käsemann, 'Differences and Unity in the New Testament', op. cit., 57: 'After Easter, the mission of the Gentiles is the distinguishing mark of the Church.'
162. Cf. the observations of James Barr, 171 above, note 64. — See the Institution of the Magisterium in the Roman Catholic tradition: The Magisterium has indeed been closely associated with Scripture and Tradition by Vatican Council II; but it finds itself repeatedly in the temptation to become hermeneutically autonomous. On the definition of the Magisterium cf. Dei Verbum 9 and 10, in Austin Flannery, ed., *Vatican Council II, Conciliar and Post-conciliar Documents* (Pennsylvania: Scholarly Resources, 1981), 755f. On the Magisterium's tendency to become autonomous cf. Schillebeeckx, *Ministry: A Case for Change*, tr. John Bowden (London: SCM, 1981), 100-104, as also idem, *God is New Each Moment*, tr. David Smith (Edinburgh: T. & T. Clark, 1983), 79-90.
163. Gadamer, TM, 429.

164. On the role of the Johannine prologue in the early Christian tradition cf. Jaroslav Pelikan, *The Christian Tradition: A History of the Development of Doctrine, Vol. 1: The Emergence of the Catholic Tradition (100-600)*, (Chicago and London: University of Chicago Press, 1971), 186-200, also Bernhard Lohse, *Epochen der Dogmengeschichte*, 3rd edn (Stuttgart: Kreuz, 1974), 46-51.
165. Cf. 68-72 above.
166. Certainly the collection of laws in the Pentateuch is susceptible of being received through juristic reading genres. Nevertheless these reading genres should not be posited in an absolute fashion but, rather, in the last analysis it must be acknowledged that the juristic text genres in the Pentateuch also require a theological reading perspective which must naturally include juristic reading genres.
167. However, none of these reading genres may be absolutely posited.
168. 'Individually' aims here at the possible reading functions in which theological reading takes place and forms, in each case, its style.
169. Jauß points out the possibility of an ethical relevance of reading. He does not, however, recognise that every instance of reading *must* be seen in an ethical context and does not simply have an effective ethical significance. Jauß, 'Literaturgeschichte als Provokation der Literaturwissenschaft', op. cit., 150f.

Chapter III, pp. 129-53

1. Tracy, *Blessed Rage for Order: The New Pluralism in Theology* (New York: Seabury, 1975), abbreviated in the following as BRO.
2. Idem., *The Analogical Imagination: Christian Theology and the Culture of Pluralism* (New York: Crossroad, 1981, and London: SCM, 1982), abbreviated in the following as AI.
3. Tracy's theological thinking does not, however, consist in methodical discourse alone. Rather, in each case the first parts of the works quoted serve the purpose of methododological self-relfection, which is then followed in BRO by a systematic discussion of the God-question and in AI by a systematic discussion of Christology. The extent of abstraction, nevertheless, of the systematic discussions, gives rise occasionally to the misconception that Tracy would be only concerned with methodology. Cf. on this point the criticism of William O'Brien and Tracy's reply to this criticism in 'Review Symposium', *Horizons* 9 (1982), 313-39, especially 326-330.
4. Cf. AI, 62-4.   5. Cf. BRO, 43-56 and 72-9.   6. Cf. AI, 64-9.
7. On the difference between Fundamental Theology and Systematic Theology cf. also AI, 183, note 26, and 241f., note 1.
8. Cf. AI, 69-79.
9. Cf. AI, 78: '... there is never an authentic disclosure of truth which is not also transformative'.
10. AI, 97, note 111: 'Methodologically, ... practical theologies continue to need the correctives of fundamental theology as much as the latter needs sublation into the praxis concreteness of practical theology. Thought implies action; action already includes thought'.
11. On the discussion of this three-fold task area of the theologian's work cf. AI, 3-31.

12. AI, 85, note 28.
13. David Tracy, 'Project "X": Retrospect and Prospect', *Concilium* 170 (1983), 32.
14. Ibid. (emphasis in the original).
15. Cf. AI, 100.
16. 'Project "X": Retrospect and Prospect', op. cit. 33.
17. AI, 104.
18. Ibid.
19. This is also emphasised by Ted Peters: 'Methode und System in der heutigen amerikanischen Theologie', *Kerygma und Dogma* 29 (1983), 2-46; cf. especially 8f.
20. AI, 108.
21. Cf. TM, 89. Cf. on this point Tracy, AI, 111.
22. AI, 106f.
23. David Tracy, 'On Thinking with the Classics', *Criterion* 22 (1983), 9-10, here 10.
24. AI, 119. Cf. also Tracy, 'Creativity in the Interpretation of Religion: The Question of Radical Pluralism', *New Literary History* 15 (1983-84), 296: 'When interpreting any classic text in the Western traditions, for example, we may note that these texts bear a certain permanence and excess of meaning that resists a definitive interpretation.'
25. Cf. AI, 132. 26. Cf. AI, 126-30.
27. This fact is not expressed with sufficient clarity in Tracy. See also 140ff. below.
28. For a concise summary of Tracy's theory of interpretation cf. also his contribution to *A Short History of the Interpretation of the Bible*, ed. Robert M. Grant with David Tracy, 2nd edition (Philadelphia: Fortress, 1984), especially 154-66.
29. Cf. AI, 101f.
30. Cf. AI, 118.
31. AI, 113f.: 'In playing, I lose myself in the play. I do not passively lose myself. In fact, I actively gain another self by allowing myself fully to enter the game. Thus do I allow myself to be played by the game. I move into the 'rules' of the game, into the back-and-forth movement, the experienced internal relationships of the game itself. The game becomes not an object over against a self-conscious subject but an experienced relational and releasing mode of being in the world distinct from the ordinary, nonplayful one. In every game, I enter the world where I play so fully that finally the game plays me.'
32. AI, 121. 33. Ibid.
34. AI, 113: 'Every classic contains its own plurality and encourages a pluralism of readings.'
35. Ibid.: 'The *only* methods disallowed should be those which disown the original experience of art and replace it with some other kind of experience.' (Emphasis in the original.)
36. AI, 105: 'The principal identity which both text and reader possess is the identity-in-difference of ever new and ongoing interpretation.' Tracy does not however investigate the conditions which underlie the possibility of

the text to be 'identity-in-difference'. On the absence of a text theory in Tracy see 136 below.
37. AI, 134. 38. AI, 136, note 8. 39. Cf. AI, 137, note 16.
40. AI, 128f. 41. AI, 121. 42. Cf. AI, 122.
43. Ibid. (emphasis in the original).
44. Ibid.
45. Cf. Iser's theory of the 'blanks' in *The Act of Reading*, 182ff.
46. See 56–61 above.
47. AI, 123.
48. AI, 145, note 75 (emphasis in the original).
49. AI, 146, note 80.
50. Ibid.
51. 'On Thinking with the Classics', ibid. 10 (my emphasis).
52. Also in David Tracy's Foreword to Arthur A. Cohen, *The Tremendum: A Theological Interpretation of the Holocaust* (New York: Crossroad, 1981), x, the demand for critical thinking is restricted to the consciousness of the interpreter; it does not, however, extend to the object of interpretation, the text: 'To think historically is also to evaluate. To think historically is to develop a hermeneutics of suspicion focussed upon the illusions and the not-so-innocent theories of both ourselves and our predecessors. Only through such radical suspicion is retrieval of any tradition possible.'
53. Cf. my article 'Towards a Critical Theology of Christian Praxis', *The Irish Theological Quarterly* 51 (1985), 136–45.
54. AI, 134.
55. AI, 107.
56. Cf. 'On Thinking with the Classics', op. cit., 10.
57. Mukařovský, 'Ästhetische Funktion, Norm und ästhetischer Wert als soziale Fakten, 107. Cf. also 118 above.
58. Cf. AI, 108. 59. Cf. TM, 258.
60. John B. Cobb, Jr. questions in his review of Tracy's *Analogical Imagination*, in *Religious Studies Review* 7 (1981), 281–4, whether our so-called classics can still do justice to all our requirements. This doubt appears to me to support to some extent the demand for a critique of the classic text, such as is dealt with here. I feel obliged, however, to contradict Cobb where he deduces from this critique of classical authors of past ages: 'Hermeneutical theology makes sense as long as we believe that our classics are essentially adequate to our needs.... In faithfulness to our classics we must find our true classics in the future and not in the past.'[283] But how can we recognise the power of texts from the past, the present and the future to disclose sense except in critical discussion, in interpretation, that is to say in hermeneutical activity?
61. Cf. David Tracy in *A Short History of the Interpretation of the Bible*, op. cit. 183f.: 'There is no sound scriptural or contemporary theological reason why any contemporary Christian need accept Paul's views on either women or slaves. (Indeed, an acceptance of Paul's own Christology should be sufficient to disallow those views.)' And: 'It is not only our modern preunderstanding that demands the theological hermeneutics of retrieval and suspicion; it is the scriptures themselves.' This welcome criticism of

180 *Text and Interpretation*

the text and openness to such criticism of the subject matter remains, however, without further influence on Tracy's development of a theory of interpretation.
62. Cf. 'On thinking with the Classics', ibid. 10.
63. The beginnings of a criticism, also of the subject-matter of interpretation itself such as can be integrated into the interpretation processes, are to be found in Tracy for the first time in 'Creativity in the Interpretation of Religion',op. cit., 306: 'Insofar as every classic religious text and tradition includes in the history of its effects a moral ambiguity that can become a repressed systematic distortion, there is also need for the development and use of various hermeneutics of suspicion, with their attendant critical theories, upon the religious classics.... These critical theories are employed to spot and emancipate the repressed, unconscious distortions that are also operative in the classic religious texts and in their history of effects through the classic religious traditions.'
How and when this critique is to operate in the process of interaction between text and reader is, however, not yet specified at this point.
64. See 179 above, note 51.
65. AI, 155.
66. AI, 157f.: '... the questions which religion addresses are the fundamental existential questions of the meaning and truth of individual, communal and historical existence as related to, indeed as both participating in and distanced from, what is sensed as the whole of reality.'
67. Cf. AI, 371.
68. AI, 163 (emphasis in the original).
69. Cf. AI, 174 and AI, 175: 'In principle, the religious classic expression cannot find an adequate form.' Cf. also Gerhard Ebeling, *Einführung in Theologische Sprachlehre*, op. cit., 256.
70 Cf. AI, 193.
71. AI, 195.
72. Cf. AI, 163.
73. Cf. on this point the parallel insight of Eberhard Jüngel: 'One can see the truth within our reality only to a greater or lesser extent; but truth cannot be immediately perceived; perception, to take something as true, is always dependent upon mediation. One cannot for this very reason at any stage possess truth, one cannot place onself in its possession.'
Jüngel, '"Auch das Schöne muß sterben" —Schönheit im Lichte der Wahrheit: Theologische Bemerkungen zum ästhetischen Verhältnis.' *Zeitschrift für Theologie und Kirche* 81 (1984), 122.
74. AI, 177.   75. AI, 248.   76. Ibid.
77. AI, 310. Cf., however, on this point Tracy's observation elsewhere: AI, 241, note 1 (emphasis in the original): '... still I believe the doctrine of Christ remains the major candidate for *the* Christian classic.' This conceptual uncertainty forces us to ask: Is the doctrine of Christ the classic of Christianity, or is it the event and the person of Jesus Christ himself? That Jesus Christ is a classic event is an insight which arises from the reception of the testimonies which mediate Jesus Christ to us today. Consequently it

is not very meaningful to make a distinction of reception between the event and the texts which bear testimony to it.
78. AI, 249.   79. Cf. AI, 250ff.   80. Cf. AI, 263 and 274.
81. Cf. AI, 438: Here Tracy deals with a 'Christian theological perspective'. Regarding the insight into the necessary perspectival nature of our thinking cf. also John B. Cobb's review of Tracy's *Analogical Imagination*, op. cit., 284.
82. AI, 408, 421f., 425.   83. AI, 448.
84. On the usefulness of the concept of 'Perspective' cf also: Rudolf Bultmann, 'Wissenschaft und Existenz', in Bultmann, *Glauben und Verstehen: Gesammelte Aufsätze*, Vol. 3, op. cit., 107–21, especially 111f.
85. AI, 372: '... the New Testament itself is internally pluralistic. As everyone knows, the later Christian tradition from the post-New Testament period to the present is yet more radically pluralistic in its interpretations of Christianity and often mutually contradictory.... Pluralism is not an invention of our present age. Pluralism is a reality in all the traditions.'
86. AI, 421: 'The major aim of all systematic theology is to formulate a theological understanding of the originating religious event into a theological focal meaning. The particular focal meaning chosen for that theological understanding will prove an "essentially contested concept." More exactly, the ultimate incomprehensibility of the religious event itself as well as the inability of critical intelligence to master either situation or event will yield a recognition that all theological proposals are necessarily and intrinsically inadequate.'
AI, 425: 'At the same time, each focus limits, occasionally even distorts, the vision of other major disclosures in the same paradigmatic event.'
87. AI, 423.   88. Ibid.
89. On 'manifestation, proclamation and historical action' cf. AI, 376–98.
90. Cf. Gregory Baum's review of Tracy's *Analogical Imagination*, in *Religious Studies Review* 7 (1981), 284–90, especially his insistence that the different disciplines of Christian theology distinguished by Tracy, namely Fundamental, Systematic and Practical Theology, are parts of the same politically responsible theological endeavour (p. 288). On Praxis as locus of theology and on the fundamental consequences which emerge from such a determination of the locus, see Claude Geffré, *Le Christianisme au Risque de l'Interprétation* (Paris: Cerf, 1983), 30 and 342–6.
91. AI, 376.   92. Cf. AI, 405.   93. Cf. AI, 376.   94. Cf. BRO, 43–56.
95. See 2f. above.   96. Cf. AI, 344.
97. Tracy sees such one-sidedness at work in certain traditional theological thought models, which he rejects in BRO, 24–32.
98. Cf. BRO, 71ff.
99. Tracy's concept of a 'revisionist theology' — apart from the linguistic relationship — has nothing to do with the concept of a political revisionism.
100 Cf. here the helpful explanations in Hans Küng, *Does God Exist? An Answer for Today*, tr. Edward Quinn (London: Collins, 1980), 427–41, especially 429. For a discussion on the problem of paradigm change in

182 *Text and Interpretation*

theology and its impact on interpretive perspectives see Küng's reflections in Hans Küng and David Tracy, eds., *Theologie — wohin? Auf dem Weg zu einem neuen Paradigma*, Ökumenische Theologie 11 (Zurich, Cologne: Benziger, and Gutersloh: Gerd Mohn, 1984) 19-25 and 37-75. See also Hans Küng, *Church and Change: The Irish Experience* (Dublin: Gill and Macmillan, 1986), especially 24ff.

101. AI, 51. Compare also Tracy, 'Defending the Public Character of Theology', in *Theologians in Transition: The Christian Century 'How My Mind Has Changed' Series*, ed. James M. Wall, with an Introduction by Martin E. Marty (New York: Crossroad, 1981), 119f.
102. AI, 454: 'In theology, the event is religious. The focal meaning articulated to interpret the event is theological.' — Paul Knitter has convincingly pointed out the significance of the theocentric perspective in Christian theology: 'Christianity as Religion: True and Absolute? A Roman Catholic Perspective', *Concilium* 136 (1980), 12-21.
103. On the mysterious nature of God cf. especially Eberhard Jüngel, *God as the Mystery of the World: On the Foundation of the Theology of the Crucified One in the Dispute between Theism and Atheism*, tr. Darrell L. Guder (Edinburgh: T. & T. Clark, 1983), 250-61, as also Jüngel, 'Der Tod als Geheimnis des Lebens', in *Entsprechungen: Gott — Wahrheit — Mensch: Theologische Erörterungen* (Munich: Kaiser, 1980), 330: "That which cannot be de-mystified through understanding and which nevertheless does not loses its indefinability through understanding, we call a mystery, *misterium*. Not the least difference between itself and an enigma consists in the fact that the more it is understood the more mysterious it becomes.

'In this sense God deserves to be called a mystery. The more one understands God the more mysterious God becomes. And the deeper one penetrates this mystery the more interesting it becomes.'
104. Cf. AI, 454f. and Tracy, 'Analogy and Dialectic: God-Language', in David Tracy and John B. Cobb, Jr., eds., *Talking about God: Doing Theology in the Context of Modern Pluralism*, with an Introduction by David R. Mason (New York: Seabury, 1983), 29-38.
105. It is surprising that Tracy does not also consider the texts of the Hebrew scriptures and other texts of Judaism here; for surely the theocentric perspective of Christian thinking stands in an indissoluble union with the Jewish writings and their interpretations. — On the significance of the double Canon of the Old and New Testaments see Gerhard Ebeling, *Dogmatik des Christlichen Glaubens*, Vol. I, 2nd edn (Tübingen: J.C.B. Mohr [Paul Siebeck], 1982) 27f.
106. Cf. AI, 249.   107. AI, 264.
108. Cf. Claude Geffré, *Le Christianisme au Risque de l'Interprétation*, op. cit., 62f.
109. Cf. also Ernst Fuchs, *Glaube und Erfahrung: Zum christologischen Problem im Neuen Testament* (Tübingen: J.C.B. Mohr [Paul Siebeck], 1965), 185.
110. Cf. Walter Kasper, *Die Methoden der Dogmatik: Einheit and Vielheit* (Munich: Kösel, 1967), 60: 'Theological anamnesis must accordingly always question its object in relation to the promise which it contains for the existential salvation questions of contemporary man.'

Bibliography

Anton, H., 'Interpretation', in *Historisches Wörterbuch der Philosophie*, ed. J. Ritter and K. Gründer, Basel: Schwabe, 1976, Vol. 4, col. 514-18.
Austin, John L., *How To Do Things With Words*, ed. J. O. Urmson and Marina Sbisà, Oxford: Oxford University Press, 1976.
Barr, James, *Fundamentalism*, 2nd edn. London: SCM, 1981.
——— *Holy Scripture: Canon, Authority, Criticism*. Oxford: Clarendon Press, 1983.
Barthes, Roland, *The Pleasure of the Text*, tr. Richard Miller, New York: Hill and Wang, 1975.
Baum, Gregory, review of David Tracy, *The Analogical Imagination*, in *Religious Studies Review* 7 (1981), 284-90.
Birus, Hendrik, ed., *Hermeneutische Positionen: Schleiermacher — Dilthey — Heidegger — Gadamer*, Göttingen: Vandenhoeck & Ruprecht, 1982.
Blank, Josef, *Schriftauslegung in Theorie und Praxis*, Munich: Kösel, 1969.
——— *Verändert Interpretation den Glauben?* Freiburg i. B.: Herder, 1972.
Bloch, Ernst, *Tübinger Einleitung in die Philosophie I*, 6th edn Frankfurt/M.: Suhrkamp, 1968.
Bourgeois, Patrick L. 'From Hermeneutics of Symbols to the Interpretation of Texts', in *Studies in the Philosophy of Paul Ricoeur*, ed. Charles E. Reagan, Athens, Ohio: Ohio University Press, 1979, 84-95.
Braun, Herbert, 'Vom Verstehen des Neuen Testaments', in Braun, *Gesammelte Studien zum Neuen Testament und seiner Umwelt*, 283-98, 3rd edn Tübingen: J. C. B. Mohr [Paul Siebeck], 1971.
Bubner, Rüdiger, *Dialektik und Wissenschaft*. 2nd edn Frankfurt/M.: Suhrkamp, 1974.
Bünting, Karl-Dieter, *Einführung in die Linguistik*, Frankfurt/M.: Athenäum Fischer, 1972.
Bultmann, Rudolf, *Glauben und Verstehen: Gesammelte Aufsätze*, Vol. 3, 3rd edn Tübingen: J. C. B. Mohr [Paul Siebeck], 1965.
Bußmann, Hadumod, *Lexikon der Sprachwissenschaft*, Stuttgart: Kröner, 1983.

Cobb, John B., Jr., review of David Tracy, *The Analogical Imagination*, in *Religious Studies Review* 7 (1981), 281-4.
Coseriu, Eugenio, *Textlinguistik: Eine Einführung*, Tübingen: Narr, 1980.
Dalferth, Ingolf U., *Religiöse Rede von Gott*, Munich: Kaiser, 1981.
Daneš, František, ed., *Papers on Functional Sentence Perspective*, Prague: Academia, and Den Haag, Paris: Mouton, 1974.
―――― 'Functional Sentence Perspective and the Organization of the Text', in *Papers on Functional Sentence Perspective*, 106-28, ed. František Daneš. Prague: Academia, and Den Haag, Paris: Mouton, 1974.
Denzinger, Henricus and Schönmetzer, Adolfus, eds., *Enchiridion Symbolorum: Definitionum Et Declarationum De Rebus Fidei Et Morum*, 36th edn Freiburg i. B.: Herder, 1976.
Dijk, Teun A. van, *Textwissenschaft: Eine interdisziplinäre Einführung*, tr. Christoph Sauer, Munich: DTV, 1980.
Dressler, Wolfgang, *Einführung in die Textlinguistik*, Tübingen: Niemeyer, 1972.
Dunn, James D. G., *Unity and Diversity in the New Testament*, London: SMC, 1977.
Ebeling, Gerhard, 'Hermeneutik', in *Religion in Geschichte und Gegenwart*, Vol. 3, 3rd edn, Tübingen: J. C. B. Mohr [Paul Siebeck], 1959, col. 242-62.
―――― *Einführung in Theologische Sprachlehre*, Tübingen: J. C. B. Mohr [Paul Siebeck], 1971.
―――― *Dogmatik des Christlichen Glaubens*, 3 vols. Tübingen: J. C. B. Mohr [Paul Siebeck], 1979.
Eicher, Peter. *Theologie: Eine Einführung in das Studium*, Munich: Kösel, 1980.
Eroms, Hans-Werner. 'Textlinguistisches Arbeiten aus sprachwissenschaftlicher Sicht', MS, Regensburg, 1977.
―――― 'Die dynamische Struktur der Texte', MS, Passau, 1982.
―――― 'Zur Analyse kompakter Texte', *Sprachwissenschaft* 7 (1982), 329-47.
―――― 'Komplexitätsmaße bei der Textsortendifferenzierung', in *Textsorten und litrarische Gattungen: Dokumentation des Germanistentages in Hamburg vom 1. bis 4. April 1979*, Hamburg: Erich Schmidt, 1983, 131-44.
―――― 'Stilistik', in *Kritische Stichwörter zur Sprachdidaktik*, ed. Margareta Gorschenek and Annamaria Rucktäschel, Munich: Fink, 1983, 235-46.
―――― *Funktionale Satzperspektive*, Tübingen: Niemeyer, 1986.
Fish, Stanley, *Is There a Text in This Class? The Authority of Interpre-*

tive Communities. Cambridge, Mass. and London: Harvard University Press, 1980.

Flannery, Austin, ed., *Vatican Council II, Conciliar and Post-conciliar Documents,* tr. from Latin, Pennsylvania: Scholarly Resources, 1975.

Fohrer, Georg, *Einleitung in das Alte Testament,* 11th edn Heidelberg: Quelle & Meyer, 1969.

Frank, Manfred, *Das individuelle Allgemeine: Textstrukturierung und -intepretation nach Schleiermacher,* Frankfurt/M.: Suhrkamp, 1977.

────── 'Was heißt "einen Text verstehen"?' in *Texthermeneutik: Aktualität, Geschichte, Kritik,* ed. Ulrich Nassen, Paderborn: Schöningh, 1979, 58-77.

────── *Das Sagbare und das Unsagbare: Studien zur neuesten französischen Hermeneutik und Texttheorie,* Frankfurt/M.: Suhrkamp, 1980.

Frege, Gottlob, *Funktion, Begriff, Bedeutung: Fünf logische Studien,* ed. Günther Patzig, 5th edn Göttingen: Vandenhoeck & Ruprecht, 1980.

Fuchs, Ernst, *Hermeneutik,* 2nd edn Bad Cannstatt: Müllerschön, 1958.

────── *Glaube und Erfahrung: Zum christologischen Problem im Neuen Testament,* Tübingen: J. C. B. Mohr [Paul Siebeck], 1965.

Gadamer, Hans-Georg, *Kleine Schriften III: Idee und Sprache,* Tübingen: J. C. B. Mohr [Paul Siebeck], 1972.

────── *Wahrheit und Methode: Grundzüge einer philosophischen Hermeneutik,* 4th edn Tübingen: J. C. B. Mohr [Paul Siebeck], 1975.

────── *Truth and Method,* translation ed. Garret Barden and John Cumming from the 2nd (1965) edition, New York: Seabury, 1975.

────── *Kleine Schriften I: Philosophie-Hermeneutik,* 2nd edn Tübingen: J. C. B. Mohr [Paul Siebeck], 1976.

────── *Philosophical Hermeneutics,* tr. and ed. David E. Linge, Berkeley, Los Angeles, London: University of California Press, 1976.

────── *Kleine Schriften IV: Variationen,* Tübingen: J. C. B. Mohr [Paul Siebeck], 1977.

────── *Kleine Schriften II: Interpretationen,* 2nd edn Tübingen: J. C. B. Mohr [Paul Siebeck], 1979.

────── *Reason in the Age of Science,* tr. Frederick G. Lawrence, Cambridge, Mass. and London: MIT Press, 1981.

Gadamer, Hans-Georg and Boehm, Gottfried, eds., *Seminar: Die Hermeneutik und die Wissenschaften,* Frankfurt/M.: Suhrkamp, 1978.

Gadamer, Hans-Georg and Boehm, Gottfried, eds., *Seminar: Philosophische Hermeneutik,* 2nd edn Frankfurt/M.: Suhrkamp, 1979.

Geffré, Claude, *Le Christianisme au Risque de l'Interprétation,* Paris: Cerf, 1983.

Gobyn, Luc, 'Differenzierungskriterien für Textsorten', in *Sprache:*

Formen und Strukturen. Akten des 15. Linguistischen Kolloquiums, Münster 1980, Vol. 1, ed. M. Kohl and J. Lenerz, Tübingen: Niemeyer, 1981, 269–80.

Grant, Robert M., with Tracy, David, *A Short History of the Interpretation of the Bible*, 2nd edn Philadelphia: Fortress, 1984.

Gülich, Elisabeth and Raible, Wolfgang, *Linguistische Textmodelle: Grundlagen und Möglichkeiten*, Munich: Fink, 1977.

Habermas, Jürgen, *Knowledge and Human Interests*, tr. Jeremy J. Shapiro, 2nd edn London: Heinemann, 1978.

――― *Technik und Wissenschaft als 'Ideologie'*. 11th edn Frankfurt/M.: Suhrkamp, 1981.

――― *Theorie des kommunikativen Handelns*, 2 Vols., Frankfurt/M.: Suhrkamp, 1981.

Harweg, Roland, *Pronomina und Textkonstitution*, 2nd edn Munich: Fink, 1979.

Heidegger, Martin, *Being and Time*, tr. John Maquarrie and Edward Robinson, Oxford: Blackwell, 1962.

Hellholm, David, *Das Visionenbuch des Hermas als Apokalypse: Formgeschichtliche und texttheoretische Studien zu einer literarischen Gattung I*, Lund: Liber Läromedel, 1980.

Henrichs, Norbert, *Bibliographie der Hermeneutik und ihrer Anwendungsgebiete seit Schleiermacher*, 2nd edn Düsseldorf: Philosophia, 1972.

Hermeneutik und Ideologiekritik: Mit Beiträgen von Karl-Otto Apel, Claus v. Bormann, Rüdiger Bubner, Hans-Georg Gadamer, Hans Joachim Giegel, Jürgen Habermas, Theorie Diskussion, Frankfurt/M.: Suhrkamp, 1971.

Hirsch, E. D., Jr., *Validity in Interpretation*, New Haven, London: Yale University Press, 1967.

――― *The Aims of Interpretation*, Chicago, London: University of Chicago Press, 1976.

Iser, Wolfgang, *The Implied Reader: Patterns of Communication in Prose Fiction from Bunyan to Beckett*, Baltimore: John Hopkins University Press, 1974.

――― *Der Akt des Lesens: Theorie ästhetischer Wirkung*, Munich: Fink, 1976.

――― *The Act of Reading: A Theory of Aesthetic Response*, Baltimore: Johns Hopkins University Press, 1978.

Jauß, Hans Robert, 'Literaturgeschichte als Provokation', in *Rezeptionsästhetik: Theorie und Praxis*, ed. Rainer Warning, 2nd edn Munich: Fink, 1979, 126–62.

Jeanrond, Werner G., 'Biblical Interpretation as Appropriation of Texts: The Need for a Closer Cooperation between Biblical Exegetes

and Systematic Theologians', *Proceedings of the Irish Biblical Association* 6 (1982) 1-18.
——— 'The Theological Understanding of Texts and Linguistic Explication', *Modern Theology* 1 (1984), 55-66.
——— 'Towards a Critical Theology of Christian Praxis'. *The Irish Theological Quarterly* 51 (1985), 136-45.
——— 'The Impact of Schleiermacher's Hermeneutics on Contemporary Interpretation Theory', in *The Interpretation of Belief: Coleridge, Schleiermacher and Romanticism*, ed. David Jasper, London: Macmillan 1986, 81-96.
Jüngel, Eberhard, *God as the Mystery of the World: On the Foundation of the Theology of the Crucified One in the Dispute between Theism and Atheism*, tr. Darrell L. Guder, Edinburgh: T. & T. Clark, 1983.
——— 'Der Tod als Geheimnis des Lebens', in *Entsprechungen: Gott — Wahrheit — Mensch. Theologische Erörterungen*, Munich: Kaiser, 1980, 327-54.
——— 'Auch das Schöne muß sterben' — Schönheit im Lichte der Wahrheit: Theologische Bemerkungen zum ästhetischen Verhältnis', *Zeitschrift für Theologie und Kirche* 81 (1984), 106-26.
Kallmeyer, W.; Klein, W.; Meyer-Hermann, R.; Netzer, K.; and Siebert, H. J., *Lektürekolleg zur Textlinguistik*, 2 Vols. Frankfurt/M.: Fischer Athenäum, 1974.
Käsemann, Ernst, ed., *Das Neue Testament als Kanon: Dokumentation und kritische Analyse zur gegenwärtigen Diskussion*, Göttingen: Vandenhoeck & Ruprecht, 1970.
——— 'Differences and Unity in the New Testament', *Concilium* 171 (1984), 55-61.
Kasper, Walter, *Die Methoden der Dogmatik: Einheit und Vielheit*, Munich: Kösel, 1967.
Klein, Wolfgang and Nassen, Ulrich, 'Textlinguistik und Textthermeneutik', in *Texthermeneutik: Aktualität, Geschichte, Kritik*, ed. Ulrich Nassen, Paderborn: Schöningh, 1979, 23-36.
Köster, Helmut, *Einführung in das Neue Testament im Rahmen der Religionsgeschichte und Kulturgeschichte der hellenistischen und römischen Zeit*, Berlin, New York: de Gruyter, 1980.
Küng, Hans, *Does God Exist: An Answer for Today*, tr. Edward Quinn, London: Collins, 1980.
——— *Church and Change: The Irish Experience*, Introduction by Seán Freyne, Dublin: Gill and Macmillan, 1986.
Küng, Hans and Tracy, David, eds., *Theologie — wohin? Auf dem Weg zu einem neuen Paradigma*, Ökumenische Theologie, 11. Zurich, Cologne: Benziger, and Gütersloh: Gerd Mohn, 1984.
Lohse, Bernhard, *Epochen der Dogmengeschichte*, 3rd edn Stuttgart: Kreuz, 1974.

Lutz, Luise, *Zum Thema 'Thema': Einführung in die Thema-Rhema-Theorie*, Hamburger Arbeiten zur Linguistik und Texttheorie, Vol. 1, Hamburg: Hamburger Buchagentur, 1981.
McCarthy, Thomas, *The Critical Theory of Jürgen Habermas*, London: Hutchinson, 1978.
McFague TeSelle, Sallie. *Speaking in Parables: A Study in Metaphor and Theology*, Philadelphia: Fortress, 1975.
——— Metaphorical Theology: *Models of God in Religious Language*, London: SMC, 1983.
Marfurt, Bernhard, 'Textrezeption und Textsorte', *wirkendes wort* 5 (1980), 293-311.
Meyer zu Schlochtern, Josef, 'Erzählung als Paradigma einer alternativen theologischen Denkform: Ansätze zu einer 'Narrativen Theologie', in *Theologische Berichte* 8, ed. Franz Furger. Zurich, Einsiedeln, Cologne: Benziger, 1979, 35-70.
Mezger, Manfred, 'Theologie als Wissenschaft', in *Ernst Bloch zu ehren*, ed. Siegfried Unseld. Frankfurt/M.: Suhrkamp, 1965, 181-207.
Millar, Alan and Riches, John K., 'Interpretation: A Theological Perspective and Some Applications', *Numen* 28 (1981), 29-53.
Mukařovský, Jan, *Kapitel aus der Ästhetik*, tr. Walter Schamschula, 3rd edn Frankfurt/M.: Suhrkamp, 1978.
——— *Structure, Sign, and Function: Selected Essays by Jan Mukařovský*, tr. and ed. John Burbank and Peter Steiner, New Haven and London: Yale University Press, 1978.
Nassen, Ulrich, ed. *Texthermeneutik: Aktualität, Geschichte, Kritik*. Paderborn: Schöningh, 1979.
Nikolaus, Kurt, 'Zur Kritik der Textlinguistik', in *Sprache: Formen und Strukturen. Akten des 15. Linguistischen Kolloquiums, Münster 1980*, Vol. 1, ed. M. Kohl and J. Lenerz, Tübingen: Niemeyer, 1981, 281-91.
Pannenberg, Wolfhart, *Theology and the Philosophy of Science*, tr. Francis McDonagh, London: Darton, Longman & Todd, 1976.
Pelikan, Jaroslav, *The Christian Tradition: A History of the Development of Doctrine*, Vol. 1: *The Emergence of the Catholic Tradition (100-600)*, Chicago, London: University of Chicago Press, 1971.
Pellauer, David, 'The Significance of the Text in Paul Ricoeur's Hermeneutical Theory', in *Studies in the Philosophy of Paul Ricoeur*, ed. Charles E. Reagan, Athens, Ohio: Ohio University Press, 1979, 98-114.
Peters, Ted, 'Methode und System in der heutigen amerikanischen Theologie', *Kerygma und Dogma* 29 (1983), 2-46.
Peukert, Helmut, *Science, Action, and Fundamental Theology: Toward*

A Theology of Communicative Action, tr. James Bohman, Cambridge, Mass. and London: MIT Press, 1984.

Rahner, Karl, *Foundations of Christian Faith: An Introduction to the Idea of Christianity*, tr. William V. Dych, London: Darton, Longman & Todd, 1978.

Rahner, Karl and Vorgrimler, Herbert, *Kleines Theologisches Wörterbuch*, 8th edn Freiburg i. B.: Herder, 1971.

Reagan, Charles E., ed., *Studies in the Philosophy of Paul Ricoeur*, Athens, Ohio: Ohio University Press, 1979.

Ricoeur, Paul, *The Symbolism of Evil*, tr. Emerson Buchanan, Boston: Beacon, 1969.

——— *Freud and Philosophy: An Essay on Interpretation*, tr. Denis Savage, New Haven and London: Yale University Press, 1970.

——— 'Qu'est-ce qu'un Texte? Expliquer et Comprendre', in *Hermeneutik und Dialektik: Aufsätze II*, ed. Rüdiger Bubner, Konrad Cramer and Reiner Wiehl, Tübingen: J. C. B. Mohr [Paul Siebeck], 1970.

——— *The Conflict of Interpretations: Essays in Hermeneutics*, ed. Don Ihde, Evanston: Northwestern University Press, 1974.

——— *The Rule of Metaphor: Multi-disciplinary Studies of the Creation of Meaning in Language*, tr. R. Czerny, London: Routledge, 1978.

——— *Interpretation Theory: Discourse and the Surplus of Meaning*, Fort Worth, Texas: Texas Christian University Press, 1976.

——— 'Schleiermacher's Hermeneutics', *The Monist* 60 (1977), 181-97.

——— *Essays on Biblical Interpretation*, edited with an Introduction by Lewis S. Mudge, Philadelphia: Fortress, 1980.

——— *Hermeneutics and the Human Sciences: Essays on Language, Action and Interpretation*, edited, translated and introduced by John B. Thompson, Cambridge: Cambridge University Press, and Paris: Editions de la Maison des Sciences de l'Homme, 1981.

The Philosophy of Paul Ricoeur: An Anthology of His Work, ed. Charles E. Reagan and David Stewart. Boston: Beacon, 1978.

Ricoeur, Paul and Jüngel, Eberhard, *Metapher: Zur Hermeneutik religiöser Sprache*, Einführung von Pierre Gisel, Sonderheft Evangelische Theologie, Munich: Kaiser, 1974.

Ritschl, Dietrich and Jones, Hugh O., *'Story' als Rohmaterial der Theologie*, Munich: Kaiser, 1976.

Robertson, John C., 'Hermeneutics of Suspicion *versus* Hermeneutics of Goodwill', *Sciences Religieuses/Studies in Religion* 8/4 (1979), 365-77.

Sandig, Barbara, *Stilistik: Sprachpragmatische Grundlegung der Stilbeschreibung*, Berlin, New York: de Gruyter, 1978.

Schapp, Wilhelm, *In Geschichten verstrickt: Zum Sein von Mensch und Ding*, 2nd edn, Wiesbaden: Heymann, 1976.
Schillebeeckx, Edward, *Ministry: A Case for Change*, tr. John Bowden, London: SCM, 1981.
——— *God is New Each Moment*, tr. David Smith, Edinburgh: T. & T. Clark, 1983.
Schmidt, Siegfried J., *Texttheorie: Probleme einer Linguistik der sprachlichen Kommunikation*, 2nd edn Munich: Fink, 1976.
Schupp, Franz, *Auf dem Weg zu einer kritischen Theologie*, Quaestiones Disputatae 64, Freiburg i.B.: Herder, 1974.
Searle, John R., *Speech Acts: An Essay in the Philosophy of Language*, London: Cambridge University Press, 1969.
Sowinski, Bernhard, *Deutsche Stilistik: Beobachtungen zur Sprachverwendung und Sprachgestaltung im Deutschen*, 2nd edn Frankfurt/M.: Fischer, 1978.
——— *Textlinguistik: Eine Einführung*, Stuttgart: Kohlhammer, 1983.
Stobbe, Heinz Günther, *Hermeneutik — ein ökumenisches Problem: Eine Kritik der katholischen Gadamer-Rezeption*, Ökumenische Theologie 8, Zurich, Cologne: Benziger, and Gütersloh: Gerd Mohn, 1981.
Suleiman, Susan R. and Crosman, Inge, eds., *The Reader in the Text: Essays on Audience and Interpretation*, Princeton: Princeton University Press, 1980.
Thiselton, Anthony C., *The Two Horizons: New Testament Hermeneutics and Philosophical Description with Special Reference to Heidegger, Bultmann, Gadamer, and Wittgenstein*, Exeter: Paternoster Press, 1980.
Thompson, John B., *Critical Hermeneutics: A Study in the Thought of Paul Ricoeur and Jürgen Habermas*, Cambridge: Cambridge University Press, 1981.
Tracy, David, *Blessed Rage for Order: The New Pluralism in Theology*, New York: Seabury, 1975.
——— *The Analogical Imagination: Christian Theology and the Culture of Pluralism*, New York: Crossroad, 1981.
——— Foreword to Arthur A. Cohen, *The Tremendum: A Theological Interpretation of the Holocaust*, New York: Crossroad, 1981, and London: SCM, 1982, vii–xiii.
——— 'Defending the Public Character of Theology', in *Theologians in Transition: The Christian Century 'How My Mind Has Changed' Series*, 113–24, ed. James M. Wall, Introduction by Martin E. Marty, New York: Crossroad, 1981.
——— 'On Thinking with the Classics', *Criterion* 22 (1983), 9–10.
——— 'Project "X": Retrospect and Prospect', *Concilium* 170 (1983), 30–36.

——— 'Creativity in the Interpretation of Religion: The Question of Radical Pluralism', *New Literary History* 15 (1983-1984), 289-309.

Tracy, David and Cobb, John B., Jr., *Talking About God: Doing Theology in the Context of Modern Pluralism*, Introduction by David R. Mason, New York: Seabury, 1983.

Turk, Horst, 'Wahrheit oder Methode? H.-G. Gadamers 'Grundzüge einer philosophischen Hermeneutik', in *Hermeneutische Positionen: Schleiermacher — Dilthey — Heidegger — Gadamer*, ed. Hendrik Birus, Göttingen: Vandenhoeck & Ruprecht, 1982, 120-50.

Wacker, Bernd, *Narrative Theologie?* Munich: Kösel, 1977.

Warning, Rainer, ed., *Rezeptionsästhetik: Theorie und Praxis*, 2nd edn Munich: Fink, 1979.

Weinrich, Harald, *Sprache in Texten*, Stuttgart: Kohlhammer, 1976.

——— *Tempus: Besprochene und erzählte Welt*, 3rd edn Stuttgart: Kohlhammer, 1977.

Wilson, Thomas J., 'The Text-model: A Key to Heidegger's Thought?', *The Irish Theological Quarterly*, 47 (1980), 286-95.

——— *Sein als Text: Vom Textmodell als Martin Heideggers Denkmodell. Eine funktionalistische Interpretation.* Freiburg, Munich: Alber, 1981.

Zemb, Jean-Marie, *Métagrammaire: La Proposition.* Paris: OCDL, 1972.

Name Index

Ammann, Hermann, 170 n. 43
Anton, H., 162 nn. 169, 170
Aristotle, 95
Augustine, 5
Austin, John, 76

Barr, James, 74 n. 1, 92 n. 63, 122 n. 162
Barth, Karl, 8
Barthes, Roland, 106 n. 102, 135
Baum, Gregory, 181 n. 90
Beardsley, Monroe, 43
Blank, Josef, 157-8 n. 19
Bloch, Ernst, 70f.
Boehm, Gottfried, 156 n. 6 (ch. I)
Bormann, Claus von, 160 n. 108
Bourgeois, Patrick, 40 and 163 n. 189
Bubner, Rüdiger, 167 n. 282
Bühler, Karl, 84
Bünting, Karl-Dieter, 168 n. 7
Bultmann, Rudolf, 8, 74, 180 n. 84
Bussmann, Hadumod, 76 n. 9

Campenhausen, Hans von, 92 n. 61
Cobb, John, 179 n. 60, 181 n. 81
Coseriu, Eugenio, 77, 78, 94 n. 65

Dalferth, Ingolf, 83-4 n. 36
Daneš, František, 85, 86
Denzinger, Henricus, 99
Derrida, Jacques, 175 n. 102, 135
Dijk, Teun van, 168 nn. 6, 7
Dilthey, Wilhelm, 8, 48, 57
Dressler, Wolfgang, 81 n. 32, 88 n. 54, 168 n. 7
Dunn, James, 171 n. 158

Ebeling, Gerhard, 8, 119 and 171 n. 159, 180
Eicher, Peter, xvii n. 2, 7 n. 20, 156 n. 6 (ch. I)
Eroms, Hans-Werner, 81 and 165 n. 27, 81 n. 31, 86 and 166 n. 48, 95, 96 n. 73, 99, 103 and 169 n. 99, 163 n. 7, 165 n. 30, 166 n. 43, 168 nn. 74, 79

Firbas, Jan, 87
Fish, Stanley, 106, 110-13, 120
Fohrer, Georg, 100-101 n. 94
Frank, Manfred, 79, 95 n. 66
Frege, Gottlob, 48, 165 n. 224
Freud, Sigmund, 46, 52
Fuchs, Ernst, 166-7 n. 282, 182 n. 109

Gadamer, Hans-Georg, xvi-xvii, 1, 9-38, 40, 44-6, 49, 52-5, 56, 60, 61, 64f., 66f., 68, 71, 73, 114, 129, 133, 134, 141, 151, 172-3 n. 74
Geffré, Claude, 150 n. 108, 181 n. 90
Gobyn, Luc, 173 n. 80
Greimas, Algirdas, 89
Gülich, Elisabeth, 77f.
Gunkel, Hermann, 100f.

Habermas, Jürgen, 22-7, 53, 54, 65, 162 n. 168, 174 n. 93
Harweg, Roland, 88 n. 53
Hegel, Friedrich, 18
Heidegger, Martin, xviii, 14, 23, 36, 40, 66, 158 n. 50, 162 nn. 169, 171
Hellholm, David, 101, 157 n. 16
Hirsch, E. D., 106
Husserl, Edmund, 58

Ionesco, Eugène, 160 n. 112
Irenaeus von Lyon, 5
Iser, Wolfgang, 106-10, 113, 120, 137 and 179 n. 45

Jakobson, Roman, 84
Jauss, Hans Robert, 175f. n. 147
Jüngel, Eberhard, 180 n 73, 182 n. 103

Käsemann, Ernst, 92, 119, 121, 171 n. 61, 176 nn. 158, 161
Kästner, Erich, 66, 166 n. 281
Kallmeyer, W., 88, 89, 168 n. 6, 171 nn. 55, 58
Kasper, Walter, 182 n. 110
Klein, Wolfgang, 78, 168-9 nn. 16, 17, 20

Name Index

Knitter, Paul, 182 n. 102
Köster, Helmut, 92, 171 n. 61
Küng, Hans, 148 and 181-2 n. 100

Lévi-Strauss, Claude, 50
Lohse, Bernhard, 176-7 n. 164
Luther, Martin, 5
Lutz, Luise, 87 and 171 n. 51, 170 n. 43

McCarthy, Thomas, 160-61 n. 128
McFague TeSelle, Sallie, 155 n. 1
Marfurt, Bernhard, 98 and 173 n. 79
Marx, Karl, 52
Matthesius, Vilém, 85 and 170 n. 41
Meyer zu Schlochtern, Josef, 155 n. 1
Millar, Alan, 75 and 168 n. 5
Mudge, Lewis, 40 and 163 n. 181
Mukařovský, Jan, 116f., 140

Nassen, Ulrich, 78 n. 16
Nietzsche, Friedrich, 52
Nikolaus, Kurt, 169 n. 20

O'Brien, William, 177 n. 3
O'Jones, Hugh, 155 n. 1
Origen, 5

Pannenberg, Wolfhart, 32
Pelikan, Jaroslav, 167 n. 164
Pellauer, David, 38 and 163 n. 172
Peters, Ted, 132 and 178 n. 19
Peukert, Helmut, 3f.
Plato, 142

Raible, Wolfgang, 77f.
Rahner, Karl, 8
Riches, John, 75 and 168 n. 5

Ricoeur, Paul, xvii, 1, 19 and 159 n. 88, 37-65, 68, 71, 73, 78 and 169 n. 18, 80, 95, 109, 114 and 176 n. 149, 129, 134, 135, 137, 151
Ritschl, Dietrich, 155 n. 1
Ryle, Gilbert, 43
Robertson, John, 162 n. 168

Sandig, Barbara, 95-7, 172 n. 71
Saussure, Ferdinand de, 47, 80
Schapp, Wilhelm, 175 n. 125
Schillebeeckx, Edward, 176 n. 162
Schleiermacher, Friedrich, 8, 94f., 157 n. 14, 176 n. 157
Schmidt, Siegfried, 77 n. 11, 79f., 87 and 171 n. 50, 168 n. 7
Schupp, Franz, 167 n. 287
Searle, John, 76
Sowinski, Bernhard, 96 n. 76, 168 nn. 6, 7
Stobbe, Heinz Günther, 15 n. 55, 28-34, 161 n. 158, 162 n. 164
Suleiman, Susan, 105

Thiselton, Anthony, 167 n. 4
Thompson, John, 60
Tillich, Paul, 167 n. 4
Tracy, David, 3 and 156 n. 5 (ch. I), 6 n. 15, 118 and 176 n. 157, 129-52
Turk, Horst, 33 and 162 n. 162

Vorgrimler, Herbert, 2 and 156 n. 2

Wacker, Bernd, 155 n. 1
Weinrich, Harald, 79 and 169 n. 22, 99 n. 89, 168 n. 7
Wilson, Thomas, 32 and 161 n. 157

Zemb, Jean-Marie, 170-71 n. 43

Subject Index

agreement, 30f., 66
analogy, 149
assessment (*Deuten*), xvii, 63, 64-72, 124-7, 139, *see also* interpretation
authority, 7, 13f., 24, 30, 107, 124, 141, 144
automation in the reading process, 118, 140, 141

Bible: interpretation of biblical texts, xv, xviii, 4, 5, 35, 67, 74f., 81f., 87, 92-4, 99, 100-103, 117, 118-28, 141, 150-53
blanks/spots of indeterminacy (*Leerstellen im Text/Unbestimmtheitsbeträge*), 110f.

canon: aesthetic, 116; biblical, 2, 92-4, 103, 117f., 122, 125, 145, 149
Church, 2, 93f., 98, 100, 119, 122, 131, 141
Church history, 130, *see also* theology, historical
classic, classical: in general, 13, 132; perspectives, 142; texts, 118, 133-5, 140-42; religious, 143-5
communication: in general, 77-80, 82, 83f., 89, 90-92, 96-9, 103, 107, 108, 109; competence, 23, 100; pseudo-, 23; distorted, 23-7, 54, 55, 65, 67, 135
criticism in the process of interpretation, *see* interpretation

deconstructionism, 106, 134
delivery, manner of (*Vortragsweise*), 157 n. 13
dialectic between text and reading, xviii, 33, 108f., 113f., 135
disclosure, *see* sense
dogma, 99, 103
dogmatics, *see* theology

effective history/historical consciousness, 15f., 18, 22, 33, 103, 106, 129, 143
enlightenment, 5, 36

epistemology/knowledge, 8, 11f., 13f., 23f., 32f., 37, 49, 56, 58, 133
ethics of interpretation, *see* interpretation
exegesis, historical-critical, 6f., 37, 75f., 100, 130, 152
experience: in general, 130, 134; aesthetic, 12, 20f., 100f., 116f., 118, 120, 133; religious, 130, 144, 150, 152
explanation (*Erklären*), *see* interpretation

faith community (*Glaubensgemeinschaft*), *see* Church
formalism, xviii, 79, 95, 137
functional sentence perspective, *see* theme-rheme structure
fundamentalism, 93, 162 nn. 1, 2

genre theory (*Gattungstheorie*), 94, 100f.
God, xv, xvi, 2, 3, 82f., 91, 102, 119, 121, 127, 144f., 148f., 150-53

handing on/transmission (*Überlieferung*), 2, 3, 7, 12, 13, 15, 17f., 20, 21, 29, 30, 31, 52, 102, 119, 121
hermeneutics/hermeneutical: in general, *see* interpretation, theory of; experience, 8, 9-12, 18-21, 25, 53, 140; universality of, 8, 11, 20, 22, 23, 26, 36, 37, 41, 56, 64, 71f.; conversation, 9, 12, 14, 18f., 31f., 65f., 133f., 137f., 142, 143, 147, 150, 152; circle (*hermeneutischer Zirkel*), 14f., 61f.; philosophical, xvi, xviii, 1, 8-64, 73, 129; theological, 4, 7, 67f., 141; depth, 23, 55; *see also* interpretation, theory of
heterodoxy, 93
history/historicality, 18, 47, 112, 134, 152, 75 n. 231
historiography (*Geschichtswissenschaft*), 17

Subject Index

horizons, fusion of (*Horizontverschmelzung*), xvii, 15f., 22, 27, 31, 32, 45, 65, 75, 139

idealism, 59, 64, 142
ideology, critique of, 24, 26f., 35, 53f., 68, 139, 142
interpretation: and reflection on praxis (*Handlungsbesinnung*), 2f., 7, 35, 54f., 120; criticism in the process of, 34–6, 42, 52–5, 61, 64–71, 110, 112, 113f., 138–40, 141f.; dimensions of, 68f., 71, 73, 139; ethics of, 67–71, 74, 120–28, 134, 136f., 139f.; perspectives of, *see* reading perspectives; pluralism of, 62f., 74, 93, 105, 112, 113f., 118, 119, 120–28, 134, 151; prejudice/understanding in, 13–15, 23f., 26, 29, 35, 66, 107, 114, 125, 134; theory of, xvi–xviii, 1, 6, 8–72, 73, 111, 131f., *see also* reading; interpreters, self-understanding of
interpreters: community of, 111–13, 114, 119, 120, 134f., 142; responsibility of, xvii, 70, 74, 95, 114, 119, 121, 125, 126, 127f., 129, 139f., 151f., 153; self-understanding of, 39, 52–4, 56, 59, 61f., 63, 67, 72, 107–10, 122, 135, 145, 149, 150, 152, 179 n. 52
isotopic levels, 89

Jesus Christ, 2, 3, 82, 98, 99, 103, 121, 125, 127, 145f., 148–50

language: in general, 19f., 22, 25f., 30f., 32, 39, 40f., 43, 46–8, 56f., 66f., 75f., 112, 117, 130, 150f.; polysemy in, ambiguities of, 34, 41–3, 45, 51, 89, 122, 150
linguistics, linguistic theory, xviii–xix, 73, 75–8

metaphor, 42–4
methodological problem in interpretation theory, 9–14, 20, 27–38, 53f., 57, 60, 101, 148
misunderstanding, 16, 22–31
myth, 40

norms: of interpretation, 92, 102, 104, 113, 115–18, 124, 133, 141, 149; stylistic, 96f.

ontology, 34, 37f., 40–49, 56, 71, 140
orthodoxy, 93

paradigmatic shift, 148
phenomenology, 58, 105, 108, 130, 133, 138, 148
philology, 129
philosophy, 8, 9, 10, 39, 112, 129
play, 20f., 31, 134f., 166 n. 278
pluralism, *see* interpretation, pluralism of
polysemy, *see* language
praxis, 35, 146f.
prejudice/understanding in interpretation, *see* interpretation
proclamation, 146

reading, xvii, 4f., 48f., 54, 61, 73f., 83f.
reading perspectives, 7, 62f., 93, 114f., 125f., 139, 143, 144f., 148f., 151f.
reason (*Vernunft*), 9, 13, 24
reference, *see* sense and meaning
religion, 117, 132, 143
rheme, *see* theme-rheme structure
rhetoric, 27, 105

self-understanding of the interpreter, *see* interpreters
sense, disclosure/understanding of sense (*Sinn/Sinnerschliessung Sinnverstehen/Textsinn*), 13, 14f., 17, 19, 20, 23, 29f., 41f., 51, 56–61, 62, 69, 76, 78, 83, 89, 93, 98, 102, 104, 109, 110, 115, 116, 119 n. 160, 136f., 142f., 153, 176 n. 60, 178 n. 24
sense and meaning/reference (*Sinn und Bedeutung*), 17, 46–52, 56–61, 63, 78–83, 88f., 109, 136f., 146
spots of indeterminacy, *see* blanks
structuralism, 46
style/stylistic, in general, 87, 94–7, 117, 134, 151f.; reading, xviii, 105, 114f., 121, 125, 136, 140, 151; competence, 100, 174 n. 93; textual, 46, 94–7, 101, 114f., 120, 136, 151
symbol, 40–42

text: coherence of, 86; hierarchy of functions in, 100f.; hierarchy of perspectives, 91f.; oral nature of (*Mündlichkeit*), 45, 48, 78, 121, 155 n. 3; autonomy, 19, 44–52, 54, 62, 112; theory, xviiif., 43f., 56f., 63f., 66, 73,

75-103, 133f., 139f.; textuality of, xv, 7, 45f., 59f., 70, 75, 76-8, 81, 88, 90; written nature of, xvii, 19, 44, 50, 51, 56, 78, 94f., 105, 112, 121, 129
text genres, (*Textsorten*): in general, xviii, 94-101, 105, 111, 116, 120, 136; theological, 100-103, 151
text linguistics, xv, 75-94, 136, 174 n. 97
textual composition, *see* textualisation
textual reception, *see* reading; interpretation
textualisation, xv, 46, 83-90, 94-6, 98, 103
theme-rheme structure, 85-90, 91, 98, 107f., 139
theology: in general, xv, 1, 2, 3, 73-5, 100f., 127f., 130, 148f., 151-3; as textual science, xv-xix, 1f., 74f., 101f., 129; division of labour (*Arbeitsteilung*), 6f., 75, 131; dogmatic, 74f., 99, 182 n. 110; fundamental, 3f., 130, 144, 156 n. 6, 181 n. 90; hermeneutical nature of, 130-32, 147, 150f.; historical, 131; method of, 130, 147, 156 n. 1; narrative, 155 n. 1; practical, 6, 131, 146, 181 n. 90; revisionist, 142-9; systematic, 6, 75, 130, 132, 146, 181 n. 86
theory and practice/praxis, 129, 177 n. 10
tradition, 2, 7, 13, 14, 22f., 30, 33, 62, 93, 96, 112f., 119, 124, 130, 131, 132, 138, 142f., 152
transformation, 131, 134, 135, 140, 142, 143f., 147, 150f.
transmission, *see* handing on
truth, xviii, 20, 21, 24, 27, 28, 32, 36, 41, 49, 58, 60, 67f., 74, 119, 130, 133, 134, 140, 142, 144, 151

understanding, *see* interpretation, interpreters, self-understanding of

www.ingramcontent.com/pod-product-compliance
Lightning Source LLC
Chambersburg PA
CBHW070323230426
43663CB00011B/2205